ANGER
MANAGEMENT

PUBLISHER'S NOTE

This publication is designed to provide accurate and authoritative information in regard to the subject matter covered. It is sold with the understanding that the publisher is not engaged in rendering psychological, medical, or other professional service.

Books in The Practical Therapist Series® *present authoritative answers to the question, "What-do-I-do-now-and-how-do-I-do-it?" in the practice of psychotherapy, bringing the wisdom and experience of expert mentors to the practicing therapist. A book, however, is no substitute for thorough professional training and adherence to ethical and legal standards. At minimum:*

- ☛ *The practitioner must be qualified to practice psychotherapy.*
- ☛ *Clients participate in psychotherapy only with informed consent.*
- ☛ *The practitioner must not "guarantee" a specific outcome.*

— Robert E. Alberti, Ph.D., Editor

REVIEWER COMMENTS ON
Anger Management: The Complete Guidebook For Practitioners

"One of the most difficult problems for therapists to tackle is a patient's anger. The angry client, in addition to requiring help, often elicits feelings of resentment and hopelessness in the clinician, further contributing to the difficulty in treating these individuals. Now we can have hope, because *Anger Management: The Complete Treatment Guidebook for Practitioners* will help the clinician as much as it will help the patient.

"Kassinove and Tafrate provide an excellent guide to understanding and modifying anger. I was impressed with their five-stage *Anger Episode Model,* since they integrate theory and empirical research with highly practical and insightful guidelines for treating angry patients. The clinician helps the patient analyze triggers, negative appraisals, experiences, patterns of expression and their outcomes. Each step in the model provides an opportunity to better understand and modify angry behavior. This is a highly practical book, with many powerful clinical interventions, written by two leading experts on anger who show great clinical sensitivity. I highly recommend this thought-provoking and very useful book."

— **Robert L. Leahy, Ph.D.**
Director, American Institute for Cognitive Therapy, New York, NY 10022
Editor, *Journal of Cognitive Psychotherapy: An International Quarterly*
President-Elect, International Association for Cognitive Psychotherapy
Clinical Associate Professor, Department of Psychiatry, Cornell
University Medical College, New York Hospital

"Howard Kassinove and Raymond Chip Tafrate describe their book as "the complete guidebook for practitioners.". . . I think they are right. . . . this guidebook for practitioners is much more thoroughgoing than other books on the subject and it covers the complex field of the psychological treatment of anger remarkably well.

"All eighteen chapters include exceptionally relevant and important materials from which any practitioner is likely to benefit. Moreover, the materials presented by the authors are written in clear cut, highly readable language, with their main points accurately presented. Good — in fact, great!

". . . this guidebook describes useful multimodal and comprehensive approaches for teaching clients and others how to reduce and manage anger. Remarkably well done and very worthwhile reading."

— **Albert Ellis, Ph.D.**
(1913-2007)
(From the Foreword)

"This is an absolutely great practitioners' book by two well-known scholars in the field of anger management. As Drs. Kassinove and Tafrate note, anger, unlike some other disorders, affects most people at some time, making this guidebook particularly useful. They have written what is probably the definitive therapist book on anger control."

"There are chapters on conceptual models of anger, anger awareness, methods of change, and relapse prevention, with numerous case examples and actual client-therapist dialogue included. There are also several very useful client information sheets. I was especially gratified to see the superb chapter on forgiveness, a topic not normally considered by mental health practitioners."

"I recommend this book highly for all therapists who deal with anger management - their own or their clients. In the end, that really includes almost everyone!"

— **E. Thomas Dowd, Ph.D., ABPP**
Professor of Psychology
Kent State University
President, American Board of Behavioral Psychology

"A well-written guidebook which can be utilized by the novice to the most experienced clinician. The authors nicely integrate theory into clinical practice which can be used with diverse clinical populations."

— **Ann Marie Kopeck, LCSW, BCD, CAC**

"This is a must book for the practitioner aiming to expand one's practice to anger — the modern day disorder of major proportions. The book is an excellent source of practical knowledge for conducting assessments and designing workable intervention programs. The step-by-step approach overlooks nothing as it comprehensively addresses how to help people gain control over this emotion — from increasing motivation, to developing self-control strategies, to adjusting to aversive realities, to relapse prevention. This program does it all."

— **Richard Suinn, Ph.D., ABPP**
Emeritus Professor
Colorado State University
Past President, American Psychological Association

The Practical Therapist Series®

ANGER MANAGEMENT

THE COMPLETE TREATMENT GUIDEBOOK FOR PRACTITIONERS

HOWARD KASSINOVE, PH.D., ABPP
RAYMOND CHIP TAFRATE, PH.D.

FOREWORD BY ALBERT ELLIS, PH.D.

Impact Publishers®
ATASCADERO, CALIFORNIA

Seventh Printing, September 2009

ATTENTION ORGANIZATIONS AND CORPORATIONS:
This book is available at quantity discounts on bulk purchases for educational,
business, or sales promotional use. For further information, please contact
Impact Publishers, P.O. Box 6016, Atascadero, California 93423-6016. Phone:
1-800-246-7228, e-mail: sales@impactpublishers.com

Library of Congress Cataloging-in-Publication Data

Kassinove, Howard
   Anger management : the complete treatment guidebook for
practitioners / Howard Kassinove, Raymond Chip Tafrate
     p. cm. — (The practical therapist series)
   Includes bibliographical references and index.
   ISBN 1-886230-45-5 (alk. paper)
  1. Anger. 2. Conflict management. I. Tafrate, Raymond Chip.
     II. Title. III. Series.

BF575.A5 K37 2002
152.4'7—dc21

2002073678

Impact Publishers and colophon are registered trademarks of Impact
Publishers, Inc.

Cover Design by Gayle Downs, Gayle Force Design, Atascadero, California.
Printed in the United States of America on acid-free, recycled paper.
Published by **Impact 🕮 Publishers**®
     POST OFFICE BOX 6016
  ATASCADERO, CALIFORNIA 93423-6016
     www.impactpublishers.com

Dedicated to:

Tina Kassinove, my wife and best friend. She is the most supportive, rational, and accepting woman I know. For so many years she has graciously shared me with "Tillie" and "Tallulah," two of my many computers.

Andrew Kassinove, M.D. and Jeffrey Kassinove, Ph.D., my sons, and my mother Judith Kassinove, who have taught me so much about life.

— Howard Kassinove

Lauren Tafrate, my wife, who by her eloquent example has taught me patience, understanding, and selflessness.

Jacob Tafrate, my son, who serves as a reminder that the time spent with those you love is life's most valuable gift.

— R. Chip Tafrate

Contents

Section 5: Maintaining Change

Section 6: Working On Our Own Anger

Section 7: Sample Treatment Programs

Acknowledgements

P ractitioners and scientists do not work in isolation. Whether it is in a clinic, hospital, prison, school, university, or other setting, each of us engages in collaborative efforts to develop intervention programs that will be of help to members of our community and society. Therefore, we would like to give mention, and say "thank you" to those colleagues who have collaborated with us over the years and have shaped much of our thinking. These include:

Jerry Deffenbacher, Ph.D., ABPP	Professor of Psychology Colorado State University
Raymond DiGiuseppe, Ph.D., ABPP	Professor of Psychology St. John's University
Christopher I. Eckhardt, Ph.D.	Assistant Professor of Psychology Southern Methodist University
Albert Ellis, Ph.D., ABPP	Executive Director Albert Ellis Institute
Eva Feindler, Ph.D.	Professor of Psychology C.W. Post College
J. Ryan Fuller, M.A.	Doctoral Candidate Hofstra University
J. Christopher Muran, Ph.D.	Director, Psychotherapy Research Project Beth Israel Hospital
Usha Ram, Ph.D.	Reader University of Pune, India
Kurt Salzinger, Ph.D.	Director, Science Directorate American Psychological Association
Charles Spielberger, Ph.D., ABPP	Distinguished Research Professor University of South Florida
Denis G. Sukhodolsky, Ph.D	Post Doctoral Fellow Yale University
Junko Tanaka-Matsumi, Ph.D.	Professor of Psychology Kwansei Gakuin University, Kobe City,Japan

Sergei V. Tsytsarev, Ph.D.	Associate Professor of Psychology
	Hofstra University
Julia R. Vane, Ph.D, ABPP (deceased)	Professor of Psychology
	Hofstra University
Joseph Wolpe, M.D. (deceased)	Professor, Pepperdine University and
	Temple University Medical School
	Temple University School of Medicine

We also thank the many other students, colleagues, family members, and clients/patients who provided thoughtful suggestions about anger and anger disorders during interactions at professional and scientific meetings, during our workshops on anger, and in psychotherapy sessions. Although they are too numerous to mention by name, we are most grateful.

Special mention goes to Jeffrey I. Kassinove, Ph.D., Assistant Professor of Psychology at Monmouth University, Joseph Netto, M.A., doctoral candidate at Hofstra University, and Joseph Scardapane, Ph.D., Director of Hofstra's Psychological Evaluation and Research Clinic, for the thoughtful suggestions they gave when reading parts of the manuscript. Jeff spent many hours reading and giving comments, which we resisted at first, but which turned out to be exceptionally helpful as the manuscript moved toward its final form. We also had highly supportive and insightful input from our editor, Bob Alberti, Ph.D., himself a psychologist and an expert in assertiveness and social skills. He worked closely with us, from beginning to end, and we truly appreciated his base of knowledge, energy, and timely feedback. We also thank Carriann Mulcahy of Central Connecticut State University, Sharon Skinner and Jean Trumbull at Impact Publishers, Kathy Richardson and Kathleen White at K.A. White Design for their very important "behind the scenes" support.

Scientists generate and test hypotheses about anger, sometimes in sterile laboratory environments. In contrast, therapist-practitioners are on the front line in the war against dysfunctional anger. They use the knowledge and techniques generated by scientists to develop individualized treatment plans. In turn, the scientists use feedback from therapist-practitioners to refine those intervention techniques which require improvement. To those practitioners and scientists who have shaped our thinking, and to those practitioners who work so hard to reduce anger in our society, we extend our heartfelt thanks for trying to make this world a better place.

Foreword

Howard Kassinove and Raymond Chip Tafrate describe their book as "the complete guidebook for practitioners." I think they are right. Although I have written two books on anger management myself, including the newly revised edition of *Anger: How To Live With It and Without It* (New York: Citadel Press, 2002), I must admit that *Anger Management: The Complete Guidebook for Practitioners* goes beyond them in some respects. While it is hardly "perfectly" complete, this guidebook for practitioners is much more thoroughgoing than other books on the subject, and it covers the complex field of the psychological treatment of anger remarkably well.

As the authors (experienced clinicians who have published some excellent research studies on anger management themselves) note, *Anger Management* includes seven detailed sections which cover the basics of anger and the anger episode model; preparing for change; changing; accepting, adapting, and adjusting; maintaining change; working on the therapist's own anger; and provide sample anger management treatment programs. Each of these sections of the guidebook are quite thoroughgoing and complete.

All eighteen chapters include exceptionally relevant and important materials from which any practitioner is likely to benefit. Moreover, the materials presented by the authors are written in clear-cut, highly readable language, with their main points accurately presented. Good — in fact, great!

As the founder of Rational Emotive Behavior Therapy (REBT), the first major cognitive behavior therapy, and the first to stress that anger management had better include thinking, feeling, and behavioral methods, I was naturally drawn to chapters 13 and 14 of this guidebook. Chapter 13 describes Aaron Beck's techniques of Cognitive Therapy (CT) and chapter 14 presents some of the main techniques of REBT in helping people minimize their anger. Both are well-written chapters and show the many similarities, as well as the main differences, between these approaches. As Kassinove and Tafrate state, the Beckian approach helps clients to more accurately perceive the triggers of their anger, while the Ellisonian approach "is the most elegant of approaches, since the goal is to develop a lowered level of angry reactivity through a philosophical shift about the world." I would agree with this main difference in the two approaches. But, I would also like to point out that the REBT approach distinctly stresses emotional-evocative-experiential techniques more than does Cognitive Therapy. I think the highly emotive aspects of REBT and its' approach to anger management are quite important for the practitioner.

The rest of the chapters of the guidebook, as I noted above, cover many different and important methods and show how therapists, counselors, teachers, and trainers can effectively use them. Let me especially note that chapter 16, Relapse Prevention, and chapter 17, Anger Reduction for Practitioners, include some important points from which every anger therapist can appreciably benefit.

Once again, this guidebook describes useful multimodal and comprehensive approaches for teaching clients and others how to reduce and manage anger. Remarkably well done and very worthwhile reading.

Albert Ellis, Ph.D.
(1913-2007)

Introduction

Mental health practitioners usually have little personal experience with the problems they treat. They may provide interventions for phobias, without ever having suffered with the limitations of being phobic. They may provide counseling to prison inmates, without having been incarcerated themselves. Or, they may focus on marriage counseling while living in a stress-free, happy, loving bond with a spouse.

Anger is different! It is a very common human response, experienced frequently by persons of all ages, backgrounds, and occupations. Hardly a person exists who has not experienced anger. Marriage counselors, social workers, psychologists, medical doctors, prison and school personnel, and practitioners in industry have all had first-hand anger experiences. And, practitioners have often been the target of another person's anger, including their clients' anger.

Chon (2000) noted that anger appears in both Western and Eastern cultures, that it has been a part of ancient as well as contemporary theories of emotion, and that it has been included in Confucian as well as Indian writings (Aquinas, 1225-1274; Averill, 1987; Ekman, 1992; Hahn & Chon, 1991; Izard, 1992, Plutchik, 1980, 1994, 2000; Schweder, 1993; Shaver, Schwartz, Kirson, & O'Conner, 1987). Because it is so widespread and appears in almost every emotion theory, Chon (2000) concluded, ". . . anger appears to be a fundamental and vital human emotion, the experience of which appears to be universal" (p. 148).

Unfortunately, for some people anger becomes highly problematic and they may be judged to have an *anger disorder.* When judged objectively, their anger is *excessive in frequency and duration,* and is *disproportionate to the event or person* who triggered it. For these people, anger leads to highly negative outcomes and an anger management program is appropriate. In this book, our goal is to provide practitioners with an understanding of the "basics" of anger and with a management plan that can be selectively modified for use in independent practice and institutional settings.

Anger management refers to the reduction of disruptive, excessive angry arousal and expression. The goal is to teach clients to react to the stressors of life with minimal and infrequent anger and, when it is experienced, to

1

express the anger appropriately. We believe this is best accomplished by a combination of *knowledge development* and *behavioral practice*. Thus, it is first important for clients to *understand* exactly what anger is, how it is related to other emotions, when it is adaptive or maladaptive, and why it is important to reduce maladaptive anger. Then, with the help of mental health professionals, clients engage in office-based and *in-vivo* practice to develop more adaptive reactions to the stressors of life.

We believe that it is *critical for clients and practitioners to share the same base of knowledge* about anger. The knowledge base inc ludes:

- A shared definition of "anger," to allow for its differentiation from other emotional states,
- Awareness of the stimuli which are likely to trigger anger reactions,
- Understanding the anger experience itself and the ways that anger may be expressed,
- Understanding the difference between normal, or adaptive, and maladaptive anger reactions,
- Recognition of the many (but mostly negative) consequences associated with intense, frequent, and persistent anger, and
- Recognition that, irrespective of the external cause, the client contributes significantly to his or her own anger experiences

An understanding of these ideas provides the foundation for the *anger management program*. Once presented by the practitioner, and accepted by the client, this knowledge base is likely to increase the motivation of clients to develop healthier reactions to aversive situations. The program, thus, is based on two principles:

- *With knowledge about the causes of anger and the many problems associated with frequent, strong, and persistent anger, motivation to change increases.*
- *Change itself comes from practitioner-guided, reinforced practice of new behaviors.*

The chapters are organized into six sections. In section 1, *The Basics*, we first address the relationship of angry arousal to cognitive and motor performance. We then formally define anger and differentiate it from the related concepts and experiences of hostility and aggression. Next, we present our *anger episode model* that consists of five dimensions: *triggers, appraisals, experiences, expressive patterns,* and *outcomes*. Consideration is given to the difference between healthy and problematic anger, and to the outcomes that follow anger episodes. We hope this information will serve as a common base of knowledge for practitioners and clients, and we encourage discussion and sharing during the early phase of treatment. A collaboratively planned anger intervention program, wherein the practitioner and client work as a team, holds the greatest likelihood for success. We then discuss anger assessment and diagnosis. Elements of anger assessment are presented as they are related to the anger script. That is, the combination of private thoughts and the overt behaviors that we define as "anger." In the final chapter of Section 1, we present an overview of the anger management program.

In section 2, *Preparing for Change*, consideration is given to the factors that underlie change. We discuss motivation and the therapeutic alliance, and present some ideas about increasing client awareness of anger. These are critical elements to an anger management program, since many angry clients initially have low motivation to change.

Clients can be self-referred, referred by friends or colleagues or family members, or a teacher or the criminal justice system may mandate them for treatment. The best treatment outcomes are likely with self-referred clients, as they recognize their problems and possess the greatest motivation to change. The poorest outcomes are likely for mandated clients from the school or criminal justice system (e.g., "See the school psychologist for counseling or you will be suspended for three weeks," or "Attend a ten-session anger management program or go to jail for two months"). In the middle are clients who are referred by others. For them, motivation is typically marginal or variable.

Referral by others is common in anger management clients. After a suggestion by a friend, family member, or colleague, or an employee assistance program, the referred client arrives voluntarily but with a good deal of skepticism. He or she may not yet agree that a real problem exists and may not be committed to attending a multiple-session and perhaps costly program. The client may be ambivalent about change and not understand the negative effects of anger. And, unfortunately, the client may believe that a little insight, as opposed to a lot of practice, is what will lead to improvement. Therefore, the preparation phase concerns the underlying interpersonal and motivational factors that increase the likelihood of success.

Section 3 presents strategies to help clients change, so they can deal better with their anger triggers. Clients and practitioners often agree that change is the goal. However, each party often sees "change" differently. Practitioners recognize that the world is a pretty difficult place that is filled with disappointment, conflict, frustration, violence and evil. They want clients to change by developing better skills to solve problems so that less anger will emerge. In contrast, clients typically want others to change. In their view, all of their frustrations, anger and bitterness, and problems would disappear if only their spouse, or child, or boss, or colleague, or friends, or political leaders, would change. Once clients realize that they themselves have to act better, they become more ready to learn how and when to avoid or escape from difficult situations when a "cooling off" period may be helpful, to manage their own bodily arousal, to develop new life skills to achieve their goals, and to become less reactive by practicing relaxation and coping skills while purposely exposing themselves to problems.

In contrast, Section 4 focuses on adjustment strategies to help clients accept the often unpleasant realities of life. After all, no matter how many skills we have, many circumstances are beyond our control. Aversive triggers such as a job loss, strong disagreements with others, or neglect, will occur no matter how good our skills. Much anger, it turns out, is caused by errors in cognitive processing of aversive triggers. Clients jump to conclusions and see the world inaccurately, or they minimize their personal ability to cope with perceived adversity while maximizing the seriousness of the difficulty being faced. Thus, we present techniques to help clients interpret reality accurately, to accept reality and adjust to it, and to forgive and move forward as an alternative to ongoing rumination. It is important for the practitioner to help clients differentiate letting go of the past, living in the present, and preparing for the future.

Finally, in Section 5, we conclude the formal anger management program as we discuss the maintenance of change and *relapse prevention*. The literature in the area of addictions and habit disorders has shown that change is not linear. Clients take two steps forward and one backward. When they take the backward step they often conclude that no "real" improvement has occurred and total failure is imminent, and they may "give up" working on their anger. In addition, from the literature on learning and conditioning we understand that after bad habits are eliminated there is typically a period of spontaneous recovery. That is, unwanted anger reemerges. In relapse prevention clients are given the awareness that change is an "up and down" process. Then, they develop skills to deal with the down moments so that continued slippage or program abandonment will not occur.

We conclude with "Anger Reduction for Practitioners" (chapter 17) and "Sample Anger Management Programs" (chapter 18). Anger is such a common part of life that practitioners also often become angry. In fact, one of the triggers for practitioner anger is client behavior. Thus, we offer some ideas about anger reduction for practitioners themselves. After all, it is best if we can model good behavior for clients. And, by reducing our own anger we, also, are likely to live better lives. We then briefly present some possible session-by-session programs for use in special situations.

A note is in order about terminology. These days, many terms are used for the recipient of professional mental health services. The same individual may be called a *client, consumer, group member, inmate, offender, participant, patient, service recipient, student,* or yet another label. Throughout most of this book we refer to "clients," since it is a broad term that is used in many settings. When it seemed appropriate, because the setting would dictate treatment modifications, we have used other terms such as "offender-client." Of course, the scientific principles and treatment procedures are generic and apply equally, no matter how the individual is labeled.

Anger has been experienced to varying degrees by all of us. Nevertheless, when compared to anxiety and depression, it has been relatively ignored in the scientific and professional literature. Thus, we hope this book will provide knowledge and techniques, useful for both clients and practitioners, to help all of us deal more effectively with problematic anger.

Howard Kassinove, PhD, ABPP
Raymond Chip Tafrate, PhD

1 ❖

THE BASICS

Anger

Holding on to anger is like grasping a hot coal with the intent of throwing it at someone else; you are the one who gets burned.
— Buddha

Buddha was right! Like holding a hot coal, it is often the person, or the family or group that gets burned by anger. We can give a personal example. Following a heated and "unfair" ping-pong match between two of our adolescent sons, the younger boy became very angry and threw the paddle against the sheet rock wall, causing a gaping hole. He was punished, there was friction in the family, and it was costly to repair the wall. No one benefited from the anger. Nevertheless, anger is a pervasive social response that may be both useful and normal or disruptive and abnormal. When anger is low to moderate in intensity, and the problem at hand is relatively easy, anger may be useful. Anger triggered by a disrespectful salesperson might motivate us to talk to the store manager or write a letter of complaint, which is usually an easy task to accomplish. Or, if people are talking loudly in a movie theater we may become annoyed and request that they quiet down. Again, this is usually a relatively easy task to accomplish.

In contrast, when anger is strong, and the task is complex, it often leads to problems. It would certainly be difficult to successfully repair the tiny mechanism of a fine old watch while infuriated by the insults of a coworker. As a pianist, it would be difficult to play Liszt's *Hungarian Rhapsody #2* at the finest level while in an agitated state of brooding about a recent argument with a friend. And, tennis players are unlikely to play at their optimal level while in a state of rage. In addition to inferior motor performance, there are also cognitive consequences of anger. Thus, it is unlikely that spouses will see all of the conflict resolution possibilities to repair a deteriorating relationship while screaming at each other. And, teachers who are angry with their students, in response to very poor performance on a test, are unlikely to consider all of the possibilities to help educate them better. Problems emerge when anger reactions are too strong, when anger occurs too frequently, and when the task is complex. Anger also creates problems when it endures and remains unresolved. Under such conditions, we become overpowered and unable to handle the intellectual and behavioral challenges that would otherwise be easily managed.

❖ *Angry Arousal and Performance*

If your heart is a volcano, how shall you expect flowers to bloom?
— Kahlil Gibran

Known to scholars and professionals as the Yerkes-Dodson Law (1908), one of the first points of knowledge for angry clients to learn is that they are more likely to cope effectively with the stressors of daily life if their angry arousal is low to moderate rather than extreme (Figure 1-1).

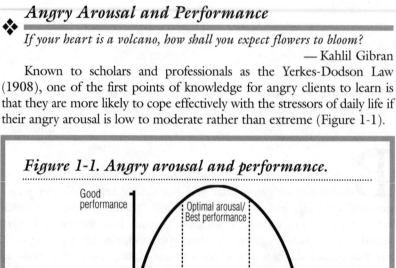

Figure 1-1. Angry arousal and performance.

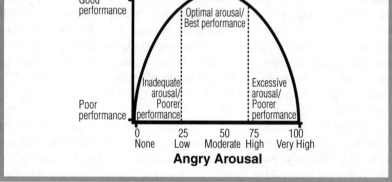

Consider, Robert, a 17-year-old high school senior who is sleeping and, thus, is near the zero level of arousal. His muscles are relaxed and his cerebral cortex and sympathetic autonomic nervous system are inactive. In this state there is little response to ordinary stimulation. It is 7:00 a.m.

Suddenly, the alarm clock rings. Robert automatically turns it off, and rolls over in bed. Ten minutes later his mother yells, "Get up! You're going to be late for school, again! What's wrong with you anyway? You're about to apply to college and need good grades. You won't be accepted anywhere. Please! Get up, now!" The yelling is a strong stimulus. His muscles and glands respond automatically, and their secretions lead to more bodily feedback. Robert is now awake and annoyed. He yells, "Leave me alone! I'll make it on time. You know, you really don't know what you are talking about." After more shouting, he takes a shower, gets dressed, eats breakfast, and sleepily goes off to school.

It is now 10:30 a.m. Robert's body has reached an optimal level of arousal. He is alert and is responding efficiently to his teachers and friends. However, he hasn't forgotten the way his mother treated him — and he hasn't forgiven her. He tells three friends about the argument, thus mentally rehearsing it. In class, he ruminates about his mother's words and misses some of the lecture material.

After lunch, and two more classes, Robert goes to the school library to find a book required to complete an important term paper. But, it is missing from the shelf. The term paper is difficult, intellectually complex, and challenging. It requires that Robert integrate materials from the past two months of classroom lectures in his History and Spanish classes. The paper is due in two days! It is now 2:15 p.m. He asks the librarian for help but she calmly says, "It seems to be missing. I don't know where it is. We'll just have to wait and see if it turns up." This new frustration produces an increment in his agitation, which was primed by the earlier interaction with his mother. As he listens to the words of the librarian he feels angry. He thinks, "That bitch! She doesn't care!" He returns to the shelves, to continue to search for the book.

As he looks at the books, he ruminates about the lack of help provided by the librarian, and thinks of how critical the report is for his grade and his future. And, it is due in just two days! Maybe his mother was right. Maybe he won't get into a good college. He blames the librarian and begins to catastrophize about the problem. "It's not my fault that I can't find the book," he thinks, "Some dumb jerk didn't return it, or some dumb clerk didn't return it to its proper shelf. That stupid librarian probably flunked her own courses in college. And, anyhow, she is really ugly!" He thinks, "This is the end. My mother was right." His anger and agitation increase.

After 30 minutes of frustration, rumination, blame, and self-doubt, Robert leaves, then meets up with a group of friends, including Vanessa, a girl he would like to impress. Wanting to join them, he says, "Hi, where are you going?" Without answering, one friend starts to tease him about his hair cut. He wonders, self-consciously, if it is as bad as the friend is implying. He becomes furious, curses under his breath at his friend, and is ready to react strongly to any new problem. Thinking of the girl, he becomes quite angry at the friend — way out of proportion to the tease. Suddenly, Robert recalls a pimple on his nose that he saw in the mirror earlier in the morning. Is it still there? Did she see it? Are they laughing at him behind his back? What about his hair? Robert slinks away, very angry and embarrassed.

Robert was supposed to spend the rest of the afternoon working on the term paper. But, at this point he is so mad that his cognitive processes consist of a stream of distorted and angry thoughts about his mother, the librarian, his so-called friend, the girl he wanted to impress, etc. He is filled with a combination of anger, blame, self-doubt and pessimism. His capacity for creative thinking and the generation of alternate solutions regarding the paper is totally blocked. Robert probably couldn't find the library book now if it was right under his nose, and he is convinced his chances with the girl are ruined. The optimal level of arousal he experienced at 10:30 a.m. has disappeared, replaced by disruptive anger based disorganization. In this state of brooding, rumination, anger, and embarrassment, he is ready to argue with anyone unfortunate enough to cross his path.

With regard to emotions such as anger, the Yerkes-Dodson Law notes:

1. *Optimal cognitive and motor performance is generally associated with a moderate level of arousal.*

Unfortunately, Robert's arousal is already too high. Primed by the morning interaction with his mother, and fueled by the frustration in the library and the teasing by his friend, Robert's angry arousal is much greater than optimal. He is unlikely to make decisions in a rational and thoughtful manner. And, it is probably wise for others to stay out of his way. Any provocation at this point could easily lead to a verbal or physical assault.

2. *Optimal arousal depends on the difficulty of the task.*

Anger is less likely to interfere if the task is easy and well-practiced, as with making a telephone call to a friend one has called 100 times before. Anger is more likely to interfere in unfamiliar or complex situations that require concentration and thinking about multiple possibilities.

Robert's present task (the term paper) is complex and difficult. Even with moderate anger he is likely to make mistakes, including inadequate decisions about which materials to include in the paper. He may forget to run his paper through the spell checker of his word processor, potentially leading to a poorer grade. He may become confused about the due date of the paper. His grade may be lowered if he hands it in a day or two late. He may prepare it on time, but forget to bring it to school (after yet another negative interaction with his mother). Or, in a fit of agitation and rage, he may be unable to locate the project on his computer or might inadvertently delete it from his hard drive. *In a state of strong anger and rage, Murphy's Law is likely to take hold — anything bad that might happen, will!*

Robert would do better if he could reduce his strong anger-based agitation to a milder state of annoyance. His present situation is clearly not good. True, his mother was disrespectful to him. True, the book is not available. True, his good friend teased him. And true, there was a pimple on his face. At this point, it would certainly be inappropriate to be happy. At the same time, strong anger, fury and rage are not helpful. Robert's task is to learn to respond to the accumulating aversive situations in his life with moderate arousal (i.e., annoyance).

Why do we perform better at lower levels of angry arousal? The cue-utilization hypothesis suggests that we use cues from the environment to solve problems and complete other complex tasks (Easterbrook, 1959). When under-aroused we pay little attention to cues, as when Robert was waking up from his night's sleep. At moderate levels of arousal, we optimally process the cues around us and select those that are most relevant. However, as angry arousal increases we again attend to fewer cues and, instead, focus only on specific (anger) triggers. Performance then deteriorates, since we don't attend to all of the available possibilities to solve the problem at hand. Robert's needed library book, for example, might be purchased at a local bookstore, or on the internet, or it might be found in the community library. It might be even lying on a cart next to the librarian's desk, waiting to be re-shelved. But, with increased angry arousal, he is focused only on the bookshelves — where it is *supposed* to be! He may not attend to the visual stimulus (the book) on the library cart, and he doesn't generate alternative solutions.

Does this sound improbable? Consider those times when you've been unable to find the keys to the car, especially when you're late for work and others are waiting. You search your desk, or the pants or coat you wore yesterday, to no avail. As you become frantic, your spouse joins in the search – only to discover the keys are on the desk under a piece of paper that you didn't think to move. The answer was right in front of you! This scenario has happened to both authors more than once.

As anger increases, we neglect cues, do not engage in thoughtful and systematic examination of problems, and do not generate solutions. For example, how might Robert's teacher react if he asked for a time extension so that he could locate the book? Perhaps negatively or maybe quite positively. He won't know unless he asks. And, he has to generate "asking for help" as a possible solution. The authors of this manual are both university professors. Both have seen cases where we would have responded positively to students — had they only explained their problems in a timely fashion. Instead, they became overwhelmed, frustrated and angry, and came to us *after* course deadlines have passed. We have also worked with many highly intelligent clients who have made poor decisions about their marriages, children or jobs because angry arousal interfered with their usual good thinking. For people of all ages, backgrounds and community standing, the ability to solve problems rapidly diminishes as angry arousal increases.

❖ *Definitions*

Everything that is in agreement with our personal desires seems true. Everything that is not puts us in a rage.

— Andre Maurois

Since we believe that it is important for practitioners and clients to share the same base of information, we now present some formal definitions. We define *anger* and differentiate it from *hostility* and *aggression*, as a prelude to introducing the anger management program.

Anger. Kassinove and Sukhodolsky (1995) defined anger as a *felt emotional state*. This private state varies in intensity and duration, as well as frequency, and is associated with cognitive distortions, verbal and motor behaviors, and patterns of physical arousal. Although anger may emerge spontaneously, another person is typically seen as the cause of anger. And, it usually includes a perception of blameworthiness.

Anger is not a form of aggression, and most often does not lead to aggression! Rather, it is a felt experience that typically follows unwanted, aversive interactions with close friends, colleagues, and family members. Although anger is common, and sometimes useful, it can become an independent problem with many negative consequences, requiring treatment in the context of individual, couples, or family therapy in private practice or institutional settings.

Intensity. Some anger episodes are mild, while others are quite strong. In addition, the intensity of anger varies within any single episode. This is reflected in the observation that anger may build as more and more "fuel is put on the fire." Alternatively, anger may begin suddenly at a relatively high level and then taper off. Anger outbursts, which begin at a very high intensity, are common for some people and may result from minor triggers. For example, in one case, office workers became uncomfortable when the temperature reached 72º and they repeatedly turned the thermostat down to 68º to increase the air conditioning flow. When the boss, Bert, noticed this, he would immediately explode in an angry rage, shouting and cursing for about 30 seconds that he was in charge and didn't want to waste the firms' money. Then, he immediately returned to his calm state and, to the surprise of those who didn't know him, would talk in a very composed manner. We have also worked with clients who would become intensely angry at the slightest indication of negative feedback, believing that we weren't on their side regarding some conflict in their lives. Some clients have raised their voices, criticized us strongly and, on occasion, have even cursed at us. These clients usually distorted our feedback and attached unique, personal meaning to our attempts to help them to see the situation from a different perspective. Unfortunately for them, this pattern also occurred outside of counseling and created damage to their work and social relationships.

At lower intensity levels, angry feeling states are identified by words such as "irritated, annoyed, goaded, bothered, (and) displeased." At the middle range the experience may be labeled directly as "angered, aggravated, antagonized, indignant, (or) mad." At very strong levels it is often called "crazed, enraged, rabid, unhinged, (or) wild." Words at the lower level of intensity often reflect only the internal, phenomenological feeling state. In contrast, words at higher levels of intensity may also reflect behavioral disorganization. Unfortunately, after much examination of the issue, we have concluded that there is little agreement as to the intensity of feeling represented by various anger words. While most readers would probably agree that "annoyed" represents a less intense state than "rage," there is less agreement about words such as "mad" and "indignant." Which of the two is a more intense state? It turns out that verbal labels are rather imprecise and are not strongly related to specific motor behavior or physiological reactivity. Nevertheless, words are important as they serve to anchor practitioners and clients to a common understanding of the world. For this reason, we discuss below the importance of developing a shared *anger vocabulary*, partially based on an anger thermometer, so that practitioners and clients develop a common meaning to anger words.

Of course, some clients act as though they will achieve more of their goals with hyperbole (e.g., "My wife spends *all* of her time with her friend Rebecca. And, she is *never* home and *never* cleans the house. I'm absolutely *furious!*") than with realistic identification of the intensity of their anger (e.g., "My wife spends *many* afternoons with her friend Rebecca. I feel really *annoyed* and *jealous*. She's *often* not home when I arrive at 6 p.m., and the house *often* looks like it hasn't been cleaned at all"). Of course, few angry clients think in advance about the goal of their communications to others. In this example, hopefully, the assertive expression of feeling would lead to improved communication and a plan for spending time together. Hyperbolic, catastrophizing, blaming communications remind us of the little boy who continually cried "Wolf." Eventually, these communications lose meaning and lead to less responding from significant others.

Duration: Some anger episodes are fleeting. The anger emerges and the person may explode with great intensity. Then, as suddenly as it came, it is over. This was true in the case of Bert, mentioned above, who might have been diagnosed with an "intermittent explosive disorder."

At the other extreme some clients *seethe* for days, months, or even years. They have a kind of *festering, ruminative anger* that is truly enduring and problematic. The initial intensity may be low, moderate, or high and the anger may build over time. For some, little annoyances are remembered and repeatedly rehearsed. After their anger finally emerges, these clients have a whole "laundry list" of annoyances that may seem trivial to the listener. For the client, however, they have become very important.

In other cases, the initial event may have truly been traumatic and overpowering, such as clients who have suffered rape, physical abuse, or torture. Although it is enduring, these clients may not talk about their anger for years, until they finally work with a competent understanding practitioner or are otherwise encouraged to speak up. For example, after filming *Schindler's List,* Steven Spielberg established the 1994 Survivors of the Shoah Visual History Foundation to preserve the testimonies of Holocaust survivors. More than 50,000 eyewitness testimonies have been collected. Many of these survivors, filled with anger and rage for many years, would not have come forth except for Spielberg's project. Another example is provided by the South African Truth and Reconciliation Commission established to help deal with the violence and human rights abuses under apartheid which occurred between 1960 and 1994. As noted by Dullah Omar, former Minister of Justice, *"... a commission is a necessary exercise to enable South Africans to come to terms with their past on a morally accepted basis and to advance the cause of reconciliation."* One goal is to restore dignity and formulate recommendations for rehabilitation and healing of survivors, their families and communities at large. The overall function of the commission has been to ensure non-repetition, healing and healthy co-existence. Without this commission, some victims may have suffered in angry silence, for years, with little possibility of putting past experiences in perspective and moving forward.

Frequency: Some people, high on anger as a personality trait, experience it frequently in response to many different triggers or problems, and in many different environments. These clients seem primed to become angry in almost any situation and others quickly learn to avoid them. In contrast, clients low on the anger trait experience it much less often. Their anger emerges only in response to a limited set of triggers, such as criticisms about their body, or their family, or their academic or work performance. Their anger may appear only in limited circumstances such as at home, at work, or in school. For example, we have always had informal relationships with our student assistants at the university and these have often included free-flowing, humorous teasing. In one recent case, however, a student made it very clear that while he *generally* enjoyed this kind of informal relationship, he did not want it to include any references to his mother. Although he was low on the anger trait, teasing about his mother was a specific and strong anger trigger.

Body Changes: Physiological changes are also associated with anger. Angry clients may sweat, become jittery or tremble, and feel their hearts race out of control during specific episodes of anger. They may experience muscle tension, tight jaws and headaches. In addition, they may observe their own clenched fists and other anger-related motor behaviors, such as a raised voice, or slamming a book on a desk. In all likelihood, as noted by James and Lange (see James, 1984), part of the experience of anger emerges from self-observations of these physiological reactions and motor behaviors.

Since it is almost impossible to be relaxed and angry at the same time, one of the first interventions we recommend is aimed at physical arousal reduction. Indeed, techniques such as deep muscle relaxation, meditation, and mindfulness training are among the most validated interventions for a wide variety of disorders (e.g., Alexander, Rainforth, & Gelderloos, 1991; Clum, Clum, & Surls, 1993; Dua & Swinden, 1992; Eppley, Abrams, & Shear, 1989; Hermann, Kim, & Blanchard, 1995; Jacobson, 1938; Johnston, & Voegele, 1993; Linden & Chambers, 1994; Speca, Carlson, Goodey, & Angen, 2000; Schopen & Freeman, 1992). As we note in chapter 9, these techniques have the benefits of being quickly learned, with no known side effects, thus increasing the credibility of the practitioner.

Distortions and Deficits: Anger is associated with well-recognized cognitive or perceptual distortions and deficiencies. These distorted ways of thinking lead clients to become, according to Beck (1999), "Prisoners of Hate." For example, John Gupta, a supervisor at the local shoe manufacturing plant was called upon to terminate an employee because of poor work performance. Although Mr. Gupta handled this unpleasant situation quite well by objective standards, the employee was very angry and wrongly believed that the termination occurred because Mr. Gupta didn't like employees of certain ethnic backgrounds. He told his family and friends that he "hated" Mr. Gupta. Yet, there was little Mr. Gupta could do to reduce the employee's anger, since it was based on *biased attributional thinking* about the cause of the termination. In another case, an angry employee who was terminated from his job engaged in *magnified disproportional thinking* by believing that the termination was the "worst thing that could happen" and believing that he would "never" get another job. In a third case, based on *demandingness* and *low tolerance for discordant events,* a father became enraged when his very bright, but poorly achieving son announced that he was quitting school. He told himself, "I can't believe it. He must be crazy to quit. I've got to get him to understand that he'll never get anywhere without an education! He really *has* to stay in school." Failure to understand the world from the perspective of others (a deficit), combined with distortions and inaccurate beliefs, magnify disappointment and anger out of proportion to the objective event. Once the anger is present, fewer options for problem solution are generated.

❖ The Big Picture: Anger is a Social Script

To this point, we have described *individual* elements of anger including frequency, intensity, duration, bodily arousal, and distorted thinking patterns. However, there may be a better and more global way to define anger. According to constructivists, anger is a role or a *socially constructed, reinforced behavioral script* that we learn to play. It consists of private thoughts, physiological reactions, and observable verbal and motor behaviors (e.g., Averill, 1982, 1983; Wessler, 1992). In the larger society, and in subgroups, multiple anger behaviors are learned and they typically appear together. In other words, we learn "how" and "when" to be angry. According to this view, anger is not a "thing" which exists and which can be easily deconstructed into its elements. Rather, anger is a relatively organized but *fuzzy concept* which, like other emotions, cannot be defined with absolute clarity (Russell & Fehr, 1994). Indeed, there is disagreement among scholars as to whether anger must always contain the element of blame or have a physiological or a behavioral component. Not everyone agrees on the subcategories of anger (e.g., annoyance, fury, etc.) or whether anger is different from hostility and aggression. A full discussion of these academic debates is well beyond the scope of this book. Suffice it to say that as it is used in everyday life, and in this manual, *anger refers to a mostly learned passion or emotion that is privately experienced and publicly shown by a person who lives in a certain culture.* Anger consists of an organized script that is partially inborn, but mostly develops as a function of learning in the family and at school, in religious training, through modeling of characters we observe on TV and elsewhere.

Although this social constructivist perspective may at first seem unfamiliar, in actuality *we all learn how to act when "angry"* and *we learn when to become angry.* For example, consider various broad differences among cultures. In some Arab cultures men learn to become angry if a woman just shows her face in public. In contrast, in France and Monaco it is quite usual for women to appear bare-breasted on the beach and this behavior elicits no anger at all. In the United States one is likely to become angry to discover that one's spouse has a lover. In contrast, other cultures allow for polygamy and their members have little reaction, not even annoyance, when the spouse is having sex with another person. Thus, "anger" is learned in terms of the specific people, objects, and behaviors to which we react.

Practitioners can expect *verbal* differences in the anger script as a function of gender, socioeconomic level, age, regional background, or country of origin. In Russian, for example, a mild and perhaps childish verbal way to exhibit anger to others would be to say, "Ti tupoi kak pyen." This means, "You are stupid as a tree stump." If an adolescent or adult were moderately angry, the phrase "Ti gandon!" might be shouted. This means, "You are a condom!" and it implies stupidity without evil intent. Finally, a very strong expression of anger would be, "Ti peerdaras!" That is, "You are a child molester." However, there would be no implication of a sexual offense in this phrase. Rather, it is simply a very strong expression of anger. The important point is that Americans in the United States would use none of these phrases. Americans, however, have phrases to express angry displeasure that do not exist elsewhere. Most clients from other countries, for example, have difficulty with the phrase, "You're as dumb as a doornail!" Such idiomatic differences suggest that there are learned, cultural norms in the verbal portion of the anger script.

There are also differences in the *behavioral* construction of the anger script. Some evidence, for example, suggests that women are more likely to cry when angry while boys and men may be more likely to be aggressive when angry (Averill, 1982; Kassinove, et. al, 1997; Buntaine & Costenbader, 1997). Lower socio-economic status clients and teenagers may be more likely to use profanity (Martin, 1997). Clients from the southern part of the United States may be more likely to aggress while angry (Nisbett, 1993) and Japanese-Americans may be less direct in their expressions than others (Komahashi, Ganesan, Ohmori, et. al. 1997; Aune & Aune, 1996). Certainly, North Americans seem cool and reserved to many persons from more expressive Latin cultures. At the same time, North and South Americans may seem overly warm and inappropriately expressive to persons from Asian cultures.

Part of the anger script is inborn and developed in our evolutionary past as part of the useful "flight or fight" motor reaction. In animals, this part consists of motor behaviors and may include squirting fowl smelling liquids (skunks), making noises (rattle snakes), shooting quills (porcupines), etc. As further described in chapter 9, we carry much of this animal past in our behavior and this is certainly true for angry behavior. Our facial expressions seem to be universal and have been retained from our evolutionary history along with some motor behaviors (e.g., Biehl, Matsumoto, Ekman, et. al, 1997). Cartoonists have been particularly able to capture these non-verbal aspects of our anger script. As shown in Figure 1-2, they are experts in depicting the facial expressions, motor behaviors, and fantasies associated with anger. The ease with which we recognize anger in cartoons confirms the identifiable and cohesive nature of the script.

Figure 1-2. Expressions of the anger script.

The human anger script is both innately programmed *and* learned. Facial expressions and responses to some triggers may be universal, but we also learn what is supposed to be unacceptable and aversive, when it is appropriate to act with anger, when to shout and point our fingers, or what the likely interpersonal consequences will be in any given situation. This anger script includes *cognitive distortions* as reflected in inflammatory and demeaning thoughts about the person or situation leading to the anger (e.g., "That stupid bastard. He never tried to understand me and has always been out to get me. I can't stand him"), *arousal* (e.g., increased heart rate, sweating, etc.), *expressive motor behaviors* (e.g., pointing a finger at an offending person, slamming a telephone into its' cradle, clenched fists, a tight mouth), and *verbal anger labels* reflecting the specificity and intensity of our subjective feeling (e.g., annoyed, enraged, etc.). These labels are often generated by reading our own bodies (e.g., noticing that we are yelling) and are reflected in statements such as "I feel totally enraged!" or "I feel agitated and confused."

Other parts of the anger script are:

- Raised voice: i.e., well beyond the norm for the client.

- Accusatory content: e.g., "You did it on purpose, didn't you? Why don't you tell me the truth?"

- Sarcastic content: e.g., "You're a *real* genius, huh?"

- Harsh tone: e.g., "Why didn't you think of the effect of your actions had on me?" (said sharply)

- Profanity: e.g., "You bastard!"

- Gestures: e.g., pointing a finger

- Body posture: e.g., leaning forward; looking down at the target of the anger

- Strong words   e.g., "I absolutely *hate* her and will *never* forgive her!"

Figure 1-3. The anger script.

The script also defines what is *not* a part of anger. For example, we don't put a finger in our ear or laugh or scratch our kneecap when angry. And, although we may do so with sarcasm, we don't honestly complement the target of our anger. These behaviors don't fit the typical anger script.

It is the whole constellation of responses that defines anger. No single part of the script alone is a sure sign of anger as there are *individual, group,* and *cultural differences* in the experience and expression of anger. When angry, some people scream while others pout. Some have aggressive fantasies, while others do not. Some demean the target of their anger, but others do not. Not all clients will raise their voices when angry and not all will use profanity. In fact, some clients will lower their voice when they become angry. Some never use profanity or sarcasm. Instead, they express their anger directly. And, although many clients gesture while angry, some do not. As an example of individual differences, we know of a woman who mumbles "6-21-3-11" when she becomes angry. These numbers reflect letters of the alphabet, as in "F," etc.

In summary, anger is a privately felt emotional state of varying intensity with associated verbal and motor behaviors, bodily responses, cognitive distortions and deficits, verbal labels, and interpersonal effects. It may occur frequently or infrequently, and it may be fleeting or enduring. Given the wide variability in anger experiences, it is probably best for practitioners to begin their examination with self-reports from the client. Indeed, it is the role of the practitioner, with the help of the client, to identify the client's individual anger scripts. Such reports pave the way for an intervention program in which each client's anger script is modified by a collaborative effort of the practitioner and the angry client.

Hostility. Hostility is defined as a set of *attitudes* or semi-permanent thoughts about a person, institution or group. Clients may express hostility with phrases such as, "She's such a bitch. I can never trust her" or "I hate those damn . . . (ethnic group). They deserve to suffer." Hostile attitudes are held with varying *degrees of conviction* (Abelson, 1987). Those that are *central*, in the sense of being a defining part of the client, have typically been held for a long time, are shared by friends and family members, and the client may donate money or work for a special interest group to promote the attitudes. Centrally held beliefs, which are held with great conviction, can represent ideas defined by most members of society as positive (e.g., "Save the Whales") or negative (e.g., ideas about "NAMBLA," a group which promotes sexual activity between men and boys). Consider some of the attitudes held about Jews, Catholics, Muslims, gays and lesbians, southerners, blacks, the elderly, the physically handicapped. It is easy to imagine the anger and bitterness that can be affiliated with such attitudes. And, when they are central to a client's self-definition, reflect long-held suspicions of other people or groups, and have been reinforced by family and peers for long periods of time, they can be almost impossible to change. For example, in some countries in the Middle East people have maintained deeply held hostile attitudes toward each other for years, leading to conflicts and wars, which go on to this day and have resisted many change efforts. The attitudes of the terrorists who planned and destroyed the World Trade towers in New York in September 2001 were certainly a critical variable in their behavior. Centrally held attitudes are difficult to change.

In contrast, *surface attitudes* are rather easily changed, often with simple logic. Young children, for example, have little experience in the world. If asked whether guns are dangerous, they may initially say "yes," based on what has been taught in school. However, if the child's parent is a gun owner or gun advocate the child's attitudes may very quickly become more positive after talking with the parent. Or, a client may have little experience with the elderly but may, nevertheless, believe they all are mentally rigid and old fashioned. Yet, after working for a few days in a home for the aged, the client may report a much more varied attitude that some elderly are indeed rigid in their thinking, while others may now be seen as modern and "sharp as a tack." Since the initial attitudes were not well formed, or central, they were easily changed.

Changing negative attitudes about specific co-workers, spouses, children, or teachers, may be part of an anger management program. Sometimes, it is helpful to work on general attitudes such as those about the police, teachers, or specific groups of people. At other times, it is an attitude about a specific person that requires change. The best way to change attitudes is through *contact, knowledge,* and *interaction.* When gays and lesbians were "in the closet" and when we had little contact with people from the former Soviet Union, it was quite easy to maintain negative attitudes toward these groups. Change came through interaction. As we became aware that some of our co-workers were gay, or that our neighbors came from the former USSR, many people changed their attitudes. The same process has held true for attitudes towards blacks, Jews, southerners, Indians, the handicapped, the learning disabled, etc. Contact and interaction with members of these groups challenges pre-existing beliefs and leads to change.

Unfortunately, there is a corresponding counterforce. When we have hostile attitudes toward persons or groups, we tend to avoid them. Thus, we sometimes find clients have long held negative attitudes that have never been challenged because it was relatively easy to avoid that cousin or neighbor or former friend who is "known" to really be a "snake in the grass!"

Clinically, hostility and negative attitudes set the stage for anger. These attitudes are much like the gray or brown lens in sunglasses. When we put on these lenses the world seems darker. In contrast, skiers prefer yellow lenses, as they make the snow covered mountain easier to see when the sun goes down. In a similar way, negative attitudes serve as filters that predispose clients to be intolerant and to quickly interpret neutral or mildly problematic behaviors in a highly negative way, without a critical evaluation of the factors involved. This leads to anger responses and to enduring anger episodes.

Aggression. Aggression is defined as *motor behavior.* It refers to a *physical* action *intended* to hurt or harm another person, or sometimes to destroy property (Figure 1-4). *Intent* is central to the definition, as

Figure 1-4.
The motor response
of aggression.

we do not include harm caused by the unintentional acts of others in the definition. Accidents that lead to harm do occur, but they are not aggressive in intent.

If the motor behavior intended to harm is directed against the source, it is labeled *direct* aggression. This would include a husband who hits his wife in response to her insults during an argument. It would also include a mother who hits her young child when she discovers he wrote with crayons on the bedroom wall. If the behavior is not aimed directly at the target it is labeled *indirect* aggression. For example, rather than hitting his partner a man might break dishes, throw a planter against a wall, or kick the proverbial dog. The goal is to hurt the partner, but the means is indirect. The partner has to clean up the mess or soothe the dog, and feels both vulnerable and threatened. In the example of Robert given above, the actual goal might be to aggress against his mother, or against the unhelpful school librarian. However, since there are social proscriptions against such behavior, it was easier for Robert to aggress against a school friend. It would be wise to avoid Robert until he cools down, lest an unknowing person become the target of his indirect aggression.

Aggressive behavior can emerge from anger and/or from hostility, or it can be a planned and calculated means to achieve a desired goal with little or no anger at all. If the aggression emerges from anger it is labeled *hostile* or *emotional* aggression. Hostile aggression is unplanned and impulsive. It simply erupts as part of an *hostile attitude + anger →* *aggression* chain. The specific consequences are likely to be unknown in advance, even to the perpetrator. Hostile aggression often reaches unintended targets and may become much more severe than expected. We saw one case of emotional aggression, in which a 27-year-old man went to his girlfriend's house without first calling her. Finding a strange car in the driveway, he peeked into the window and discovered that she was sexually involved with another man. He became enraged, drove to his apartment in a fury, and got his gun. He then returned and shot both of them to death! Obviously, it is wise that practitioners use caution when working with clients who have a history of hostile aggression.

Aggression can also be *instrumental*. This type of aggression is carefully planned, and may even be sanctioned by society. Thus, we might say that a veterinarian who euthanizes a sickly dog is aggressive since killing the dog is a motor act intended to harm. And, we would say that a physician hired to put a convicted killer to death by lethal injection is engaging in instrumental aggression, as are the members of a government-sanctioned military operation. In these cases we pay people to kill, much as a "hit man" might be hired to kill a pre-identified victim. The instrumental aggressor may even feel no anger or hostility, and may even feel compassion, as in the case of the veterinarian. Since there is little or no anger, there is much time for planning and forethought before the aggression occurs. The aggressive act, therefore, is carried out at a planned time and in a thoughtful, deliberative, and measured manner.

Aversive Verbalizations. Many authors label verbal expressions of anger, such as yelling or shouting or cursing, as "verbal aggression," especially when intentionally directed at another person. We do not find this to be a useful characterization of verbal behavior for two reasons. First, motor behavior has a relatively predictable effect on each of us. If punched in the nose, we bleed. If pushed down the stairs, we fall and suffer with painful black and blue bruises. Although young people may suffer milder consequences than the elderly, the effects are generally the same.

In contrast, the effects of verbal behavior are variable. If another person calls you "fat," or "stupid," you may, or may not, react. If you are skinny, you might think there is something wrong with the person who calls you "fat." If a young 4-year-old child calls you "stupid," you will likely have a very different reaction than if a supervisor at work uses that term in the presence of your co-workers.

Consider how you might respond if you hear a slur involving your own racial background. If someone not of your race makes the remark, you may have a strong reaction and feel infuriated! However, if the person who makes the remark is of your race, then your reaction may be only of annoyance, or you may have no reaction at all. As but another example, consider the case of professional actors and actresses. They may play roles where they are the recipients of repeated aversive verbalizations. In Hollywood they may have to shoot a scene repeatedly and on Broadway they may play the role for many nights. Yet, they hold no animosity toward the person who delivers the aversive verbalizations, for that person is also only "playing a role." Finally, we often have a more extreme reaction to verbal insults when we are fatigued or upset with something or someone else. Remember, for example, that Robert was less able to tolerate teasing by his friend after the incidents with his mother and the librarian. Again, the effects of aversive motor behavior, such as being hit or kicked, do not depend on our mood or our relationship with the other person or whether it occurs on or off Broadway. A physically aversive stimulus, such as a kick, has its own unyielding predictable effects based on its intensity and location. In contrast, responses to aversive verbalizations from others are quite variable.

There is a second reason to avoid the term "verbal aggression." As a motor behavior, aggression produces harm such as bruises, bleeding, redness, broken bones, etc. We have no choice but to respond in these ways to motor aggression. We cannot choose to not bleed when stabbed, or learn to not develop bruises when punched. However, that is not the case with aversive verbal assaults. In fact, *one of the goals of anger management is to become less responsive to the aversive verbalizations of others through knowledge development and behavioral practice.* Motor aggression produces an invariable effect on a person's body, irrespective of mood, color, religion, age, or relationship with the aggressor. In contrast, aversive verbalizations (so called, "verbal aggression") lead to varied responses depending on many factors and, of importance to practitioners, the responses may be modified in an anger management program.

So, we use these terms:
• *anger* labels a person's (mostly learned) internal experiences such as thoughts, fantasies, and images, verbal behaviors, and bodily responses to the aversive behavior of others; these vary in intensity, frequency, and duration
• *hostility* refers to enduring negative attitudes or thoughts that predispose people to experience anger
• *aggression* is motor behavior intended to cause harm
• *aversive verbalizations* is our term for words and statements, usually negative, that have variable effects, and may or may not lead to anger in others.

We again note that the aversive verbal behavior of other people (i.e., yelling, cursing, berating, etc.) may be intended to cause distress. However, it may or may not do so depending on factors such as the interpreted meaning of the verbalization and the belief that such negative verbalizations can or cannot be tolerated. After all, aversive words are just words and, "Sticks and stones can break our bones, but words can never hurt us" — unless we allow them to!

❖ *Emotional Vocabulary Development*

Anger is a *subjectively labeled* experience. It is a word we use to identify our thoughts, physiological responses, and behavioral reactions. In the ideal cases, different words would be used to identify different feelings, intensities and, perhaps, durations. Unfortunately, clients often mislabel their feeling states. They may wrongly label short-term and milder levels of arousal as anger or infuriation, rather than annoyance. Frances, an older woman who lived in a nursing home, labeled every minor inconvenience such as a late arriving meal as "awful." She often belittled the staff ("They are so stupid"), and in a blaming way would report, "They got me so incredibly angry today." This behavior led to needless arousal that was not only problematic for her own health, but it also led the staff to dislike her. Another problem occurs when clients use labels with less specific meaning, such as "upset," to describe their felt emotional state. In such cases, practitioners do not know if it is anger or anxiety or something else which is being experienced, nor is the intensity clear. Thus, helping clients develop a clear *emotional vocabulary* is important for any anger reduction program and many clients benefit from a discussion of how to label the full range of their emotional experiences.

Anger has consistently been identified as one of the basic human emotions and is occasionally felt by almost everyone. Although variation exists among scholars, other basic feelings are typically labeled as fear, joy, sadness, acceptance, disgust, expectation and surprise. Plutchik (1980, 1994, 2000; Figure 1-5) organized the basic emotions in the form of a half sphere. His model shows that each of the basic slices, including anger, varies in intensity. In the case of anger, the three

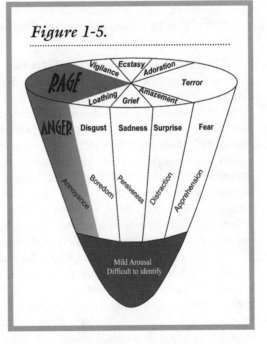

Figure 1-5.

basic intensity labels are rage, anger, and annoyance. His theory also posits that specific emotions are most clearly identifiable at the "equator," at the strongest level. As feelings get weaker, we are less able to identify exactly what is experienced.

Certainly, practitioners have observed clients who are mildly and vaguely "upset" but cannot clearly label their feeling state. Some practitioners talk of one emotion lurking under another. To them, depression is really anger, or anger is masking guilt, etc. Plutchik's view is simpler, and more acceptable. When emotions are weak they are hard to identify clearly and we often misuse labels when we share mild feelings with others. It is in these cases, when feelings are not strong enough to be clearly identified, that practitioners may project their perceptions on to the client. Care is required, however, as clients may agree with our interpretations only because of our professional status, not because what we say is true for them. *A simple clinical truth is that clients often do not know how to label their emotions.* They may use a generic word, such as "upset," or "agitated" to describe anger or they may not use any emotion word and, instead, describe a desired response or goal. Note, for example, that the following are *not* true feeling statements:
"I feel like he should listen to me," or
"I feel like she is ungrateful," or
"I feel that he could study more often than he does," or
"I feel that my boss is unfair."

Given the difficulty that many clients have with the direct and honest expression of anger, it is wise to use and define words like "annoyed," "unhappy," "angry," "pissed-off," "aggravated," "furious" and "enraged" as practitioners and clients discuss problems in session. In this way, the practitioner can model an appropriate emotional vocabulary for clients to use in their daily lives. The goal is to teach appropriate verbal labels for emotional experiences of mild, moderate and strong intensities. *Assertiveness* — the clear, direct, and appropriate expression of angry feelings, without hyperbole — can do much to improve interpersonal communication and avoid conflicts (Wolpe, 1958, 1990; Alberti & Emmons, 2001). There is much to be said for clear and positive verbal expression, which is why assertiveness training is part of anger management.

An *anger thermometer,* perhaps one that is provided in a client handout and mounted on the wall (Figure 1-6), may be helpful as anger episodes are discussed. Since clients do not automatically learn to appropriately label feeling intensities, an anger thermometer helps practitioners and clients agree on a common vocabulary. Lots of reinforced practice, to apply appropriate labels, is required. Using the thermometer, ask clients to rate how they felt *when,* for example, they were abused or otherwise mistreated, or *when* a TV program they were eager to watch was suddenly cancelled, or *when* it was discovered that someone spread a rumor about them. Stick with specific examples and use the temporal, state-oriented word "when" to reinforce the definition that *anger is a personally felt response when something happens.* Use examples likely to yield mild, moderate, or intense reactions in the clients' life and reinforce appropriate labeling.

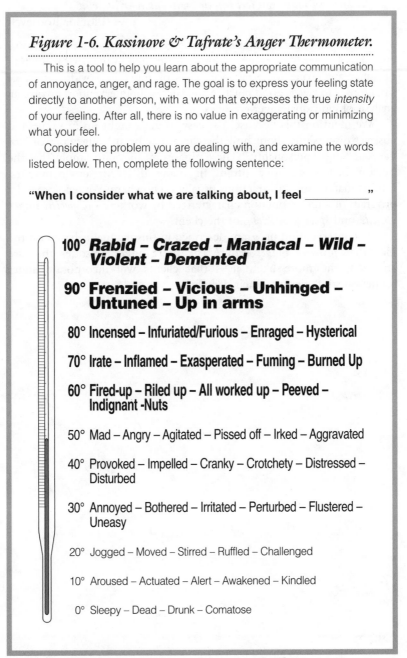

Figure 1-6. Kassinove & Tafrate's Anger Thermometer.

This is a tool to help you learn about the appropriate communication of annoyance, anger, and rage. The goal is to express your feeling state directly to another person, with a word that expresses the true *intensity* of your feeling. After all, there is no value in exaggerating or minimizing what your feel.

Consider the problem you are dealing with, and examine the words listed below. Then, complete the following sentence:

"When I consider what we are talking about, I feel _____"

100° ***Rabid – Crazed – Maniacal – Wild – Violent – Demented***

90° **Frenzied – Vicious – Unhinged – Untuned – Up in arms**

80° Incensed – Infuriated/Furious – Enraged – Hysterical

70° Irate – Inflamed – Exasperated – Fuming – Burned Up

60° Fired-up – Riled up – All worked up – Peeved – Indignant -Nuts

50° Mad – Angry – Agitated – Pissed off – Irked – Aggravated

40° Provoked – Impelled – Cranky – Crotchety – Distressed – Disturbed

30° Annoyed – Bothered – Irritated – Perturbed – Flustered – Uneasy

20° Jogged – Moved – Stirred – Ruffled – Challenged

10° Aroused – Actuated – Alert – Awakened – Kindled

0° Sleepy – Dead – Drunk – Comatose

[Howard Kassinove, Ph.D. and Raymond Chip Tafrate, Ph.D. *Anger Management: The Complete Treatment Guidebook for Practitioners* © 2002]

❖ *Episode Analysis*

No one can make you feel inferior without your consent.
— Eleanor Roosevelt

When working with angry persons it is critical to work on individual episodes of anger. We agree that some clients high in the personality trait of anger are prone to experience states of anger in a wide variety of situations. However, good practice and successful intervention involve an analysis of individual anger episodes.

We mention this because it is easy to get caught up in vague and abstract discussions about how the client may be an "angry person" or have an "angry personality." These phrases mean, quite simply, that the person becomes angry often, in many different environments. Unfortunately, such abstractions usually go nowhere. We recommend a program of anger reduction characterized by working on *specific anger episodes* and *specific problems* of the client.

The intervention program described in this manual is based on the idea that *practice makes better!* The more anger episodes that are analyzed, the more likely it is that clients will incorporate anger reduction strategies into their daily lives.

2

The Anger Episode Model

Anger begins with folly, and ends with repentance.

— H. G. Bohn

Although anger seems to begin with the personal experience, it is actually part of a larger chain of events. Helping clients understand this chain, which we call *anger episode analysis*, leads to an improved and more easily accepted intervention program. Many benefits are derived from presenting the anger episode analysis model to clients.

- Almost all clients, for example, blame the external world for their anger. This view can be modified by understanding the relationships among each component of the anger episode. *Anger is typically caused by some combination of the anger trigger and the interpretation of the trigger, along with the short-term reinforcing consequences of angry expression.* Certainly, it is wise for practitioners to also consider biological causes, since problems such as diabetes, neoplasm, drugs and alcohol can lead to displays of anger. However, most anger is caused by elements in the client's environment that precede or follow the anger display, along with the client's personal interpretations of the environment.

- *Many clients are unaware that their anger is exaggerated, beyond the scope of "normal," and are oblivious to the short and long-term costs associated with their anger.* It is these costs that make their anger problematic. We liken anger to tobacco usage or to drinking polluted water while living in an impoverished country. Even if 100% of the population engages is such behaviors, they are "bad" because of their outcomes. Tobacco use and drinking polluted water reduce life span. The costs of intense enduring and persistent anger are similar to these other problems.

- *Shared understanding of the anger episode, and the costs of anger, increases the therapeutic bond, client motivation, and the chances of successful treatment.* Through discussions with mental health practitioners, clients learn to understand more about their anger episodes by breaking them down into component parts. By gaining practice in monitoring their anger components, the model becomes part of the shared base of knowledge and, thus, expedites development of the therapeutic relationship and the intervention process. Also, because the model is simple and increases understanding, it gives clients an increased sense of mastery over their anger.

• The identification of specific features of a client's anger that repeatedly occur over the course of multiple episodes allows for treatment to be tailored to that client's patterns. In sum, *a shared base of knowledge about anger will yield a more effective intervention program.*

Our episode model has five parts: *triggers, appraisals, experiences, expressive patterns,* and *outcomes.* Each part is detailed below. In the beginning of any intervention program, in addition to spending time in discussion of this model, giving clients an informational handout is usually helpful. Alternatively, the client information sheet can be used in a waiting room to stimulate thoughts about the personal anger experiences of clients. Thus, a descriptive *Client Information Sheet* and a graphic presentation of the model (Figure 2-2) appear at the end of this chapter. Readers are granted permission to reproduce this material for use with their clients, subject to inclusion of the copyright notice on each copy reproduced.

The model emerged from studies which examined how people experience anger in their real-world environments (e.g., Averill, 1983; Deffenbacher, 1993, Kassinove & Fuller, 1999; 2000; Davidson, Golub, & Kassinove, 2000; Kassinove, Roth, Owens, & Fuller, 2002; Tafrate, Kassinove, & Dundin, 2002). Results from these studies, when combined with our professional practice experiences in mental health clinics, public schools, private practice, and consultations with prison and parole counselors, nurses, social workers, etc., provided information regarding common characteristics of anger episodes. They also allowed us to understand the anger experiences of persons high or low on the trait of anger. Other studies examined differences across cultures by comparing the anger episodes of American subjects to those of people in many other countries, including Russia, India, and Israel (Eliaz,

---

The Anger Episode Model

Triggers + Appraisals ➤ Experiences ➤ Expressive Patterns ➤ Outcomes

2001; Kassinove, Sukhodolsky, Tsytsarev, & Solovyova, 1997; Matsumoto, Kudoh, Scherer, & Wallbott, 1988; Scherer, 1997a; 1997b). Such knowledge is important given the multicultural background of clients likely to be seen by practitioners.

❖❖ ## *Triggers*

It is normal for children to test our limits — both in words and actions. Establishing independence from adult authority is a healthy way for children to find their own styles. The question is how can parents walk the tricky line between allowing their children to express their feelings while still asserting their authority as parents, and setting necessary limits.

— Nancy Samalin

Triggers are the external or internal stimuli that set the stage for the anger response. They are the actions (or inactions) of others, or the times and places, or memories or current thoughts, which begin the anger sequence.

The most commonly reported anger triggers, for adults from community and university student samples, show that *anger typically develops in response to unwanted, and sometimes unexpected, aversive interpersonal behavior.* That is, something negative done by someone else. This finding holds up across cultures. In samples of Americans, Indians, Israelis, and Russians, the vast majority (about 80%) of anger episodes were reported to be in response to the unwanted actions of other people. Most of these actions occurred during the late afternoon or evening hours, and were unexpected. However, we note that the unexpected actions of others can also lead to joy, as when an unexpected gift is received from someone who is loved. And, clients may become angry even after an expected action occurs. Thus, a parent may experience anger when a child fails an examination, even though the child had previously failed school exams many times and had told the parent that failure was likely again. Expectedness, thus, is probably not central to the formation of anger (Scherer, 1997).

The remaining anger experiences are triggered by something done by the angry person him/herself, situations related to inanimate objects (e.g., car breaking down), or some larger abstraction (e.g., "life"). These, however, are relatively infrequent. Even when anger is attributed to unfair life events, such as loss of a job due to the closing of a company or suffering physical injury, perhaps due to a building collapse, the causal attribution is usually placed on a person. That is, the job loss is blamed on senior personnel who "didn't manage the company correctly" or to a greedy contractor who "didn't build it right."

Of importance, most anger events (about 70%) are reported to involve people who "love" or "like" each other. Anger typically develops during social interactions with parents, spouses, live-in partners, colleagues at work, children, friends, etc. Anger episodes attributed to strangers, individuals who are disliked, animals, or objects are far less common. When we specifically studied high trait anger adults, identical trigger patterns emerged (Tafrate, Kassinove, & Dundin, 2002). Anger was again most frequently attributed to the unwanted and sometimes unexpected actions of others who are well-known and liked.

Thus, clients participating in anger treatment programs become angry in response to the same types of situations that we all experience from time to time. However, client reactions are likely to be more extreme and to have more problematic outcomes. Since we found no important differences in the triggering stimuli of persons who are higher or lower on the trait of anger, combined with few cross-cultural differences, we do not think that detailed cataloging of triggers is particularly useful. Rather, knowledge about the client's triggering events is important because it helps the practitioner understand the starting point of each client's anger episode and because discussion allows the client to present the facts without therapist reinforcement of the inflammatory comments.

Almost any stimulus can lead to anger and, as noted above, detailed cataloging is unnecessary. However, in a more general way, we tend to think of triggers as *negative events.* These include the verbal, visual, and motor stimuli that most of us judge to be aversive. In many cases, some kind of personal stressor, threat, unfair event, loss or potential loss is involved. Common examples of client anger triggers include:

Figure 2-1.

An aversive stimulus which could become an anger trigger.

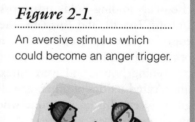

• *Verbal:* personal insults, rudeness, family or ethnic slurs, teasing, profanity, receiving disappointing news (such as learning that an expected promotion at work was not granted, or being told that your spouse wants a separation), being accused of misconduct, being told that you were "wrong," chronic complaining by family members or colleagues, criticism.

- *Motor:* being pushed shoved or hit, being spit at, having something thrown at you, being held down or having a part of your body restrained by someone else.
- *Visual:* observing inappropriately fast drivers in a school zone or inappropriately slow drivers in the passing zone on the freeway, being glared at by a stranger, being "placed under a microscope" by the constant observation of an employer or parent, observing a parent mistreat a child in the supermarket, observing mistreatment of an animal, observing someone scratch your car, seeing your young child purposely throw food on the floor.

Although almost any trigger can initiate the anger sequence, most triggers are negative, aversive, and interpersonal, are initiated by a well-known person, and are unexpected. Of course, practitioners will be faced with clients who have experienced all kinds of aversive triggers, from mild to severe.

In one of our cases, strong anger was evoked by a child who didn't listen to his mother. In another, it was elicited by a husband who tied his wife to a tree and cut her arms and legs with a razor blade. The former case is common and seems uninteresting when it is mentioned. In contrast, the latter case is quite unusual, and when it is presented to our students and supervisees they always want more of the details. We recognize that practitioners in prisons or parole offices will see more severe cases in which aggression was a triggering event. Yet, non-aggressive interpersonal behaviors are much more common triggers for anger (e.g., verbal disrespect, failure of a child to come home on time, etc.). These lead to anger in the largest number of cases seen by practitioners of all sorts. Kowalski (2001) addressed this issue of variability in the triggers of anger and came to the following conclusion:

> *"When most people think of aversive interpersonal behaviors, they think of acts of aggression or violence, such as physical abuse, murder, and rape. In fact, these extreme forms of aversive behaviors are, within the whole scheme of behaviors, relatively rare. To limit our focus to these acts of aggression or violence would be to ignore the more mundane aversive interpersonal behaviors to which most people are exposed on a much more regular basis and which in some instances may lead to more extreme aggressive actions."* (p.3).

Thus, anger is far more likely to result from triggers at work or in school or in our daily environment — such as neglect, infidelity, deception, teasing, and incompetence — than from stronger triggers. Such triggers are simply much more frequent than rape, murder, or child abuse. In practice, therefore, an anger intervention program may be called for in school, family, community, or industrial settings because of the common occurrence of such "lesser" triggers.

Figure 2-2.

A positive stimulus which could become an anger trigger.

Lois, like I said last week *and the week before,* you are a really beautiful boss.

Sometimes stimuli that would objectively be judged as *positive* can become anger triggers. Consider a working woman, perhaps a serious account executive at a major firm, who is told every day at the water cooler that she is "a good-looker." After the first few so-called compliments, she may find the positive remarks to be quite aversive and likely to lead to anger. Or, consider the woman who receives roses everyday with a card expressing affection, from a man she dislikes. The roses, along with the words of affection, which are generally considered to be positive, may become a trigger for anger. Even a promotion may be aversive. We know of a part-time staff psychologist who was offered a promotion to full-time Chief Psychologist, based on his excellent job performance. Unfortunately, due to family commitments, he was unable to take the full-time position and, for budgetary reasons, the part-time position was eliminated, along with the "promoted" psychologist. His "opportunity" for advancement led to considerable anger.

Anger, and possibly aggression, might even be triggered by positive and affectionate remarks, if made by a member of the same sex as the client. In a recent case at our university, "William" indicated his affection for, and sexual interest in, "Mark." Mark was surprised, offended and repulsed by the advances. Feeling rejected, William then murdered Mark! Obviously, this is an extreme case that illustrates the importance of appraisal and evaluation of triggers.

Negative and positive feedback can *both* lead to anger, depending upon how the client interprets the feedback. For example, when a child brings home a term paper grade of B+, it may lead to joy or anger. Did the parent *expect* an "A" or a "C"? Based upon their family and cultural backgrounds, and personal learning history, clients become angry in response to specific and often unique triggers, some of which are objectively negative and some which are objectively positive. And, they will become especially angry when those triggers appear again and again.

Initially, triggers may lead only to a general state of arousal (Berkowitz, 1993; Schacter & Singer, 1962). This arousal then transforms into a negative or positive emotion, which may initiate motor behavior such as aggression. Imagine yourself in this situation:

It is 11:00 p.m. and you are quite tired. It was a long and difficult day at work. Most of the lights in your home have been turned off; you are undressed for the evening and are relaxing in your bedroom. Suddenly, the doorbell rings. Then, it rings again. Who could it be? It's so late! Why would anyone ring the bell at this hour? You are now in a general state of arousal. Reluctantly, you put on some clothing, turn on a light, and go to the door.

- Scenario 1: You open the door and find an unknown person who wants you to sign a long petition to save the purity of the local water supply. What do you feel?
- Scenario 2: You open the door and find it is a very close friend who has been out of the country for a year. This friend greets you with a smile and says, "Surprise!" How do you feel?

This example shows how the initial general state of arousal (triggered by the doorbell) can turn into either anger or a positive feeling, such as happiness.

In summary, the most likely trigger for anger is an *unwanted, unexpected, objectively negative action by another person who is well-known, liked, or loved.* However, almost anything can set the stage for client anger responses.

❖ *Appraisals*

Men are not moved by things, but by the views which they take of them.
— Epictetus

To understand the role of appraisals in the causation of anger, consider the example of teasing. People tease each other as a form of socialization and bonding, a method to help resolve conflicts and bad feelings, a way to flirt, or just a way to pass time and "play" with each other (Keltner, et. al, 2001). Although most teasing is done in fun, it sometimes leads to a feeling of shame or humiliation and can be taken as a hostile, insulting behavior. In these instances, rather than strengthening bonds between people, it leads to anger. A playful verbalization, such as "Well, aren't you a know-it-all," can lead to laughter or anger, depending on how it is interpreted. A tease is simply a playful provocation that typically brings people who know each other even closer to each other.

However, anger emerges when such playful and ambiguous triggers are appraised as purposeful, unjust statements, which aim to demean and which could have been controlled or avoided if the other person really wanted to. So, how clients perceive the behaviors of others contributes a great deal to whether or not anger is experienced.

Anger is sometimes associated with an appraisal of the trigger as *unexpected*. More often, triggers are appraised as *preventable* and *intentional*. Consider the anger that many parents feel when their children perform poorly in school. Mrs. Carnegie was the mother of 12-year old Martin. His daily grades had dropped, leading to a poor report card and a failing grade in math. In addition to her disappointment, Mrs. Carnegie viewed Martin's performance as *unexpected* ("He has a high IQ, you know!"), and preventable ("If he would spend 15 minutes a day with his books, he would do just fine!"). She also viewed the failure as somehow *intentionally* produced ("Do you think he does it to punish me?"). These appraisals are significant contributors to the formation of her anger. Specific appraisal errors are now presented.

Misinterpretations of the trigger. Aspects of the trigger are often distorted or exaggerated by angry clients. For example, one man viewed frequent phone calls from, and visits by, his in-laws as "totally intrusive!" He believed they were motivated by a lack of trust and a desire to check-up on their daughter. Upon closer examination it became clear that the in-laws actually just enjoyed spending time with their children and grandchildren. The motivations attributed to the in-laws were actually distortions of reality. In another case, a mid-level manager in a large corporation felt anger toward his supervisor who he believed did not like him. He viewed his supervisor's abrupt manner as evidence of disinterest and dislike. However, a closer examination revealed that the supervisor acted this way with everybody and was himself under a great deal of stress. His abrupt manner was more related to his own turmoil than to any personal feelings for his subordinates. This tendency to misinterpret and make negative attributions has been well documented in angry and aggressive children and adolescents who typically show deficits in interpreting the intentions of others. They often misinterpret ambiguous or benign interactions as hostile (Dodge & Coie, 1987; Dodge, Price, Bachorowski, & Newman, 1990). Anger-prone adults possess a similar negative bias when they interpret ambiguous and potentially provocative situations.

Many misinterpretations of triggers center around the themes of *unfairness* and *disappointment*. Consider the case of Carlos, a 49-year old employee for a large telecommunications company. He began his current job at age 30 and had expected to keep his position until he retired. Unfortunately, the economic climate in the area had changed dramatically and Carlos, along with many of his colleagues, was told that his position would be eliminated within the span of a year. Carlos found the negative economic events to be unexpected (he told his counselor, "Last year we did real well and everybody got bonuses!") and preventable ("Why didn't they raise prices more? Then, I'd still have a job!"). He was very disappointed with the company, viewed himself as a dedicated and loyal employee, and believed the decision was "completely unfair." He also questioned whether his layoff was part of an intentional plan (he said, "They are just laying off better paid, older people. In two years, they know they will replace me with a younger, cheaper guy!"). He thought that, given his age, it was unfair for him to have to start over again somewhere else. Carlos had great difficulty moving beyond what he considered as unfair and undeserved treatment. So, instead of spending time and energy seeking a new position, he endlessly ruminated about the pending dismissal. Even worse, he embarked on a course of action that included passive-aggressive retaliation. For example, he would intentionally not show up for appointments, "forget" to file critical paperwork, and fail to meet even minimal requirements for satisfactory job performance. While his actions might be understandable given his view that he was treated unfairly, they were nonetheless counterproductive. Ultimately, Carlos tarnished his reputation as a hardworking and dedicated employee, making transition to a potentially new and better position difficult.

Awfulizing. This is a tendency to exaggerate the level of hardship associated with aversive life events. Legitimate difficulties are conceptualized and described by the client as "awful," "horrible," or "catastrophic" when, in fact, they may be quite manageable. When clients awfulize, it typically leads to a series of complaints about how bad the situation is, diverting time and effort away from productive problem solving. Awfulizing also reduces interpersonal attractiveness. Consider the case of Mary, a 78-year-old widow with moderate arthritis, living in a senior citizens facility. Her condition was certainly not good, as her fingers were slightly bent out of shape and she suffered with periodic pain even after taking medication. The problem was that she ruminated about the pain and would bring it up to anyone who would listen. Although she described the pain as "unbearable," other indications suggested it was of moderate intensity, as Mary was able to walk, play cards, use eating utensils, use the TV remote, brush her teeth, and handle other modest tasks of daily living. As might be imagined, soon enough no one wanted to talk to Mary. Of course, we are not minimizing her pain as we describe her plight. Rather, we note that Mary would most likely be better off if she could develop better coping skills which might increase her appeal to others.

Low Frustration Tolerance. This is a tendency to underestimate one's ability to deal with discomfort and adversity. Negative events, instead of being viewed as a normal part of life or a challenge to be solved, are instead seen as situations that the client cannot "stand," "take," or "tolerate." Again, in the case of Mary noted above, she would often tell others, "I can't take it any more and that doctor doesn't do anything for me." of course, Mary did tolerate the pain for years, thus diminishing her credibility with others.

There is a relationship between awfulizing and low frustration tolerance. As triggers are elevated to awful or even catastrophic events, the client is less and less likely to believe the trigger can be tolerated. In spite of their bluster, many clients who experience frequent and intense anger have a poor view of their own ability to handle difficult or challenging situations.

A variation on this type of thinking is the idea that one is very important or busy or special, and therefore should not be burdened with such trivial and ordinary negative life events. Charles, a 50-year-old vice-president for marketing, began to see himself as a critically important person. Previously available to help others, he began to experience anger when members of his work team would ask basic questions about the product line. He began to believe that it was awful that the company was hiring such people and told his wife, "I just can't take it anymore." At home, typical household inconveniences such as a broken appliance or leaking plumbing also led to considerable anger. He would complain about how he could not handle such situations on top of his demanding job. Of course, he did tolerate these types of daily hassles, albeit with a great deal of anger and frustration. His views regarding minor inconveniences led to his anger and to nightly complaints to his wife. This of course had a negative impact on his marriage.

Demandingness. The most common anger-related belief is that persons who are viewed as the source of anger "should" have acted differently, and could have if they wanted to. Thus, the trigger is conceived to be a person who could have controlled his or her behavior but didn't want to. Remember Mary, the 78-year-old widow? Although the doctor prescribed mild and strong analgesics, and gave her nerve blocks, Mary continued to believe that he "should" be able to relieve her pain. Clients engaged in demandingness elevate their personal wishes to dictates or rules that are then imposed on the self, others, and the world. Demandingness can be detected by carefully listening for words like "should," "must," "ought," and "have to" in client verbalizations. Helping clients replace demanding and inflexible beliefs (e.g., "My husband should be more appreciative of what I do") with a more preference-based view (e.g., "It would be nice if my husband were more appreciative of what I do") is covered in more detail in chapter 14.

Negative Ratings of others. When angered, there is a tendency to view the offending person in extreme terms. This often involves condemning an individual's complete existence based on one or a few behavioral acts. For example, we have worked with clients who commonly engage in this type of thinking while driving. They make very specific statements, either aloud or to themselves, of complete condemnation of other drivers (e.g., "What a moron! He should get the hell out of the passing lane," "Who does this jackass think he is anyway?"). Of course in these situations, clients really do not have enough information about the people that they speak of, and cannot accurately make such sweeping generalizations. Many clients will readily acknowledge that they themselves are not always perfect drivers. Certainly, they would not describe themselves in such overly negatively broad terms when they commit such indiscretions.

Negative Ratings of Self. This refers to a tendency to blame or condemn oneself. So, not only are angry clients likely to be harsh when thinking about others, they may be equally prone to self-criticism and self-denigration and are thus vulnerable to experiencing other negative emotions following anger episodes.

Adults high on the trait of anger are more prone to experience anger in multiple situations and to engage more often in a variety of cognitive misappraisals. Thus, correction of inappropriate appraisals becomes a key element of the anger management program.

❖ *Experiences*

Anger will never disappear so long as thoughts of resentment are cherished in the mind.

— Buddha

The "experiences" part of the anger episode model refers to the client's internal awareness of anger, as verbally shared with the practitioner. This internal awareness is a *private event* (Skinner, 1974), since it is known only to the client. When it is reported to the practitioner, it is based on the client's self-perceived physiological reactions (e.g., heart rate increase), self-observation of spontaneous motor behavior (e.g., a clenched fist, shouting), and self-awareness of anger-related thoughts. Of course, as a private event the anger experience may or may not be shared with others.

We agree with Berkowitz (1993) that private anger experiences are often not goal directed. That is, the client may or may not have specific directed thoughts, such as this: "I'll show her. I really want to get even! She'll pay for what she did to me!" Instead, the thought associated with bodily arousal may simply be of this general nature: "I'm really pissed! I can't believe what happened!" Nevertheless, the private anger event is almost always unpleasant and it has short- and long-term negative consequences for the client. In contrast to anger, *aggression* is almost always goal directed and has the aim of harm to a specific person or object.

Anger experiences are quite common. In Scherer and Wolbert's (1994) study, for example, respondents from 73 countries recalled events in which they experienced anger, joy, sadness, fear, guilt, shame, and disgust. Uniformly, anger experiences were quite frequent: "almost half of the respondents need to think back only days or weeks to remember an appropriate episode" (p. 318). Our own data and clinical experience show that approximately half of normal adults report that they become angry once per week or more. In contrast, less than 20% report that they rarely or never become angry. In addition, anger experiences are often short-lived. Approximately 50% of the episodes last less than an hour. In contrast, approximately 30% of anger episodes are enduring and last more than a day.

From a clinical perspective, individuals high on the trait of anger have more problematic anger episodes. They experience anger that is more frequent, intense, and enduring. For example, 86% of our high trait anger adults reported that they have anger experiences at a rate of several times per week or more. Anger intensity ratings were also higher than reported by low trait anger adults. Also, in persons high on trait anger, close to half of the specific episodes reported lasted for more than a day. This was true for only 17% of low trait anger adults. Practitioners can expect clients with anger problems to have frequent episodes, many of which will be in the moderate to extreme range of intensity, and many will be enduring.

In terms of specific identifiable aspects of the anger experience, clients may report their:

- angry thoughts (e.g., "She's such a bitch for doing that!" "I hate her guts!" "I'm boiling!"),
- perceived body sensations (e.g., increase heart rate, sweating, muscle tension, shaking, etc), and/or
- fantasies and vindictive action tendencies (e.g., "I'd like to kill him." "I'm

Figure 2-3.

Angry thoughts and vindictive fantasies.

I shouldn't have to stay late to do this work. My boss is a real jerk! I'll get even with her next week.

gonna teach her a lesson she'll never forget!" "I just want to get even with that devil." "I had a dream and she was dead!").

Thought patterns during and after the experience, as discussed above, are typically related to inflammatory evaluations of the trigger. However, there are also self-statements about the magnitude of the client's reaction ("I am so pissed . . .I'm fuming," etc.). In terms of physical sensations, rapid heart rate, muscle tension and trembling are among the most commonly reported symptoms associated with anger. Gastrointestinal symptoms (e.g., upset stomach, indigestion, and diarrhea) are reported among some adults with stronger anger reactions. Head-related sensations (e.g., headaches and dizziness) are more prominent in anger experiences of high trait-anger adults.

When anger is experienced, people generally have a variety of *desires*, only some of which are aggressive in nature. Most often they report *wanting* to yell, argue, complain, or be sarcastic. Some want to fight. However, about one-third are also aware of desires to resolve the problem. They want to compromise, cool down, and get rid of their anger.

Clients high on trait anger are more likely to want to show their anger outwardly in both verbal and physical ways and to have desires to use illegal drugs. As noted above, their anger is more frequent and intense, and lasts longer than would be desirable. High anger persons also report more physical distress such as muscle tension, trembling, headache, sweating, etc. Surprisingly, they also want to hold their anger in more than low trait anger persons. The picture of the typical client is complex. However, the most common report likely to be given to a practitioner is that of an intense and enduring pattern of anger experience which is associated with angry thoughts (e.g., "I've been really, really, mad at him for more than a month!"), verbal desires ("I just feel like telling him off once and for all!") and unpleasant body experiences ("Whenever I think of what he did, I start to shake and have to run to the bathroom!"). It remains the task of the practitioner to assess each client's anger experiences for unreported anger held in, desires for aggressive revenge, and willingness to compromise and solve the problem.

❖ *Expressive Patterns*

Violence in the voice is often only the death rattle of reason in the throat.
— John F. Boyes

The private experience of anger, in turn, often leads to a pattern of *observable* verbal and motor expression. This expressive pattern may consist of descriptive words ("I'm so pissed!"), demeaning, blaming words ("That dope, Sally, acted like such a jerk. She really made me angry"), or direct expressions directed at the target person ("Keep your nose out of my business!"). It may include overt motor behaviors such as pushing, shoving, and throwing objects. And, such behaviors may be very aggressive — as in cases of murder, torture, group violence, politically motivated bombing — and they may be driven by hostile attitudes and angry thoughts and images. The actual pattern of anger expression shown by a client is determined by a combination of (1) overall socio-cultural factors which prescribe appropriate and accepted ways to express anger, and (2) the unique social learning history of each client.

A client's learning history consists of *directly reinforced anger behaviors*, as well as *anger behaviors modeled by others*. Directly reinforced expressions are based on the actual behavior of the client. For example, when a child engages in angry yelling in response to frustration, it may lead to attention by parents. For that child, this attention by the parent increases the likelihood of yelling in the future. Or, as is common in adolescence, shouting and use of profanity in school is often reinforced by peers, increasing the use of these behaviors when anger triggers reappear. Angry clients often come from angry families, where much attention is given to angry patterns of expression. Gang members also receive much reinforcement for the expression of anger.

In contrast, learning by modeling comes from the direct observation

Figure 2-4.
....
Attempts at anger control.

of angry behavior exhibited by family members or friends, on TV and in movies, from reading comic books or novels in which the characters become angry, from religious books (e.g., the King James Bible, the Koran, or the Talmud) or sermons which teach about the role and expression of anger, and from video games and stories told by teachers or colleagues or peers. There are many opportunities for all of us to learn about anger from such means. Learned anger is then coded into verbal rules, such as "I become furious and throw things when I don't get what I want!" These coded rules can be assessed in discussions or by use of various assessment instruments, as described in the next chapter.

Common patterns of anger expression include:

Anger-in. For some clients, anger is typically held in. Experientially, they may be quite aware of their angry feelings, but they judge expression to be inappropriate and thus show few external behaviors. They easily remain unexpressive and their suppressed anger may eventually dissipate. Alternatively, the client may express the anger at a later time or may initiate efforts to resolve the triggering problem. We found no differences in the degree to which anger was held in for high trait anger versus low trait anger people. For individuals seen in treatment settings, outward expressiveness is the more common and immediate concern.

As a side note, we report that although we all know of people who keep their anger in, the multinational study of Scherer and Wolbert (1994) found that anger was expressed relatively frequently. They found that to be surprising since "it is often surmised that there are socio-cultural norms inhibiting the expression of anger" (p. 391). Of course, some cultures (e.g., in some Asian countries) promote suppression more than others, suggesting that practitioners take this variable into account as they work in multicultural environments.

Indirect anger expression (passive-aggressive actions and covert sabotage). Some clients may express their anger indirectly. They may engage in destruction and sabotage of property, or verbal attack, without ever confronting the target of their anger. Many organizations have to deal with the angry but unsigned memo that appears in mailboxes from such persons. Another common method of indirect expression is to deliberately disrupt social or work relationships. Gossip or spreading misinformation may be destructive to the target of a client's anger. Finally, angry clients may passively resist demands to function at expected levels in jobs and relationships. They may not follow rules, not carry their weight in team projects, or intentionally ignore requests made by romantic partners or other important persons in their lives. Practitioners may forget to assess for these indirect means of anger expression. However, we have found these types of behaviors to be rather common among angry clients, particularly in correctional and outpatient settings.

Outward expression (verbal, physical, and bodily expressions). Most typically, anger is expressed outwardly by yelling, accusing, pouting, cursing, sarcasm, throwing something, slamming doors, demanding, etc. Many clients feel very comfortable with these kinds of expressions. Anger is also associated with increases in speech tempo and the production of more and longer utterances (Scherer & Wallcott, 1994).

Anger-out individuals may have observed such behavior in their families of origin and have come to see these expressions as a normal way to respond to frustration, disagreement, unfairness, or

Figure 2-5.
....
Expressed anger.

disappointment. The angry eruption may last a while and then some form of problem resolution may follow, without intervention of any sort. Of course, persistent patterns such as these call for an anger management program.

As we have noted, in general community samples anger is most often shown in verbal or non-confrontational motor behaviors. That is, most anger is shown by yelling, making nasty, sarcastic, or verbally abusive remarks, and overt bodily expressions (e.g., rolling eyes, shaking the head, crossing arms, etc.). Most anger episodes do not involve pushing, hitting, or destroying. High profile cases make the newspapers and give a false picture of anger associated with aggression such as murder, rape, or assault (Kowalski (2001).

However, what is likely to be found in clinical practice may be different. Adults high on trait anger report aggressive behaviors at three times the rate of normal non-angry adults. Clients high on the anger trait *are* more likely to fight, hit, kick, shove, break, throw, or destroy property. And, when angry, they *are* more likely to use alcohol and illicit and prescription drugs, which may further increase aggression (Deffenbacher, 1993; Tafrate, Kassinove, & Dundin, 2002). We fully recognize that practitioners in some settings (e.g., prison counselors) will see more of these cases. Most anger, however, is independent of aggression and anger interventions are best targeted to the thoughts, fantasies, and desired verbal and motor behaviors that are unique to anger. At the same time, persons high on the trait of anger or who have already become involved with the criminal justice system may have to be assessed more carefully for aggression.

On the surface, anger-out responding seems to be positive since resolution may follow, the client has "let it out," and nothing is being hidden. Unfortunately, as we show below, people high on anger expressed outwardly are likely to endure a variety of negative consequences, including an increased risk of serious medical disorders as they go through life. There is little benefit to a lifetime of anger, even if it is expressed.

Anger control. Some people spend a lot of effort monitoring their anger and trying to control its' expression. Spielberger (1999) labeled this behavior pattern as *anger control,* and noted that efforts may be placed either on control of the outward expression of felt experiences *or* on the minimization of such experiences. When emphasis is placed on minimizing outward expression, there is likely to be rumination and long-term vigilance to make sure it is not expressed. Such efforts at control may also lead to passivity, brooding, and holding grudges, which prevent acceptance, forgiveness, and problem resolution. Such vigilance and grudge-holding sets the stage for future anger episodes, and possibly aggression. These clients/patients set up negative filters with which they view the actions of others. Scared to express it, and unable to resolve it, there is unremitting cognitive and physiological arousal. Alternatively, attempts may be made to minimize the inner experience and to try to calm down as soon as possible. Although at first glance this may seem better, such minimization may reduce the drive to deal assertively with the target. And, as is true for clients who let their anger out, clients high on anger control have been shown to have an increased risk of serious medical problems as they go through life.

❖ *Outcomes*

How much more grievous are the consequences of anger than the causes of it.

— Marcus Aurelius

Outcomes are a critical part of the anger model, since behaviorists have shown quite clearly that *future behavior is a function of past consequences* (Hill, 1985; Skinner, 1953; 1968, 1974). Angry behavior that has typically been followed by positive events — such as attention, behavioral compliance by others, positive bodily experiences, sexual arousal, food, admiration by others — is strengthened and is more likely to reappear in the future. Angry behavior that typically has not been followed by positive events — as when it is ignored — is weakened and is less likely to reappear. Angry behavior that has been punished may be suppressed, as when a child is "grounded," and the anger may not appear in the same situation. However, it is still in the client's repertoire of behavior and may reappear in other circumstances. The outcomes that follow anger displays have a determining effect on whether or not the anger experience and expressive reaction will be repeated in similar situations.

Anger episodes can be thought of as leading to short-term and long-term outcomes. Short-term outcomes appear either during the anger episode itself (as in the case of a spouse who immediately complies with the angry demands of his partner) or in the period of a few hours to a few days after the anger episode. These have the greatest likelihood of affecting the angry behavior, since consequences close in time are more likely to have positive or negative controlling effects. Long-term outcomes do not appear until weeks or months after anger episodes have occurred and, thus, may have less of a controlling effect. However, clear and well-documented negative long-term outcomes are associated with years of living a life filled with frequent and intense anger.

Certainly, anger displays served an adaptive function in our evolutionary history, have always been part of our existence, and have some positive outcomes and reinforcing effects. An occasional episode of anger that is minimal in intensity, frequency, and duration seems to be part of the normal human experience. In contrast, anger that is frequent, intense, and enduring is problematic for adaptive functioning in modern society. Intense reactions, such as rage and infuriation, frequent anger reactions to a wide variety of minor provocations, festering fantasies of revenge and aggression, and other such manifestations of strong anger are harmful to the self and others. Although the intrapersonal and interpersonal consequences are generally negative in the short and long term, elements of reinforcement keep the anger alive.

Consider the case of a family argument. While it is going on, the participants are likely to make rash, blame-oriented, profane, sarcastic, and/or inflammatory remarks that are unlikely to lead to problem resolution (e.g., "You *never* change. How could you be so *stupid*? I've told you the same thing *over and over*, and you still don't listen. What the hell is *wrong* with you?"). However, as soon as the argument is over there is some gratification (i.e., reinforcing consequences) because the yelling may lead to overt behavioral compliance by the recipient of the anger. In a parent-child interaction, for example, screaming and demanding that a child complete homework "right now" may lead to a reinforcing consequence: the child may sit at the kitchen table and attempt some part of the homework assignment. The parent feels some degree of satisfaction. Unfortunately, the child's internally experienced tension and distress limit the amount of homework that is actually done — and what is done is often done poorly since the child is ruminating about the argument. The parent feels little sympathy for the child while in this angry, demanding mode. This diminishes the parent-child bond, and the parent has modeled poor problem-solving skills. The child doesn't want to ask the parent for further help with assignments, knowing it will come only at the price of some belittling comment. The anger festers. Although some amount of immediate compliance is achieved, the overall outcome is poor.

The reader can well imagine similar scenarios in the world of *business* (where an employee might be demeaned by a supervisor), *on the road* (where another driver yells and flips "the finger"), or *at home* (when a spouse yells that a partner has spent "too much money"). In each case *part* of the anger display (the short-term outcome) is reinforcing for the angry person. The worker may sit at the desk and do the work expected by the supervisor, the driver who received the flipped finger may back away, and the spouse may apologize.

Aside from some degree of behavioral compliance, there are other documented reinforcing outcomes for anger outbursts. For example, Stosny (1995) offered an explanation based on chemical reinforcement. During anger episodes the brain releases both epinephrine and norepinephrine. The epinephrine yields a surge of energy. Thus, in a situation where the client may have first felt demeaned and powerless, there is now a feeling of power, which accompanies an adrenaline rush. At the same time, the norepinephrine acts as an analgesic to numb discomfort. Thus, these two hormones reinforce the experience and expression of anger. The angry client becomes empowered, able to deal with situations previously found to be problematic, and is reinforced to become angry again in the future.

The immediate, reinforcing hormonal effects of anger are followed by other outcomes that emerge some time after the anger episode. These longer term outcomes appear after the immediate episode has ended and they may be positive or negative. For example, in the community resident and college student samples studied by Averill (1982; 1983), and Kassinove and colleagues (1997), one-half to two-thirds of respondents were generally "happy" about the outcome of their anger episodes. Participants reported that they understood the other person better, recognized that there are other ways to look at the situation in question, felt as close to the person involved as they did before the anger, and gained respect for the other person. Clearly, anger experiences are sometimes followed by reinforcing resolution and adaptation responses. In spite of the negatives, these reinforcements keep the anger alive.

❖ *Problematic Anger Outcomes*

Clients with anger disorders experience anger *more frequently* and with *greater intensity* than do the rest of us. Such clients hold on to their anger for a long time and *ruminate,* until it causes even greater distress than it did at first. As noted above, adults who are high on the trait of anger report more physical aggression, negative verbal responses, drug use, and negative anger-related consequences. Thus, clinically important anger outcomes may emerge as a function of the anger trait.

In the short term, in spite of some positive outcomes such as compliance by others and feeling energized, the anger of high-trait-anger clients does more than energize behavior — it disrupts behavior. Their anger serves more than a communication function — it threatens others. Their anger does more than give a sense of control by evoking fantasies of revenge — it instigates aggressive behavior. For these reasons, clients with frequent, intense and enduring anger reactions are likely to have problems associated with their anger.

In the longer term, in spite of some positive outcomes such as compliance by others and feeling energized, there are *many more negatives associated with anger than positives.* Some of the negatives appear during or immediately after the anger episode. Some emerge a few hours to a few months after the events. Others, however, do not appear for many years. Like the longer-term effects of cigarette smoking, exposure to asbestos, or water pollution, these anger outcomes are a function of years of agitation, argument and discord. Unfortunately, these outcomes may not be linked to anger in the eyes of clients since they take so long to emerge.

The negative outcomes associated with anger reactions include:

Interpersonal relationship problems. Angry clients are prone to arguments; they "come on" strong, and do not see the other side of issues. Thus, Scherer and Wolbert (1994) proposed that anger has a distancing effect. Angry clients are more likely to blame a social mishap on other people and to judge their actions as "unfair" and "purposeful," leading to a desire for retribution or revenge. Anger is likely to negatively bias perceptions, to cause clients to rely on very simple cues (e.g., sex, religious affiliation, skin color, country of origin, etc.) as they interpret social situations, and to be guided by stereotypes ("He's really tall and quite good looking and probably gets everything he wants" or, "All older women are like that!"). When angry, clients are more likely to be sarcastic, blaming, and to use profanity. This is unpleasant for others and may lead to verbal conflict, avoidance and even rejection. Given their argumentative nature, unwillingness to see the opinion of others, and their tendency to blame, angry clients are often viewed negatively in work and social relationships. Thus, they become seen as persons with diminished value.

Workplace problems. The stage is set for anger when workers experience unwanted and uncontrollable consequences caused by aversive behavior of their colleagues, supervisors, or subordinates. The angry worker typically blames others, thinks that he or she has been treated disrespectfully and unfairly, projects blame onto others, and has fantasies of revenge. The worker may engage in a form of self-imposed isolation, diminishing team performance, or may try to enlist the help of others to agree that the workplace is "evil," that the company is "greedy," etc. The anger may lead to confrontation, insubordination, challenge to company policies, misuse of company property such as telephones or computers, or to outright thievery. At work, the angry employee may become agitated, irritable and unreliable, making excuses as to why work cannot be accomplished (Miller, 1999). Observers may notice secretive behavior, withdrawal, changes in grooming, mood swings, and preoccupation with another person or company policy. There may be rumination, sleep disturbance, loss of interest in the goals of the company, increased use of medical or counseling programs. Diminished job performance, of course, leads to decreased productivity and profitability. Thus, workplace anger is harmful to both the individual and the company.

Poor decision making and increased risk taking. Anger causes clients to engage in self-defeating actions, to underachieve, and to suffer penalties in their attempt to be "victorious" over others. Typical patterns of rational decision making are suspended, trust is diminished, needless competition is increased, and interpersonal situations are seen as "battles" to be won at any cost. Needless and self-sabotaging risks are taken in order to achieve goals that later seem small and unworthy of such risks.

Substance Abuse. Anger is associated with substance use and leads to relapse in clients who have eliminated drug or alcohol dependence. Indeed, the typical relapse prevention model (for treating clients with maladaptive habits such as pathological gambling, drug addiction, or alcoholism assumes that treatment has two phases: (1) elimination of bad behavioral habits and (2) training clients to deal with situations in which emotional stress (such as anger) is high, leading to a renewed drive to drink, or smoke, or gamble again (Marlatt & Gordon, 1985; Parks, & Marlatt, 1999). It is in these highly emotional situations that clients are likely to make poor decisions, such as "to try my luck in the casino just this one time" or "to take a drink just this time" because "Given all of the crap I have gone through tonight, I deserve it!"

Disruption of motor behavior. As noted in chapter 1, when angry, there is likely to be increased difficulty with complex motor tasks, such as playing musical instruments to a high level of proficiency. Anger is also associated with poorer performance in physical activities that require "coolness" in the face of danger, even though we may be highly skilled at such tasks when not angry. Few building industry workers can learn to operate a crane, or use other heavy machinery, while highly angry.

Perhaps the most important motor behavior for the largest number of clients is driving an automobile. The relationship of anger to driving has become important because of the frustration caused by congested roadways and longer travel times. These are likely to impact mood and behavior, both while in the car and upon arrival at home. Anger may well be a response to slow drivers, discourteous drivers, rush hour traffic, being signaled or yelled at by another driver, and other antics of the road. It seems to be a precursor to traffic violations, accidents, and other risky behaviors associated with inattention to the roadway or impulsiveness. Drivers high in the trait of anger report more risky behaviors, close calls and minor accidents, and less controlled forms of anger expression. Men report more intense anger and more aggressive behavior than do women, and anger is associated with increased speeding and risky driving in adolescent drivers. There is also a link between the experience of anger in non-driving situations and reports of near accidents where the driver was to blame. Anger was also linked to mild social deviance and the commission of driving violations (Arnett, et al., 1997, Deffenbacher and associates, 1994, 2000; Underwood and associates, 1999). It has been known for a long time that young — especially male — drivers are most at risk for accidents and anger may play a role in their driving behavior.

Rumination, fantasies of revenge, and interpersonal-occupational maladjustment. Anger rumination consists of memories about a past anger trigger, placing a focus on the immediate anger experience, and distorted thoughts that are contrary to what actually happened (Sukhodolsky, Golub, & Cromwell, 2001). When angry, there is ruminating condemnation of others, holding grudges, and engaging in revenge based thoughts and behaviors. Thus, the anger rumination itself sustains and increases the original anger experience, without further transgression by the offender. Ruminative thoughts lead to further unhappiness, erode interpersonal relationships, diminish work productivity, and decrease the likelihood of occupational and educational success.

Additional negative feelings. High-trait-anger individuals report more negative feelings such as depression, disgust, foolishness, and guilt/shame following their anger episodes (Tafrate, Kassinove, & Dundin, 2002). We have routinely seen clients in treatment and also research subjects who, when angry, have behaved in ways that they later regretted. For example, one 40-year-old male client got into an argument with a clerk at a local grocery store. He became increasingly abusive toward the clerk who was much younger. The clerk eventually called the police, who subdued the man and took him away in handcuffs. The client felt a great deal of embarrassment and shame over the incident and has avoided that supermarket ever since. Thus, among clients seeking anger treatment, it is likely that many will experience other negative emotional consequences requiring attention by the practitioner.

Aggression. Although some clients and professionals think of anger and aggression as a unified problem, we have made the case that they are separate. Aggression is one of the negative outcomes that *may* emerge from general arousal and anger. Anger may set the stage for the occurrence of many types of aggression, ranging from minor property destruction and physical assaults to major felonies such as murders committed as "crimes of passion." Interpersonal violence remains a leading cause of death among Americans and anger readies us for focused action and mediates aggressive behavior. Individuals whose anger is problematic engage in more aggressive behaviors, as compared with individuals who are not anger-prone (Tafrate, Kassinove, & Dundin, 2002; Tsytsarev & Grodnitzky, 1995).

This readiness to aggress occurs as a function of the rise in general arousal. The anger serves as a filter to increase the level of "crankiness." That is, we are uncomfortable and irritable (cranky) when aroused. We are likely to turn teases, minor insults, and beliefs that we have been disrespected, into major issues. Our awareness that this kind of crankiness exists is reflected in advice such as, "Don't make it into a federal case!" or "Don't make a mole hill into a mountain." Once events are interpreted as major issues, depending on the learning history and social script of the client, they may trigger retaliation in the form of aggression. This model has been advanced by a number of theorists including Berkowitz in 1984 (Cognitive Neoassociation Theory), Zillman in 1983 (Excitation Transfer Theory), and Anderson and associates in 2000 (General Affective Aggression Model).

A drive for retaliation and vengeance is but one reason people may aggress when angry. It implies a sense of retributive justice in the form of, "if you offend me, I will offend you." However, there are other reasons why people become aggressive when angry. Anger is a negative felt state; anger is uncomfortable. Few people wake up in the morning with self-talk such as "I hope I get really angry today. I'd like to spend the day in a pissed-off mood." So, since anger is unpleasant and to be avoided, one possibility is that clients become aggressive to repair their angry mood. Unfortunately, the catharsis hypothesis is false. Hitting a punching bag or a spouse or a wall does not let aggression out. After becoming aggressive people do not become less aggressive. In fact, people often become *more* aggressive after engaging in aggression (e.g., Bushman, Baumeister, & Stack, 1999; Bushman, Baumeister, & Phillips, 2001, Geen & Quanty, 1977; Kassinove 1995).

After acting aggressively people report feeling some degree of pleasure. They may say, for example, "It really felt good to hit that wall!" This may be due to the effects of epinephrine and norepinephrine mentioned above. But, there is a major downside! People who report that they like hitting things, that it feels good, are the ones who act most aggressively later on. The conclusion is that when people face negative life events and feel angry, they may *want* to act aggressively and they may *actually* do so. Following the aggression they may even feel better. However, because the aggression feels good it reinforces the likelihood of acting aggressively in the future (Bandura, 1969). This is clearly a negative pattern.

Medical Problems. Anger, along with anxiety, is "hazardous to health" (Suinn, 2001, p. 27). Since anger is directly related to arousal of the autonomic nervous system and to the functioning of the immune system, it likely increases overall *vulnerability to illness.* For example, in 1993, Kiecolt-Glaser and colleagues videotaped 90 recently married couples as they spent 30 minutes trying to resolve marital conflict issues. The results were very interesting, in that couples high in anger showed decreases in macrophages (which initiate immune activity), neutrophil activity (important for fighting bacteria), and compromised responses to latent viruses. These responses can lead to a number of different medical problems. As a long-term outcome, it seems that health is diminished by high anger. In contrast, if high anger is not experienced in the first place, or if is assertively expressed when it does appear, the negative effects may be diminished

We now present some of the known relationships of anger to health issues, with documentation for the interested reader.

Cholesterol. Cholesterol levels are markers for many important diseases and some evidence suggests that anger is related to blood cholesterol. Waldstein, et. al (1990) investigated this relationship in 29 healthy white men. Using Spielberger's STAXI (1988; see chapter 3), they found that both high trait anger and anger-out were related to high cholesterol levels ($r = .44$ and $r = .46$ respectively). In 1992, Johnson and associates examined this relationship in 39 healthy Black American men who were free of hypertension and heart disease. Although they did not find significant relationships between anger and cholesterol levels, trait anger was significantly related to the LDL-HDL ratio ($r = .46$).

Coronary Heart Disease. Williams and her associates (2000) completed a large-scale prospective study of the relationship of trait anger to cardiovascular heart disease (CHD). A cohort ($n = 12,986$) of middle-aged men and women were followed for a mean of 53 months. They were initially free of CHD and had normal blood pressure. Trait anger was assessed by Spielberger's (1988) STAXI and other known risk factors were also evaluated including weight, presence of diabetes, alcohol and cigarette consumption and educational attainment. The study specifically examined the relationship of trait anger to combined CHD (acute myocardial infarction [MI], fatal CHD, silent MI, and cardiac revascularization procedures) and to "hard" events only (acute MI and fatal CHD). Results indicated that among adults with normal blood pressure, "the risk of combined CHD and of 'hard' events increased monotonically with increasing levels of trait anger" (p. 2034). In addition, "for combined CHD ...high anger scorers were 2.61 times more likely to have an event than low anger scorers" and "the risk of 'hard' events among high anger normotensive individuals... was nearly 3 times that of their low anger counterparts" (p. 2036). The risk posed by high trait anger was concluded to be independent of other established biological risk factors. This study is of particular importance since it was prospective in design and the subjects were free of heart disease at the beginning of measurement. The authors concluded that, "in addition to any adverse personal and social consequences that may accrue from having frequent and intense anger, there may be unfavorable cardiovascular-related outcomes as well. Anger proneness as a personality trait may place normotensive middle-aged men and women at significant risk for CHD morbidity and death independent of the established biological risk factors" (p. 2038).

A similar study on hostility was conducted by Iribarren (2000). Known as the Coronary Artery Risk Development in Young Adults Study, the participants were 374 men and women, black and white, from four major cities in Alabama, Illinois, Minnesota and California. After 10 years, their coronary artery calcification was assessed using electron-beam instrumentation. Results from the Cook-Medley Hostility scale showed a clear and direct relationship between hostility and coronary artery blockage.

Numerous other research studies have found that anger and hostility are associated with death from cardiovascular disease. For example, Barefoot and colleagues (Barefoot, et al., 1989; Barefoot, Dahlstrom, & William, 1983; Barefoot, Larsen, von der Lieth, & Schroll, 1995; Barefoot et al., 1987) demonstrated a significant association between Cook-Medley Hostility scores and cardiovascular disease incidence and deaths in law students (followed for almost 30 years), medical school students (followed for 25 years), older adults (followed for 15 years), and Danish older adults (followed for 27 years). Some of the data showed these results held even when age, health status, and traditional risk factors such as smoking, lipid levels, and blood pressure were controlled.

Finally, there is evidence that episodes of anger (as opposed to anger as a trait) may trigger myocardial infarctions. In one study, 1623 patients were interviewed an average of four days after they had a heart attack and were give an anger onset scale and the state anger scale of the STAXI. Based on the anger onset scale, it was concluded that, "the relative risk of myocardial infarction in the 2 hours after an episode of anger was 2.3" and "the state anger scale corroborated these findings with a relative risk of 1.9" (Mittleman, et al, 1995, p. 1720).

Stroke: Stroke is another problem that has been linked to anger. In a prospective epidemiological study, Everson and her colleagues (1999) assessed anger expression style in 2074 Finnish men with Spielberger's Anger Expression Scale (1985). As part of an ischemic heart study, they followed these men for a mean of 8.3 years to assess their probability of having a stroke. After adjusting for age, blood pressure, diabetes, smoking and alcohol use, cholesterol, and other known risk factors, they found a significant relationship between the incidence of stroke and high levels of anger expressed outwardly. According to Everson, "Men who frequently expressed their anger outwardly when provoked were twice as likely to experience a stroke in the subsequent 8 years than men who were more even tempered . . . Anger-in and anger-control were not associated with increased stroke risk. . ." (p. 526). This is strong evidence *against* the old idea of catharsis, that letting anger out is healthy.

Cancer. In 1994, Eysenck concluded that there is a cancer prone personality type (Type C), characterized by a tendency to suppress emotions such as anger and anxiety. He postulated that the link between anger and cancer is a function of the bodily changes that occur after years and years of problematic anger and immune system changes. While not discounting other known causes of cancer such as pollution, smoking, and chemical hazards, it seems important to recognize the role that anger may play in this group of diseases.

Butow and her associates (2000) reviewed the evidence regarding various epidemiological factors and breast cancer. They concluded, "Seven studies show anger repression or alexithymia as predictors, the strongest evidence suggesting that younger women are at increased risk" (p. 169). In contrast, they found no evidence that a lack of social support, chronic anxiety, or depression affect breast cancer development. Disease, particularly cancer, may well result from failures in expressiveness and/or repressiveness in the expression of anger (Hiller, 1989).

Xu, Li, Han, and Liu (1995) compared 30 male and female adult stomach cancer patients to 50 normal adults (age range of 40 to 65). Among other factors, they found a relationship between anger-in and cancer, attributed to lowered functioning of the immune system.

Kune and associates (1991) assessed self-reported anger in 637 new cases of colorectal cancer. After other known risk factors such as diet, beer intake and family history were taken into account, they found an association of cancer with a personality type that included denial and repression of anger. They concluded, "colorectal cancer patients have a personality profile which includes the elements of denial, repression of anger, anxiety and other negative emotions . . . the avoidance of conflict, and the suppression of reactions which may offend others. . . " (p. 39). Their colorectal patients tried to fake good (i.e., to maintain the appearance of a "nice" or "good" person) which Kune and colleagues believe may contribute to the clinical expression of colorectal cancer.

Pain. Evidence suggests that anger-out is negatively related to pain and to the ability to lift objects in chronic pain patients (Burns, et. al, 1996; 1998). Kerns, Rosenberg, & Jacob (1994) examined anger expression and pain reports in 142 chronic pain patients. Their mean age was 50 and they had suffered with pain (mostly, low back pain) for approximately 12 years. Almost half had surgery for their pain, almost half were on disability, and more than 60% were using prescribed pain medication. The results showed that patients who tended to internalize angry feelings, and thus avoid interpersonal conflict, reported higher subjective levels of pain and more expressions of pain behaviors. Suppressed anger also contributed to interference with other life activities. Kern, et al., (1994) suggest two possible mechanisms for the relationship between anger suppression and pain. First, as noted earlier by Beutler and colleagues (1986), suppressed anger may compromise the central opiod system's (i.e., endorphin and enkaphalin-like substances) ability to moderate perceived pain. Second, the relationship of anger to pain may be mediated by the peripheral nervous system. Unexpressed anger may contribute to pain mediated by muscle tension (see Schwartz, et al., 1981).

Wade, et. al (1990) studied 143 adult pain patients (mean age = 47) and also reported that anger is a critical concomitant of pain. Using psychological assessment instruments such as the MMPI and the Beck Depression Inventory, they concluded that anger and frustration are critical parts of the pain experience. Fernandez and Turk (1995) reported, "The prevalence of anger among chronic pain patients has negative consequences for the physical and psychological well being of the patient" p. (165). Of course, not all scholars agree that mood impacts on the pain experience. Given that much of the evidence is correlational, some believe that increase in pain adversely affects mood (Gaskin, Greene, Robinson & Geisser, 1992).

In summary, clients especially high on the personality trait of anger experience episodes of anger more frequently and intensely, and have more long-term negative outcomes. The more that anger is experienced, the more it is forcibly held in and left unresolved to fester, and the more it is expressed violently, the greater the likelihood that behavioral and medical problems will be faced by clients. Anger leads to impairments and losses, which results in other negative emotions such as depression, guilt, and shame. In contrast, if intense anger is not experienced in the first place, or if it is assertively expressed in a healthy manner when it is experienced, or if it is reduced in intensity by some of the techniques we present in later chapters, the negative effects may be greatly diminished.

Clients may resist this knowledge, as many of the negatives appear only in the longer term and may not be easily linked to their present anger. Interpersonally, we can all easily forgive one angry outburst, or two, or three. But, how many before lasting damage to relationships emerge? Medically, we can all tolerate some episodes of raised blood pressure or a lowered immune response. How long, however, before these take a serious toll?

The model on which our treatment program is based posits that anger episodes begin with personally relevant triggers which lead to general arousal. Based upon the learning history of the client, the initial trigger and the arousal are then interpreted in a way that leads to even greater arousal and agitation — labeled as anger or perhaps rage. These more intense feelings may be suppressed and forcefully controlled, leading to ruminative seething. Alternatively, they may be expressed outwardly in the form of verbal or motor action. These actions have consequences, some of which are quite negative in the longer term. Frequent, intense and enduring anger can even be fatal!

Client Information Sheet

The Anger Episode Model

Many people believe that anger just "happens." They don't understand why they become angry and agitated, sometimes about very little things. In fact, people who become angry often say, "I don't know. It's just me. It's the way I always react. It's not you, I get that way with everyone." Without understanding how anger develops, it is easy to feel overwhelmed and to become pessimistic about bringing the anger under control. In fact, anger usually follows a clear pathway to expression, which can be presented as a model or simplified way of thinking about anger. The anger model has five parts and applies to everyone. It is wise to ask your mental health practitioner help you understand how your own anger develops.

Triggers + Appraisals

A trigger is the first part of the sequence. It can be something another person says ("You're lazy) or does or doesn't do, as when a parent discovers that a child failed to do homework. It can be a minor event, as when an employer suddenly asks an employee to work overtime. Or, it can be a major event such as physical abuse. The trigger does not have to be an external event. It can be a memory of the past, as in the case of a daydream about a neglectful spouse, or a major event in history such as slavery or the holocaust.

Every trigger is appraised or evaluated. It is rare to "just" think about a trigger. For example, when it is discovered that a child failed a school examination or helped a neighbor with yard work, the trigger is placed into the category of "good" or "bad." When it is discovered that a friend is telling others that you are "trustworthy" or "not to be trusted," the event is also classified. Unfortunately, triggers are often over-appraised and magnified out of proportion. Anger is often caused by such over-evaluations. Consider, for example, that your friend promised to pick you up at 7p.m. to go to the movies. It is now 7:45 and the friend has not arrived. In fact, the friend never does arrive. When called, the friend claims to have forgotten about the whole thing. The friend's action can be called: excellent . . . good . . . fine . . . bad . . . absolutely disgusting . . . or . . . catastrophic. Most would agree that "bad" is the rational appraisal. However, we all know of people who magnify and say something like, "That was terrible, I can't take it anymore. My friend should have remembered. What a jerk." Such evaluations are frequent causes of anger.

Experiences + Expressions

The experience of anger is the personal part. It consists of your private thoughts and images, as well as your goals for resolution of the problem. No one knows about this "self-talk" but you. Your private anger can be anywhere from mild to intense, and you may feel angry rarely or quite frequently. In addition, each person has a unique pattern of anger expression. Some people yell, scream, and "let it all hang out." Others, mope and pout. Sometimes, it goes away in a short period of time. Some people, however, dwell on the event for hours, days, months or even years. With pride, they say, "I'm like that elephant who never forgets." Talk with your practitioner about your own style, as there are real costs to these patterns.

Outcomes

Your practitioner will ask you to examine the effect of your anger. In the short run, your family members or colleagues may do what you ask, when you act in anger. In the longer run, you may lose the respect of persons who are the target of your anger. And, you may suffer in other ways such as with medical problems. Ask what you are trying to achieve with your anger and if there is a better way to accomplish your goals. Your mental health practitioner is an expert.

[Howard Kassinove, Ph.D. and Raymond Chip Tafrate, Ph.D. *Anger Management: The Complete Treatment Guidebook for Practitioners* © 2002]

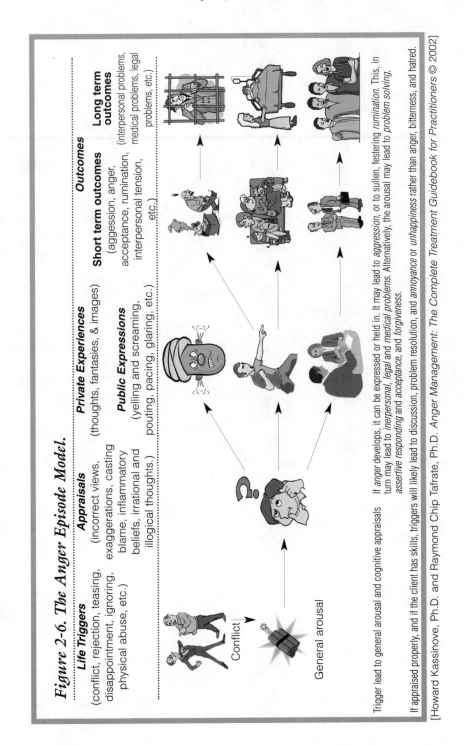

Figure 2-6. The Anger Episode Model.

[Howard Kassinove, Ph.D. and Raymond Chip Tafrate, Ph.D. *Anger Management: The Complete Treatment Guidebook for Practitioners* © 2002]

3

THE BASICS
Assessment and Diagnosis

An angry man is full of poison.
— Confucius

A good analysis of the private experience and public expression of anger is based on listening, watching, and formal testing. This analysis begins by listening to the *verbal reports* of the client that reveal some portion of the internal experience. We refer to a "portion" of the internal experience since clients filter their reports, and rarely tell us all that they are thinking or imagining. In addition, they may tell more than they have actually experienced. The practitioner's questions, in and of themselves, may encourage the client to embellish aspects of the anger experience. Thus, it is useful to have *informant reports*, when possible, to supplement client reports. They provide for a degree of reliability about the anger expression that may have actually occurred. *Observations* of the client, particularly of the client's face, add to verbal reports, and allow the practitioner to draw her or his own conclusions about the intensity of experienced anger. In contrast, *self-monitoring* helps clients/patients attend to the elements of their anger between sessions. Finally, formal *psychometric testing* completes the process and allows for a client's anger to be compared to that of a standard peer group. We do not have the space to review these elements of assessment in great depth. Nevertheless, we want to present some major points for practitioners to consider.

Verbal (Oral) Report. Ask clients what they felt during aversive interactions, especially those situations that commonly elicit anger in the majority of people. If anger is acknowledged, discussion may help both client and practitioner to understand its various dimensions (i.e., intensity, duration, attributions, etc.). If anger is denied in such interactions (e.g., "I don't care what he did," or "It doesn't matter to me," or "I'm definitely not mad"), examine the client's willingness to admit to angry feelings. It is often useful to use imagery, asking the client to close his or her eyes and, for example, to "Imagine you are in that supermarket. See

61

the aisles stacked with food. Now look at that salesclerk. Recall that you are asking for help in locating the cleaning products and the clerk responds with a curt, 'Try the other end of the store!' See the clerk's face and clothing. Now, how did you feel at that moment?"

We have no illusions that simple verbal report always leads to some kind of "truth." Distortions occur for a host of reasons. Clients may deny anger for fear that it indicates weakness or loss of control. Clients may be motivated to deny anger if they were mandated for treatment. And, of course, clients may not "know" how angry they were in a given situation.

On the other hand, it may also be a problem if a client too easily admits to anger and is too willing to discuss feelings in depth. It was shown many years ago that people sometimes "tell more than they know" (Nisbett & Wilson, 1977). That is, if asked questions such as "How angry did you feel when your wife said that?" almost all clients will give *some* answer and many will *embellish* their feelings with glory. After all, they think, it is "right" to be angry in this situation. People have been taught to answer questions and many clients believe they "should know" how they feel. Thus, they develop stories about their anger that seem quite "real" to the listener. This does not imply that they are lying. Rather, they are simply telling more than they actually know, in order to comply with the practitioner's request.

Why then, given that clients may tell more or less than they actually know, do we recommend simple discussion and listening to the verbal reports of clients? First, it allows for improvement of the therapeutic relationship. Practitioners can demonstrate empathy when clients discuss personal problems, enhancing the therapeutic relationship and increasing client compliance with the intervention program. In addition, the client's language and logic skills can be evaluated, which can be used for treatment planning. For example, a large part of intervention consists of cognitive techniques that assume some capacity for abstract reasoning. This capacity may not exist in clients of lower intelligence or those with traumatic brain dysfunction. Finally, verbal reports allow the client to tell the anger story without reinforcement from others, allowing for some degree of extinction to occur. That is, by comparison to angry friends or family members, practitioners are far less likely to respond with "Oh my gosh!... That's awful!... You must be crazed!... Don't be a jerk!... Give him hell!" These kinds of statements, often from well-meaning others, can actually intensify and extend the client's anger.

The final reason practitioners rely on verbal reports is that anger, as discussed in chapter 1, is an internal experience. Although client reports have drawbacks and may sometimes be unreliable, they are still the best way to access information regarding thoughts and personal experiences.

Simply asking clients about their inner experiences is the most efficient and informative method of obtaining information about their anger.

Of course, caution is required when verbal report is used as an assessment tool. Although the client denies anger, and none may actually exist, it is easy for practitioners to infer that a client is angry. *Projection occurs,* even in seasoned practitioners, and it may *wrongly* be assumed that a given client is feeling the anger that a practitioner thinks most of us would feel in an aversive situation. Some clients, however, truly do not feel angry, even in the most unpleasant of situations. They may be more accepting of the adversity than the practitioner would be in a similar situation. On the other hand, the practitioner may sometimes be right! In these cases, practitioners would be wise to engage clients in some form of assertiveness training and awareness enhancing exercises. In the end, there is no substitute for good clinical judgment and learning, under supervision, to understand the benefits and pitfalls of oral report.

Informant Reports. Reports by informants who know the client well, such as a best friend or spouse, can be quite helpful. For example, we have always been very respectful of parents who seem able to "read" their child's feelings. Children often deny feelings, as they haven't yet learned how to sense and express them. Yet, by looking at their actions (e.g., sulking, being inattentive to family conversation, oppositional comments by usually compliant children, etc.) parents often know they are angry. Informant reports are certainly helpful in family and group therapy, and may be used as a planned assessment technique. For example, a client and practitioner may agree that a girlfriend can be called between sessions to assess the number of anger experiences during the week. Or, a spouse or parent may be asked to fill out a rating sheet in a waiting room, prior to a treatment session. With the rise in computer technology and accessibility, we fully expect that such rating forms could be filled out online and sent to the practitioner. As always, these techniques to help the client are agreed upon collaboratively by the client and the practitioner.

Observation. As noted by Plutchik (1980, chapter 1), *anger is a basic human emotion* that varies in frequency, intensity, and duration. The common belief is that adults are generally aware of internal feeling states such as anger and can give verbal reports to practitioners, if they want to. It is certainly recognized that clients may, in some situations, "hold back." Yet, the fundamental belief is still that we are thinking creatures that are capable of sharing internal experiences through language.

We do not deny this model. We *are* verbal-cognitive animals who represent the world and our internal reactions such as anger through language. Thus, assessment through verbal report is important. However, there are also alternative observation-based assessment systems for practitioners to consider. Some are simple, as when we observe yelling and shouting, or pushing, or the use of profanity. These are obvious and frequent markers of anger.

Anger, importantly, also exists as a *recognizable facial expression* that can be observed by practitioners in the office or in field observations. Ekman (1992) has shown that the basic emotions can be seen on the face and for this reason client observation is important. Examine Figure 3-1 and label the felt emotions. Actually, it's rather easy.

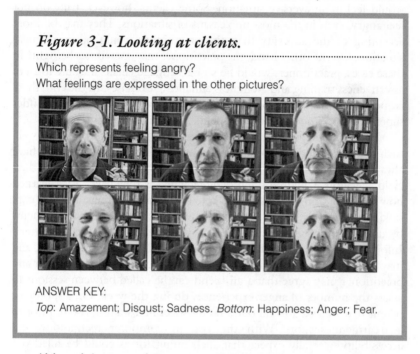

Figure 3-1. Looking at clients.

Which represents feeling angry?
What feelings are expressed in the other pictures?

ANSWER KEY:
Top: Amazement; Disgust; Sadness. *Bottom*: Happiness; Anger; Fear.

Although it seems obvious, we recommend that practitioners spend time during sessions looking at their clients during reports of situations likely to elicit anger in most people. Given the demands of employers, HMO's, and other insurance companies, it is easy to become distracted with note taking and to forget to use facial expression and other non-verbal cues as part of the assessment process.

At this point, the reader may well ask if facial expressions are as important as we are suggesting. We think so! Certainly, an angry face will inhibit empathy from others and will interfere with relationship development. Others are unlikely to approach angry-looking people and they may, thus, miss out on personal, social, and business opportunities. But, far more important evidence exists for understanding facial expressions. Rosenberg, Ekman and colleagues (2001) examined facial expressions in 115 men with coronary artery disease. They found that during stressful interviews the men who exhibited ischemia (wall motion abnormality and left ventricular ejection fraction) showed more anger expressions than men who did not exhibit ischemia. This was the first study to show, with on-line examination, that *angry facial expressions are predictive of coronary events.*

Psychotherapy in the future will certainly be more sophisticated than it is today. With regard to emotions, such as anger, the reader may be surprised to know that computer programs already exist that analyze muscle movements during facial expressions. These movement patterns are then used to determine what people are feeling. One example is Ekman's Affect Interpretation Database (1992). Eventually, data from such facial movement programs will be merged with the analysis of other bodily movements, and verbal expressions, to form a comprehensive picture of client anger experiences and expressive patterns. Until that time, we rely on the seasoned clinician to make affect judgments. The important point to remember is to *look at the client*, as there is much to be learned from the face.

Although facial identification is relatively easy, some clients are experts at keeping the proverbial "poker face." Thus, it is possible to be fooled in cases where the client consciously wants to hide the anger response. One student recently told us that he tries to inhibit the expression of all emotions. Brought up in a family from the former Soviet Union, emotional expression was considered to be dangerous and a blank face was the preferred response in interpersonal interactions. After years of practice in trying to suppress the outward expression of emotions, he now claims that his initial conscious response to negative events is always without emotion. Awareness of his emotions comes hours or days later. He does report experiencing a full range of cognitive reactions, which allows him to unemotionally talk with others about negatively charged events. However, keeping a "poker face" is his goal and he works hard to achieve it. Of course, at times even his emotions are given away on his face. We have noticed that in moments of disagreement and tension, his face becomes observably red even though he verbally denies any emotional reaction. His pattern of reactivity highlights the importance of looking at clients. Emotional reactions such as anger can be frequently detected in the face of even the most stoic clients.

Client Self-Monitoring. Simple discussion with clients is likely to yield verbal reports about past anger experiences and patterns of expression which can be distorted by memory. In contrast, client self-monitoring allows for a precise ongoing record of those current anger experiences that occur between sessions. We provide a self-monitoring form (the *Anger Episode Record*) at the end of this chapter to help clients focus on individual episodes of anger. Asking clients to fill out this form helps them attend to many facets of anger of which they may be unaware. The *Anger Episode Record* addresses the components outlined in the Anger Episode Model presented in chapter 2. One advantage of having clients complete such a record form between sessions is that they may give more accurate responses when the form is completed immediately following an episode of anger as opposed to trying to recall details about the experience at a later time. Also, the client may be more willing to "admit" to certain anger-related behaviors on paper than when being questioned in an in-person discussion.

Another advantage of asking clients to keep track of their anger episodes is to provide an indicator of treatment progress. For example, since clients are instructed to complete one record for every anger episode that they experience, the number of episodes that clients reported early in treatment can serve as a baseline from which improvement can be measured. Other dimensions of anger can also serve as indicators of progress, depending on areas that the practitioner wishes to target. These might include average intensity of anger episodes, duration, number of episodes containing aversive verbalizations or aggressive behaviors, and number of episodes containing negative consequences. Thus, a *Client Progress Record* is also included at the end of this chapter to help practitioners better monitor the course of treatment.

It is recommended that the first *Anger Episode Record* be completed with the client so that the practitioner is available to answer questions. Clients can then be asked to complete the record as homework and responses can be discussed in the next session. In terms of the *Progress Record*, the practitioner records the dimensions of anger that are being tracked during each session and shares the feedback with the client.

Standardized Anger Instruments. Paper and pencil tests are expected to have four characteristics. They are to be based on a good theory of anger, to be reliable and valid, and to have adequate normative data to support their use. One form of reliability suggests that the scores will be very similar if the same person takes the test for a second time. Validity suggests that the responses given on the paper are predictive of the frequency or intensity or duration of anger in the real world. Tests that are worthwhile have established "norms." That is, the test has been given to a reasonably large and representative group of subjects, so that clients' scores can be compared to a reference group and put in perspective. We begin with a review of these characteristics, since many "tests" of anger can be found on the internet or in popular magazines. We do not recommend them since they do not meet basic psychometric criteria and are likely to provide misleading information. Interpretations made by instruments without established reliability and validity can be harmful to clients since they may signal a problem where none exists or may overlook a real anger problem. This is a case of "caveat emptor" – let the practitioner beware!

In contrast, instruments do exist that are acceptable for clinical use. Some anger scales are embedded in instruments that are designed to assess a full range of psychopathology, such as the Minnesota Multiphasic Personality Inventory (MMPI). In such broad measures of psychopathology, anger is viewed as one dimension or subscale of a larger picture. We prefer specialty scales that are specifically designed to measure aspects of client anger experiences. The most comprehensive and well-validated assessment tool currently available to practitioners is Spielberger's (1999) *State-Trait Anger Expression Inventory 2* (STAXI-2).

STAXI-2 scores yield very useful information about individual clients. The instrument is based on a clear model that is consonant with our own anger episode model. First, anger is conceptualized and measured as a *trait*, defined as *the likelihood of experiencing anger over time*. High scores on the trait portion of the scale predict a continued sense of frustration and continued anger, unless intervention is successful. Further, trait anger is seen as either a very general temperament or a reaction pattern. Clients who score high on trait anger/temperament are quick-tempered and impulsive, and are prone to experience anger, without specific provocation, in a very wide variety of situations. However, they are not necessarily vicious and may actually use their anger to simply intimidate or consciously control others. In contrast, clients who are high on trait anger/reaction are highly sensitive and become angry in response to what they perceive as specific provocations related to criticisms or insults or negative evaluations. Thus, the triggers for clients high on trait anger/reaction are likely to be more easily identifiable and they are probably better candidates for concrete interventions. Since clients high on trait anger/temperament readily become angry almost without clear provocation, they are probably better candidates for abstract, philosophically based interventions.

Second, anger is also conceived of, and measured as, *a state of arousal at a moment in time*. Clients with high scores on the state portion of the scale are experiencing more intense anger at the time of testing and this may be a cautionary signal for the practitioner. Aggression may be imminent. In addition, an intervention that seeks to change the client's perspective about family, job, or friends, for example, is less likely to work when angry arousal is too high. Further, the state of anger may simply consist of undifferentiated arousal or it may be associated with a drive to express the angry arousal verbally (e.g., shouting or screaming) or physically (e.g., breaking or throwing objects). Each of these factors is assessed on the STAXI-2. When high state anger is combined with low trait anger it suggests infrequent and transient anger. However, when clients score high on both the state and trait of anger, the anger is likely to be chronic and associated with maladaptive interpersonal and health outcomes.

In addition to examining anger as a trait and a state, the STAXI-2 assesses the client's style of *anger expression*. Consonant with the distinction in our model between experience and expression, STAXI theory suggests that when it is experienced anger may or may not be expressed. When clients are high on *anger expression/out*, they are likely to shout, slam doors, and use extreme profanity, insults, sarcasm and/or threats. They are also more likely to be aggressive and respond to their internal experience with motor actions. In contrast, clients high on *anger expression/in* typically experience their anger consciously but do not express it. Conscious suppression, for them, is the norm and they may disagree with the notion of learning skills to "properly" express even annoyance. *Anger control* takes the concept of anger expression/in even further. Control implies not only a belief that anger is best kept in, but also that monitoring and work are required. Clients high on *anger control/out* are frequently monitoring their own anger and working to prevent expression. This takes a lot of energy and such efforts at control may lead to passivity and withdrawal when assertive expression might be better. In contrast, clients high on *anger control/in* work to calm down and reduce experienced anger.

The STAXI-2 provides norms for adolescents, adults, and psychiatric patients for both sexes. It is a reliable scale and the scores are predictive of important behaviors and physiological changes in the body. STAXI-2 scores can be used to supplement clinical judgments based on verbal reports of the client, informant reports, and questionnaire responses. The normative data allow practitioners to compare client responses to those of thousands of others, thus minimizing subjective practitioner conclusions.

❖ *Anger Disorder Diagnoses*

Anyone can become angry — that is easy. But to be angry with the right person, to the right degree, at the right time, for the right purpose, and in the right way — that is not easy.

— Aristotle

Given the many negative outcomes associated with frequent, intense, and/or enduring anger, it is very important that angry clients receive a recognized diagnosis and be eligible for treatment by knowledgeable practitioners. Usually, diagnosis follows assessment and this is where the problem lies. The often used *Diagnostic and Statistical Manual of Mental Disorders* (*DSM IV*; American Psychiatric Association, 1994/2000) does not contain any formal anger diagnoses, nor does the *International Classifications of Diseases* (ICD 10; World Health Organization, 1999). Instead, anger is treated as a peripheral part of other diagnostic categories, such as Borderline Personality Disorder, Antisocial Personality Disorder,

Paranoid Personality Disorder, Intermittent Explosive Disorder, Schizophrenia, Conduct Disorder, Tourette's Syndrome, etc. Practitioners who work with clients who experience excessive and disruptive anger are left without specific anger diagnoses.

The lack of a formal diagnostic category for anger is problematic, however, as only limited focus has been placed on anger as an independent human problem. As a consequence of the lack of recognition, few researchers have examined the causes, processes and consequences of anger. This is especially true for research scientists who depend on federally funded grants, as some agencies will only fund projects that examine individuals suffering with officially diagnosed problems.

Those of us who work with angry clients look forward to a time when anger is officially recognized as a disorder of the emotions, along with anxiety and depression. Each of these three human problems has self-report, biophysical, and behavioral components and, given what we already know, there is little reason to ignore anger. In addition, from a pragmatic standpoint, practitioners who work with clients on a daily basis know well of the high prevalence of anger.

Fortunately, some investigators have recognized the problems associated with a lack of formal diagnoses and have put forward initial proposals. For example, in recognition of the obvious diagnostic deficit, Eckhardt and Deffenbacher (1995) proposed five anger diagnoses. These are:

1. Adjustment Disorder *with* Angry Mood
2. Situational Anger Disorder *without* Aggression
3. Situational Anger Disorder *with* Aggression
4. General Anger Disorder *without* Aggression
5. General Anger Disorder *with* Aggression

For three of these categories overt motor behavior is not necessary for the diagnosis to be made. In contrast, to make a diagnosis "with aggression," would require that the practitioner had knowledge of significant aggressive behavior. They define such behavior as being either verbal or physical, and might include (a) loud verbal outbursts, yelling, and screaming; (b) verbal threats, insults, and intimidating or highly argumentative remarks; (c) repeated sarcasm, cutting verbal remarks, or hostile humor; (d) acting in a physically threatening or intimidating manner; (e) physically assaultive behavior toward others (e.g., hitting, kicking, slapping, punching, grabbing, shoving, throwing things); (f) physically assaultive or destructive behavior against property (e.g., throwing, slamming, banging upon, pounding on, breaking); (g) actively seeking or provoking a verbally aggressive confrontation; (h) belligerent or stubborn refusal to cooperate with reasonable requests to deal with provocations; and (i) engaging in sullen or sulky withdrawal (e.g., pouting, icy stares). A brief description of the five proposed categories follows.

(We expressed our concern in chapter 1 about including verbal behavior and motor behavior in the same category and believe that the criterion for aggression is motor behavior. Nevertheless, we present the Eckhardt and Deffenbacher (1995) as one model of diagnosis.)

Adjustment Disorder with Angry Mood. Adjustment disorders are maladaptive reactions to identifiable psychosocial triggers. The disorder occurs within three months after the stressor is experienced and persists for no longer than six months. In the *DSM-IV,* three adjustment disorders are characterized by their emotional elements but none are characterized by anger alone (i.e., Adjustment Disorder with Anxiety, Depression, or Mixed emotional features). Two other adjustment disorders also exist, without focus on emotion. One is characterized by disturbance in conduct and the other by disruption of functioning. Thus, for anger to be included as part of an adjustment disorder diagnosis, it must always be mixed with other emotions (even if there is no problematic anxiety or depression), with problems of conduct (even if problematic motor behavior is minimal), or significant disruption of normal work or school activities (even if the client is functioning at an adequate level).

Thus, Eckhardt and Deffenbacher suggest that an Adjustment Disorder with Angry Mood be added to the diagnostic system to reflect a simple anger-based adjustment problem — as already exists for depression and anxiety. The defining characteristic would be periods of angry affect, irritability, sullenness, anger outbursts and/or behavioral displays not sufficient to fit conduct problems. This might include irritable complaining and "pickiness," "snappiness," making (but not acting upon) verbal or physical threats, slamming objects, or throwing things. Individuals in the midst of a divorce might show these characteristics, as might a child who is told by parents that the family is moving to another city.

Differential diagnoses would be made based on a number of factors. Thus, Adjustment Disorder with Mixed Emotional Features would be more appropriate when anger is observed with other emotional excesses but where anger is not the primary reaction. Adjustment Disorder with Angry Mood would also be distinguished from Adjustment Disorder with Disturbance of Conduct and Mixed Disturbance of Emotions and Conduct, if deterioration of work or school performance were the primary problem. However, when anger is the primary problematic response to an identifiable psychosocial stressor, Adjustment Disorder with Angry Mood would be the best diagnosis.

Clients who fit this diagnosis may have been quite well adjusted prior to the emergence of the trigger. As such, they may often appear in private practices, clinics, religious or community-based agencies, and they may represent quite positive prognoses.

Situational Anger Disorder without Aggression. This diagnosis describes a persistent (six months or more), consistent, and strong anger reaction to a circumscribed trigger or situation (e.g., in response to a critical parent or discourteous drivers) or to a cluster of situations that share a common theme (e.g., being teased or having one's authority challenged). The anger is not experienced as an ever-present chronic mood (as in trait anger/temperament), or as a pervasive response pattern to many differing stimuli (as in trait anger/reaction). Although the client becomes experientially angry, there is minimal aggressive (motor) behavior. A client who becomes angry primarily when driving, even in response to relatively minor driving hassles, but only curses internally at the offender and has fantasies of retaliation, would fit this diagnosis, as might a parent who becomes physically aroused and engages in angry self-talk when chores are not completed, but does not yell at or act aggressively toward the child. At the same time, the situational anger reaction may lead to rumination and arousal, and self-perceived distress, as well as a disruption in social, work, or school activities. Clients who fit this diagnosis may strongly disagree that they even have a problem, since the reaction is limited to a specific trigger (s), and there is little or no aggression.

Situational Anger Disorder with Aggression. This diagnosis involves both elevated anger *and* aggressive motor behavior as a response to circumscribed triggers. For example, the client may not only become experientially angry in traffic, but also may drive menacingly very close to other cars and may curse aloud and make obscene gestures at such drivers. Other examples would include an angry employee who, after being "beeped" repeatedly, becomes highly agitated and also throws beepers against the wall, or a parent who becomes internally angry, yells and screams in a belittling fashion when undone chores are encountered, and may push or hit the child or throw objects on the floor or against the wall. To make the diagnosis, it would be shown that the client routinely responds with experienced anger and aggressive motor behaviors when encountering a specific and recurring provocative situation. Clients who fit this diagnosis may be even more likely to agree that they have a problem since the reaction involves some degree of aggression, although their triggers are limited and they may have periods with little or no disruptive anger.

General Anger Disorder without Aggression. This diagnosis describes a high trait anger client who experiences chronic and pervasive anger in response to a wide range of triggers or situations, but is typically not overtly (motorically) aggressive. The anger is experienced as a fairly chronic mood state and/or in response to a wide range of triggers. The experienced anger may be triggered by three factors: external situations that do not appear thematic in nature; internal psychological states (e.g., fantasies of disappointment, thoughts of being unappreciated, ruminations about past mistreatment or injustices, prior failures); and/or aversive physiological states such as physical fatigue, pain, or sleeplessness. Although they seem to be perpetually angry, and may say so, these clients only occasionally behave with motor aggression. As with the situational anger disorders, the experienced anger leads to a sense of personal distress that interferes with normal routines, social activities, relationships, and school or occupational functioning. Clients with this diagnosis will often be seen in clinics and community agencies or by private practitioners. They may even be self-referred as their experienced anger may be personally distasteful. Many such clients, however, will be referred by others, who may more readily see the problem.

General Anger Disorder with Aggression. This diagnosis involves both frequent periods of experienced anger and aggressive motor behavior. Clients with this diagnosis are frequently in an angry mood, are sarcastic and verbally threatening or demeaning of others, and/or elevate discussions to yelling matches. The client might withdraw into an angry sullenness and also have a tendency to throw or slam things, or may frequently push, grab, shove, slap others, or may even use severe forms of physical aggression such as closed-fist blows or choking. These clients display a specific habitual pattern of aggressive behavior that disrupts life. Clients with this diagnosis will likely appear more frequently in interactions with correctional counselors or probation officers, although they may also be seen in the community. Many, unfortunately, will have been mandated for treatment because of their aggression, and such cases can be problematic.

We applaud the work of scholars such as Eckhardt and Deffenbacher. Their work has added clarity to the field. We also look forward to continued efforts by others to formally recognize anger as a debilitating problem.

In summary, a variety of assessment options are available to practitioners to better understand client anger experiences. These include simple verbal reports from clients, verbal reports from others, observing client reactions, client self-monitoring, and standardized anger scales. Since problematic anger can be experienced in a number of different ways and angry clients may present with different patterns, considering diagnostic types can be useful in developing intervention strategies. Thus, good assessment and a well-documented and recognized diagnosis can be helpful as a prelude to effective treatment.

Anger Episode Record: *Triggers + Appraisals->Experiences->Expressive Patterns->Outcomes*

Directions: Fill out one record, completely, for each episode of anger that you experience.

Triggers Describe the event(s)

This anger episode occured on:
Monday   Tuesday   Wednesday
Thursday   Friday   Saturday   Sunday

This anger episode occurred in the
Morning   Afternoon
Evening   Late at night

This anger episode occurred:
At home   At work
Other _____

The target of my anger was: _____
The situation surrounding my anger was: _____

+

Appraisals Place a check next to each thought that you have/had about the trigger.

___ Awfulizing (e.g., I thought this was one of the worst things that could be happening)

___ Low frustration tolerance (e.g., I thought I could not handle or deal with this situation)

___ Demandingness (e.g., I thought the other person should have acted differently)

___ Other rating (e.g., I thought the other person was "bad," "worthless," or, an "asshole," "#@*%&," etc.)

___ Self-rating (e.g., Deep down I thought I was less important or whorthwhile)

___ Distortion (e.g., My thinking became distorted I didn't see things clearly)

___ Unfairness (e.g., I thought the other person acted unfairly)

___ Revenge (e.g., I thought the other deserved to suffer or be punished)

___ Other _____
___ Other _____

Experiences

How intense was your anger in this situation?
0......... mild .... moderate .... strong 100
none   extreme

How *long* did the anger last? ___ minutes ___ hours ___ days

What physical sensations did you experience? (place a check next to each physical sensation you experienced):

___ Muscle tension   ___ Upset stomach   ___ Diarrhea   ___ Positive energy   ___ Feelings of unreality   ___ Rapid breathing   ___ Fatigue   ___ Nausea   ___ Dizziness
___ Rapid heart rate   ___ Flushing   ___ Fluttering in stomach   ___ Tingling sensations   ___ Sweating
___ Headache   ___ Trembling   ___ Indigestion

Expressive Patterns

(Place a check next to each behavior you engaged in during this anger episode.)

___ *Aversive verbalizations* (e.g., yelling, screaming, arguing, threatening, making sarcastic, nasty or abusive remarks)

___ *Bodily expressions* (e.g., rolling eyes, crossing arms, glaring, frowning, giving a stern look)

___ *Physical aggression* (e.g., fight, hit, kick, push, or shove, someone; break, throw, slam, or destroy an object)

___ *Passive retaliation* (e.g., say something bad or do something secretly harmful to the person; deliberately not follow rules)

___ *Hold anger in* (e.g., keep things in and boil inside; harbor grudges and not tell anyone)

___ *Avoidance* (e.g., escape or withdraw from the situation; distract myself by reading, watching TV, or listening to music, etc.)

___ *Try to resolve the situation* (e.g., compromise, discuss, or come to some agreement with the person)

___ *Substance use* (e.g., drink beer or alcohol; take medications; aspirin, valium, etc.; take other drugs - marijuana, cocaine, etc.)

___ *Other* _____

Outcomes

How did you feel after the anger passed? (check all that apply)

___ Irritated/Annoyed	___ Relieved	___ Depressed
___ Satisfied	___ Disgusted	___ Happy
___ Sad	___ Triumphant	___ Concerned
___ Joyous	___ Guilty/Ashamed	
___ Foolish	___ Anxious/Fearful	

What other feelings did you have after the anger passed?

_____

List the positive short-term outcomes of the anger episode:

_____

List the positive long-term outcomes of the anger episode:

_____

How did this anger episode affect relationship(s) with others?

This episode had a (check one) ___ negative ___ positive impact on a:

___ Work/professional relationship
___ Social/friendship
___ Romantic relationship
___ Family relationship
___ Other

List the negative short-term outcomes of the anger episode:

_____

List the negative long-term outcomes of the anger episode:

_____

Client's Progress Record

Anger Dimension

	1	2	3	4	5	6	7	8	9	10	11	12	13	14	15	16	17	18	19	20
# of anger episodes																				
Average intensity of anger episode(s) *0=No Emotional Arousal 100=Maximum Arousal*																				
Average duration of anger episodes *(in minutes)*																				
# of episodes containing aversive verbalizations																				
# of episodes containing aggressive motor behaviors																				
# of episodes that had negative consequences																				
Other:																				

[Howard Kassinove, Ph.D. and Raymond Chip Tafrate, Ph.D. *Anger Management: The Complete Treatment Guidebook for Practitioners* © 2002]

THE BASICS

Overview of the Anger Management Program

It's far easier to make war than to make peace
— George Clemenceau

A formal program, in which practitioners plan in advance to use specific evidence-based clinical interventions to reduce anger, is probably the best way to treat anger-disordered clients. Indeed, formally planned programs are probably best when treating most problems (e.g., Hope, Heimberg, Juster, & Turk, 2000; Wilson, 1998; Beckfield, 1998; Daley & Marlatt, 1997). The program presented in this guide will help you: prepare clients to work on their problem anger; teach them strategies for change (how to reduce arousal, build social skills, and adapt to anger triggers); develop their cognitive coping abilities (acceptance, rational responding, forgiveness); and help them to avoid relapse into maladaptive anger.

At the same time, we recognize that no program is ideal for *every* angry client. Because of the breadth of triggers that lead to anger responses in children, adolescents, and adults, and given the wide variety of prior learning experiences that clients have had in different cultures before they come to a practitioner, a "one-size-fits-all" program is unwise. For these reasons, we decided not to develop a session-by-session treatment manual. Rather, our anger management program is organized into four *menu-based* sections. Within each section, we present a series of interventions for practitioners to choose from and use, as seems appropriate to accomplish the specific goals agreed upon by the client and practitioner. We recognize that clients are different, that the constraints of various professional settings are different, and that each practitioner will be more comfortable with some techniques as compared to others.

Thus, although it is important to follow a carefully planned treatment approach, we advocate a plan flexible enough to recognize the client's individuality. An effective plan can only be developed after thorough *assessment of the unique client* who has arrived for treatment. Differences in client characteristics (e.g., age, background, marital and family status, socioeconomic status, culture, etc.), as well as length and severity of the trigger and consequences of the angry behavior, lead to modifications to enhance the efficacy of the treatment plan.

Settings are also important. School and college counselors are limited by institutional policies and the time constraints of class schedules that do not apply to therapists in private practice. Hospital based counselors may be required to keep records in ways that are different from outpatient mental health clinic counselors. To emphasize the powerful effect of setting, we know of one correctional counselor who was required to work with clients who were handcuffed! When the counselor complained, it was agreed as an accommodation that his clients could be shackled with the cuffs in front, rather than behind, their backs.

(It is worth noting again, in this discussion of settings, that the person for whom interventions are designed may be referred to as the "client" in some settings, and the "patient" in others. The principles are equally applicable, regardless of the label you apply to those you serve.)

Finally, after working with practitioners for many years, it has become apparent that all therapists have *personal preferences* about interventions which sometimes supercede the research evidence. For example, we have worked with a well-respected and impressive psychologist who was trained in the behavioral technique of *flooding* for the treatment of anxiety. Using time-extended treatment sessions, flooding raises client anxiety to great heights. It has much empirical evidence to back up its efficacy. Nevertheless, we typically avoid flooding; we feel more comfortable with graduated approaches to the treatment of anxiety. It's a personal preference for us, since alternatives do exist. These examples point to the importance of respect for the client, setting, and practitioner as an anger management program is planned.

We have found the interventions we present to be useful for many clients with anger disorders. Thus, we ask you to carefully examine the interventions in each section with an open mind. Select those which seem reasonable to accomplish the goals of your treatment plan, and which fit with your personal preferences. Most techniques can be used with clients who are seen individually or in groups. Many can be used in family settings.

As noted in the Introduction, the anger management program has 12 components, organized into four sections. In the *preparation* section, consideration is given to client motivation, the establishment of a therapeutic alliance, and increasing client/patient awareness of their anger episodes. In the second section, the focus moves to *change* processes. Clients are taught to respond differently, with less angry arousal, to the real life provocations they face and are likely to continue to face. In addition, it is hoped that, by developing improved client response patterns, some of the triggers will change (e.g., perhaps a spouse will learn to be less demanding), leading to lowered anger. In contrast, in the next section recognition is given to the fact that sometimes change is unlikely or impossible. In such cases, the goal is to *accept, adapt* or *adjust* to the unpleasant realities of life. Finally, attention is given to *maintaining change through relapse prevention education.* The goal in this section is to help the client recognize that anger may wax and wane, increasing or decreasing over time and place, for a number of reasons. Becoming aware of, and accepting, this natural process will help practitioners get clients back on track when setbacks occur.

In the balance of this chapter, we offer an overview of each of these elements of our anger management program. Then, in the chapters which follow, we discuss each element in considerable detail.

❖ *Preparing for Change*

Assessing and increasing motivation for change. This is the first and very important step when working with anger-disordered clients. Some clients arrive for treatment with clear insight and high motivation, and are ready to work. They are aware of the problems their outbursts are causing and they want to change.

Unfortunately, such cases are in the minority. In the case of anger, many clients deny, justify, or seem blind to their own problems. They see no fault in themselves, and fail to focus on the negative consequences of their anger. Their protestations consist of such verbalizations as, "Leave me alone! I'm not interested," or "It's my mother who pisses me off," or "I can't help myself. Wouldn't you be angry if that happened to you?" In these very common cases, it is a client's spouse, partner or colleague who may be complaining and who may want the client to change. The client, however, may be perfectly happy "as is," taking no personal responsibility or blame for the anger. So, the first step is to assess and, if necessary, increase the client's insight and motivation for change. (See chapter 5.)

Developing a strong therapeutic alliance. It is important that the practitioner show empathy for the plight of clients, even if the practitioner sees the cause of the anger from a different perspective. It is also important that practitioners and clients agree both on the plan of action for anger reduction and how the plan is to be implemented. Empathy and this kind of agreement will strengthen the alliance, assuring that clients and practitioners are "on the same page." A strong alliance increases the chances of success because the client will be more ready to work cooperatively, having already agreed to the goals and methods to be used. (See chapter 6.)

Increasing awareness of anger experiences. Many clients are unaware of the situations or triggers which set their anger episodes into motion. They may also be unaware of how they act when angry and/or how others perceive their actions. Finally, they may not link other behaviors such as excessive shopping, gambling, drinking, or procrastination, to their anger. Thus, a good anger reduction program also begins with anger awareness! (See chapter 7.)

❖ *Changing*

Avoidance and Escape. On occasion, it is best to "just walk away." That is, simply not to be in situations likely to elicit anger. Certainly, being in the presence of a trigger that has repeatedly led to anger (an alcoholic cousin, an obnoxious neighbor) is only asking for trouble. Practitioners can work with clients to eliminate being caught in problematic, anger-evoking situations. This avoidance, crisis prevention strategy is also known as stimulus control. Of course, sometimes it is impossible to avoid anger-evoking situations. In these cases, it is useful to give the client escape strategies. These strategies teach clients how to leave a situation when anger has already emerged. (See chapter 8.)

Managing physical arousal. Physiological changes are a central part of the anger experience. Anger is associated with increases in heart rate and blood pressure, sweating, etc. Accordingly, when anger has been present for an extended period of time there has also been long-term reactivity of the muscles and glands. In turn, these reactions are associated with highly negative medical consequences. Thus it is useful, virtually from the outset of treatment, to teach clients relaxation techniques to use prior to, or during, anger episodes. This is a critical, easily taught skill and most clients readily learn to relax. This training immediately increases the credibility of the practitioner, since the client has learned from him or her something that is immediately useful for anger reduction. (See chapter 9.)

Building life skills. Sometimes anger can be reduced by increasing actual competence on the job, in parenting, or in marriage or other relationships. Such competence includes having skills to perform life tasks with success, and also recognizing when needed skills are absent; sometimes avoidance of, or escape from, a problem is the proper response. There is less likelihood of interpersonal conflict, thoughts of inadequacy, and feelings of shame when competence exists.

In addition, clients can be taught to make a variety of useful and helpful verbal responses in aversive situations, thereby reducing conflict and tension. There is a long history of research and professional experience which shows that responding assertively, and expressing feelings and perceptions, eases interpersonal tension. Unfortunately, clients often make verbalizations which "put down" the other person and increase tension. Thus, both motor skill enhancement and verbal skill development become part of an anger management plan to decrease the frequency of interpersonal conflict, and to reduce thoughts of inadequacy and angry feelings. There is simply less likelihood of anger in a competent person who behaves well, and who is aware of feelings and expresses the appropriately. Practitioners do an important service by teaching clients to be verbally assertive with their colleagues, family members and friends. (See chapter 10.)

Social Problem Solving. Often, clients do not conceptualize their problems clearly. Even more important, they do not think of the many different solutions which may be possible to resolve conflict or achieve other goals. Instead, they become fixated, seeing only one alternative – often an ineffective one.

Problem solving skills help clients to develop alternate models of responding to aversive situations and to imagine the consequences of different responses. This also encourages them to try out alternative behaviors, some of which may seem foreign at first, in order to improve the consequences of their actions. This increases a sense of personal responsibility, since the client has participated thoughtfully in the problem at hand. (See chapter 11.)

Exposure. In the end, we are all placed in situations that are aversive and/or filled with conflict or disappointment. Since these are unavoidable, practitioners can help clients by use of exposure techniques (both in the practitioner's office and in the natural environment) to better prepare them for the realities of daily life. Exposure to an anger-evoking stimulus may be implemented gradually or it may be of high intensity from the initial session. In both cases, the goal is to raise the client's arousal threshold, so there will be decreased reactivity to anger triggers. (See chapter 12.)

❖ *Accepting, Adapting, and Adjusting*

Fostering Cognitive Change I. No matter how hard we try, and no matter how good our actual skills are, life often continues to present us with stress, conflict, and aversive triggers. For example, companies suddenly go out of business and jobs are lost. Illness unexpectedly affects us or those we love. People misunderstand and gossip about us.

Drivers behave aggressively and often dangerously. Politicians make decisions that we dislike. Bullies threaten our children.

Many of these situations have ambiguous elements, and it is easy to misinterpret what has actually happened or the motives of other people. Clients often see things in "black and white" and have to be taught about "shades of gray." The cognitive interventions of Aaron Beck and his associates (Beck, 1976; Beck, Freeman, and associates, 1990) are aimed at teaching clients to properly assess triggers, to understand reality, and to see situations as clearly as the facts will allow. This form of cognitive change, therefore, is aimed at teaching clients to see the world as it really is, with minimal distortion, and to recognize that much anger is caused by misinterpretation of the neutral or positive behavior of others. (See chapter 13.)

Fostering Cognitive Change II. Angry clients seem to take everything *very* seriously, as if the whole world depended on them. This perspective has led them to become victims who believe that every negative event is a catastrophe (like discovering that your so-called "friend" scratched your car and did not tell you) and that they cannot possibly cope with life events.

In the cognitive change program developed by Albert Ellis and his associates (Ellis & MacLaren, 1998; Ellis & Tafrate, 1997) less emphasis is placed on figuring out "the truth" about the trigger. Instead, the goal is to create a philosophical view which increases the client's capacity to accept, adapt, adjust, and cope, even if the anger trigger *was* negative and purposeful, and could have been avoided. Typically, clients *catastrophize* when things go wrong and often believe they do not have the ability to tolerate life's aversive triggers. The proposed solution is to reconceptualize aversive triggers and to see them for what they are — highly unpleasant, problematic inconveniences. This form of cognitive change, therefore, is aimed at teaching clients to accept the world as it is perceived. Less emphasis is placed on "truth" or "fairness." Instead, the goal is to teach the empowering methods of acceptance, to help clients recognize they will not fall apart if bad things happen – because bad things *will* happen. (See chapter 14.)

Forgiveness. There used to be a common saying that went something like this — "Life stinks, and then you die." Although parts of life are truly wonderful, the phrase is actually quite true. Life *is* difficult. People of all ages and backgrounds frequently struggle and many are the victims of the bad acts. In the long run it is better to forgive the transgressions of others, to accept the reality that we are all mistake-making creatures in the face of ever-present challenges, that some offenders commit truly cruel and evil acts, and to accept the apologies of others when they realize their errors. Although it sometimes seems hard, or may even seem impossible, this intervention focuses on the role of "letting go," and further enhances the path of acceptance developed in the prior chapter.

Anger rumination and seeking revenge are past-oriented and harm both the person seeking revenge and the target of the anger. Forgiveness leads to a future orientation, to growth, and ultimately to a happier life. Of course, there are a few real "catastrophes" by comparison to the truly fleeting unpleasantness that we all face. Even in those cases, however, it is important to teach clients to see the world from the broadest possible perspective, and to laugh at themselves and others as much as possible. The truth is, in the grand scheme of things, we don't matter much. Many things in life are unpredictable and it will be a lot better if we take ourselves with a "grain of salt." (See chapter 15.)

❖ *Maintaining Change*

Relapse Prevention. Even in the best of cases, where the client has made real progress, the reality is that anger may reappear. Clients and practitioners alike continue to experience aversive events and, especially when new problematic triggers occur, old anger patterns are likely to reemerge. Seasoned practitioners know this in advance and plan for it. Helping clients prevent a relapse into the "old ways" is, therefore, the final step in a successful anger management program.

Professional experience, as well as learning theory, have shown us that spontaneous remission to older patterns of angry behavior is just part of the way we are. Thus, at the end of the anger treatment program it is important to prepare clients for that likelihood. The goal is for them to recognize that the reemergence of old patterns is likely. Such recurrence does not indicate therapeutic failure or endless backsliding into old anger habits and, with a little more practice, better management of anger reactions is likely. (See chapter 16.)

Lasting change is possible!

5

Assessing and Increasing Motivation

The starting point of all achievement is desire. Keep this constantly in mind. Weak desires bring weak results, just as a small amount of fire makes a small amount of heat.

— Napoleon Hill

U nless clients are *ready* to change, they are unlikely to work collaboratively toward a common anger reduction goal. Unfortunately, not every client wants to change! So, the first task is to assess motivation for change and increase it, if necessary. Often the client has to be shown that, although anger has some benefits, frequent and intense reactions are associated with significant personal costs.

Many clients simply do not understand that *their* anger is *their* problem. They come for help wanting *others* to change, such as their wife or child or mother or employer. They believe that all of their anger would disappear if only the other person (i.e., the boss, girlfriend, colleague, etc.) would act "better." From their perspective, others are the real cause of their anger. This is such a frequent scenario for practitioners that the very first goal is to have clients recognize that the anger problem is theirs, and theirs to resolve. Taking *responsibility* for the problem is the first step toward increasing motivation to change.

Of course, it is common for clinicians to view clinical problems differently from their clients. However, this difference is heightened in the case of anger, since clients repeatedly blame others for their distress. Practitioners realize that it is the client who has to learn to "own the problem" and it is the client who eventually has to change. Such differing viewpoints often bring up annoyance (perhaps even frustration and anger) in the practitioner, limiting the capacity for empathy. We urge clinicians to remain empathic, to accept the reality that it is important to see the problem from the client's perspective, to recognize the "self-suffering" the client perceives, and to be sympathetic in the initial stages of intervention. This kind of empathic bonding will go a long way toward heightening the chances of therapeutic success in subsequent sessions. The goal in this early preparation phase of anger treatment is to *reduce resistance* and *increase the working bond* between client and practitioner, so that the likelihood of progress will be improved.

❖ *Stages of Change*

The *Stages of Change Model* developed by Prochaska and DiClemente and their associates (1982; 1983; 1992) provides a framework for understanding why some clients accept suggested change strategies, work hard, and make progress, while others do not. Instead, these difficult clients argue, debate, insist on endless discussion, avoid behavioral practice, and make little progress. According to the stages of change model, clients do not resist because of some magical internal force or conflict. Rather, it is recognized in the model that human problems develop over time and that clients appear in clinical offices at different points in the development of a particular problem (e.g., anger).

Since personal client characteristics differ at these various stages, the specific types of interventions required depend upon the client's level of development when he or she appears for treatment. Not all clients arrive with the same degree of understanding, interest, motivation, or readiness to change. Working from a developmental stage model fosters an understanding of client characteristics at various phases; allowing the practitioner to prepare an action program that is most likely to be effective.

According to the original model there are five basic stages of client development. Based on clinical experience, others (e.g., Freeman & Dolan, 2001) have proposed enhancements to the model, and these adjunctive conceptualizations may also be useful to practitioners.

Prochaska and DiClemente's (1983) five stages are presented below:

a) *Precontemplative.* A client at this level is not even thinking about change. There is no intention to change (i.e., to reduce anger) as the client is unaware that a problem exists. Angry explosions just seem "natural and normal," with little to no awareness that other people act differently. For example, we have seen cases where young couples argue frequently and see this pattern as normal, having no awareness of other options. In contrast, friends and relatives may be very much aware of the anger problem and may talk about it in the absence of the client(s).

Freeman and Dolan (2001) suggest two additional early stages that may precede, appear concurrently, or be a part of precontemplation. These are *noncontemplation* and *anticontemplation*. In *noncontemplation* there is total unawareness and the client is oblivious to the importance of change. There is no awareness of the effect of their anger on others or the self, or the likelihood that their global level of functioning would be improved if their anger were reduced. These clients show no real active avoidance or opposition to change; they are simply not cognizant, unacquainted with, unaware of, uninformed about, and unknowing about the entire issue. This is very similar to precontemplation. In *anticontemplation,* however, the client is showing an active process of opposition to change. These clients resist and avoid, and place a great deal of blame on others. They may believe, "There's nothing wrong with me! I don't have to change. What for? I won't be a part of this therapy stuff and you can't make me do it!"

Clients in this stage do not come for help of their own volition and will resist the most well-intentioned and scientifically supported change strategies. Thus, it is wise to delay formal treatment until readiness and motivation are increased.

b) *Contemplative.* A client at this stage is evaluating the pros and cons of personal anger reduction, but has not yet made a formal decision to work at change. He or she may have received pamphlets about anger, received handouts from school or prison personnel or an employee assistance organization, or may have seen television programs about anger control. Active consideration is being given to the possible importance of change at this stage, without commitment. The client may believe, "Well, maybe it would be better if I became less angry. But, I'm not sure. And, I'm not sure I can do it." There is little or no active resistance. Rather, this is a personal questioning phase.

Again, we recommend that formal anger treatment be delayed until readiness and motivation are enhanced. Fortunately, it is much easier to move contemplative clients forward as they have more awareness of their anger problem, and its effects on others, than do clients in the precontemplative stage.

c) *Preparation.* When a client is at this stage, a clear decision to change has been made and preparations to take action are being developed. A clear intention to change is present, often within a month or so, and the client/patient is examining what the change process would entail. There may have been unsuccessful change attempts in the past, which serve to inform the client about what will truly be required for change to occur.

Freeman and Dolan call this the *action planning stage.* Clients at this stage believe, "I plan to work on my anger now." They are willing to work with, listen to, and plan a collaborative strategy with the practitioner. They are ready to change and may actively ask for change suggestions. This is the ideal case.

d) *Action.* A client at this stage has already begun to implement change strategies and is devoting time and energy to the change process. Freeman and Dolan report that one of their clients conceptualized the movement from planning and preparation to action as similar to shifting an automobile from neutral to drive. When a car is in neutral the mirror can be checked, the gas gauge and door locks can be examined, gloves can be put on or removed, etc. But none of these are actual driving behaviors. The action only begins when the car is started and placed into "drive." Often, it is an excellent situation if the client is in the action stage. The client may have read books, tried some techniques, and already found some success.

Of course, sometimes problems emerge. For example, the client may have read books which present techniques which are disagreeable to the practitioner. Or, the client may have previously worked with another practitioner and incorrectly learned a technique. Thus, the client may have wrongly concluded that relaxation or assertion or cognitive restructuring don't work, while, in truth, they may have been taught incorrectly. A thorough interview will answer many of these questions for the practitioner and will provide clues as to what direction(s) may be most promising.

There are a recurring set of problems which emerge when clients work at change. Change, after all, is not easy and the work done with practitioners is judged and evaluated by clients after they leave the practitioner's office. Thus, in a stage called *prelapse,* Freeman and Dolan note that clients may think, "Gosh, this is very hard work. Why can't I just blow off steam every so often? Is my anger really that bad? I'm getting tired of doing all of this stuff. I just want to be myself!" In *lapse* the client continues to work at change with the practitioner, but some of the behavioral skills required to continue forward movement are ignored. Such clients are not resisting. Rather, they are becoming *careless* about the hard behavioral work required for change to continue. Just as successful businesses cannot rest on their laurels, clients who begin to change cannot allow themselves much leeway before change comes to a grinding halt. Of course, if the client enters a *relapse* period, in which there has been a week or two when much anger has reemerged, immediate action is called for. Prelapse, lapse, and relapse call for a *therapeutic redirection* in which a basic question is to be answered: "How do we get back on track?" It calls for discussion, perspective-taking, and helping the client become aware of the ease with which progress can disappear. Often, motivation to continue will develop through discussions which help the client see the "light at the end of the tunnel." Of course, as the old joke notes, discussions have to help the client see that light as a new and better and more enjoyable life — not another train about to hit the client in the tunnel and make life worse. The correct perspective can only be developed through therapeutic discussion.

e) *Maintenance*. Clients at this stage have already changed (i.e., reduced their anger) and want to strengthen the changes already made. In most cases, these clients return with a very positive attitude. Further change, consolidation of treatment gains, and fine tuning of changed behaviors is relatively easy. One goal in this stage is to make the client his or her own therapist. That is, to decrease dependence on the clinician and increase self-control.

In the world of education, children are expected to learn how to add, subtract, multiply and divide with the help of their teachers and their books. Once mastered, however, these skills are expected to be useful for all of life, with no return for retraining to the elementary school teacher who imparted them. In some ways, this is the goal of maintenance. Once skills for the reduction of anger are taught, increased self-control will lead to independent adults who can better manage their lives without clinical intervention.

❖ *Increasing Motivation*

There are a number of ways to help clients move from the precontemplative or contemplative stages to the preparation and action stages. We present four possibilities here: (1) fact review; (2) recognition of the difference between short-term and long-term consequences; (3) understanding the negative role of catharsis; and (4) methods to decrease client resistance.

Fact Review; Certainly, it is useful to review the scientifically supported anger "facts" with clients. That is, as presented in the section on anger outcomes in chapter 2, to note the following:

1. Anger is associated with problematic *interpersonal conflicts* with family members, co-workers, salespeople, etc. Anger has two effects: it leads to new conflicts and it exacerbates conflicts which already exist.

2. Much evidence indicates that such *medical problems* as cardiovascular disease, stroke, and cancer appear more often in angry people. Long-term studies show clear increases in *mortality* for people who are frequently angry.

3. Anger leads to *negative evaluations* (being disliked) by others, which affect friendships, social collaborations, family happiness, job advancement, opportunity for parole, day passes from detention facilities, etc.

4. Angry people are *disliked* by others, which leads to *avoidance*, and eventually to *loneliness*. Angry people are less likely to be invited to social events, out of concern that anger-based interpersonal conflicts may develop.

5. Anger may contribute to *lowered self-evaluation*, when the negative anger outcomes are eventually recognized by the angry client.

6. Angry feelings often lead to aversive verbal and (less often) physical *assaults* on others, including persons supposedly loved and respected.

7. Anger is associated with erratic driving, and other types of erratic behavior, which may result in *altercations with the law*.

8. Anger may contribute to *property destruction*, which may be committed "automatically" in a fit of anger.

9. Anger contributes to *occupational dissatisfaction and maladjustment*, which leads to problems with coworkers as well as to lowered productivity and increased probability of job failure.

10. Some evidence indicates that anger is associated with lower pain thresholds and *lower pain tolerance*.

11. Anger leads to *inappropriate risk taking*, such as making needless risky choices which are less likely to pay off in the long run and may be quite self-defeating. It also contributes to poor decision making in social situations.

12. Angry people are often and easily lured into using *alcohol* or other *drugs* as a method of managing negative feelings.

13. Very strong anger can be highly disruptive, can cloud clear thinking, may lead us to violate our own moral norms, and can even lead to *serious crimes* such as murder or crimes of passion.

The outcome we hope to achieve by presenting these facts is a clear recognition that *the costs of holding on to anger far outweigh the benefits*.

A "Client Information Sheet" (see pages 92-93) is one way to share these facts. This sheet can be left in the practitioner's waiting room, or sent home to be reviewed in private.

Anger Outcomes - differences over time. It's important to help clients understand the difference between *short-term* and *long-term* anger outcomes. Anger reactions are often reinforcing in the short term and frequently lead clients to get what they want. Yelling angrily at a child or spouse, or at an employee, "works" — if only the immediate outcome is considered. It frequently leads to compliance, and a distorted perception of power and respect. Unfortunately, these are achieved through intimidation of the target of the anger. The target person complies only to avoid some perceived punishment (e.g., assault, embarrassment, or job loss). In such a scenario the anger is truly costly to interpersonal relations in the long run, and is likely to lead to dishonesty between friends, spouses, business partners, employers and employees.

Many angry clients don't think of the long-term/short-term distinction. Thus, we recommend *time projection* as a technique. Ask clients what their young child is likely to say after living for ten or fifteen years with a parent who is angry and often yells. Ask whether employees are likely to stay on a job where they are frequently belittled or mistreated. Ask men whether they think their wives enjoy being yelled at, and to predict what their wives will say to themselves and their friends about their husband after five or ten years of angry interactions. Ask clients if they have been the *recipient* of repeated anger. What was it like and what do they think the future holds? Also, it is quite useful to spend time educating clients about the long term medical effects of anger. As we noted in chapter 2, there is clear evidence that anger leads to increased risk of heart disease, stroke, etc. Since these outcomes take many years to develop, people often don't link them to anger. They are not well known by the general public.

Catharsis. Teach clients that *catharsis,* or "letting it out," is not a technique for good emotional health but, rather, is likely to lead to further increases in angry feelings and behaviors. This is often surprising to clients, since conventional wisdom and the popular culture encourage the ventilation of angry feelings. Decades of scientific research, however, contradict this popular view.

Figure 5-1.

Benefits of catharsis?

For example, in an early field study, Ebbesen and his colleagues (1975) interviewed 100 aerospace engineers who had been laid off by their employer. Some of them were asked a series of questions to generate anger and bitterness, based on the catharsis model, such as "What instances can you think of where the company has not been fair to you?" The catharsis model predicted that these men would show *less* anger afterwards, since they had been given an opportunity to vent their anger during the interview. However, the opposite was found. The engineers who vented their anger actually reported *more* anger as compared with those who did not vent their anger. As another example, Bushman, Baumeister and Stack (1999) found that persons who hit a punching bag as a form of catharsis were actually *more* aggressive after they did so. Indeed, they were more likely

Client Information Sheet
Anger Reduction is Important For You

Many people come for help with anger. You may be having problems with your boss, or spouse, or children, or friends, etc., and your interactions with them may often lead you to feel angry. Or, you may simply feel angry while driving, or thinking about past crises, or waiting in line. Of course, we all get annoyed and angry on occasion. However, frequent and intense anger is a real problem! Anger is toxic and it causes many more problems than it solves. Nevertheless, it is true that when you are angry people seem to listen to you and they may even do what you want — *for a while*. So, it *seems* to pay off. However, the *long-term* effects of anger are very negative and far outweigh any short-term benefits.

Your interest in anger reduction is a very positive step. By reducing your tendency to become angry, you are much more likely to live a happy, fulfilling life — and one with fewer long-term medical problems. So, congratulations on your interest and willingness to move forward to tackle this problem.

Anger-Associated Problems

1. Anger leads to conflicts with others, and increases those conflicts that already exist.
2. Anger leads others to evaluate you negatively and to dislike you. This affects family happiness, job advancement, and social opportunities. Since angry people are disliked, they are less likely to be invited to social events as hosts may fear the anger-based conflicts which are likely to occur. Anger leads to avoidance and loneliness.

3. Major medical problems, such as cardiovascular disease, stroke, and cancer, appear more often in angry people. Long-term studies show increases in death rates for people who are frequently angry. Angry people die earlier!

4. When the negative social outcomes are recognized, anger leads to low self-evaluation. In the end, it is unpleasant to come to the awareness that you have been the cause of so much family and interpersonal disruption.

5. Anger leads to aversive verbal or physical assaults, often targeted at persons supposedly loved and respected. Angry people say and do things they later regret, including name calling and inappropriate gesturing.

6. Anger is associated with erratic driving, which may lead to altercations with the law.

7. Anger may lead to property destruction, committed while "out-of-control" in a fit of anger.

8. Anger contributes to occupational dissatisfaction and maladjustment, problems with coworkers, lowered productivity, and increased probability of job failure.

9. Anger leads to poor decision making and inappropriate risk taking. In the long run, these are self defeating.

10. Very strong anger can be highly disruptive, can cloud clear thinking, and can lead to (or become a justification for) crimes of passion, committed while in an "insane" state It can also cause you to believe that you need to drink, use illegal drugs, gamble, or engage in other bad habits.

Does your anger place you at risk for any of these problems?

[Howard Kassinove, Ph.D. and Raymond Chip Tafrate, Ph.D. *Anger Management: The Complete Treatment Guidebook for Practitioners* © 2002]

to hit a punching bag again and to deliver an aversive blast of noise to their colleagues if they had been previously allowed to "vent."

"Blowing off steam," "venting," "catharting," or "giving him what he deserves" may feel good temporarily. It is likely to be reinforcing, as noted above. As targets, the children and spouses and employees will often comply with what is wanted. So, the angry person gets what is wanted and is *more* likely to act angrily the next time.

Teach clients about the bottom line! *When clients respond with anger, or act in an angry way, they are actually practicing the anger response.* This makes it more likely that they will become angry the next time around, when faced with a similar problem. Since anger seems to have "worked," it is easier to repeat the practiced pattern again. But, in fact, it does not produce a long-lasting, open, cooperative relationship in which true problem solving can occur.

At the same time, it's important to tell clients that you will be teaching them *alternative, assertive response skills,* and *relaxation,* and *cognitive restructuring* skills, so they will not have to "stuff up" their anger. The alternative to catharsis is not squashing anger. It is learning to reduce anger to a milder level of annoyance, and to express the annoyance in a way that is likely to be acceptable to the recipient.

Decrease client resistance. A presentation of the facts, including differences between short and long-term consequences and the negative role of catharsis, may not be enough to persuade some clients to want to reduce their anger. In fact, strong attempts to argue and persuade may actually backfire and increase client resistance. This is because many clients come into treatment at the contemplative stage, with ambivalence about their anger.

Ambivalence refers to having a variety of contradictory attitudes about something. For example, clients may know about the problems their anger has caused but, at the same time, may believe their anger is appropriate and justified. Thus, presentation of the facts about anger will move some clients to accept what you present. Others will rebel — no matter how wise your message may be.

Whether or not the messages presented in treatment are accepted by clients is often related to the *manner* in which they are made. For example, suppose a practitioner says, "You definitely need to work on your anger! Obviously, given what you have reported, it's very damaging to your romantic relationship. It's so clear; I'm sure that you must see it." In such a presentation, the client may feel attacked and misunderstood, and may accuse the practitioner of taking the side of the romantic partner. The statement may be perceived as limiting the client's freedom and individual choice. Thus, in an attempt to defend his viewpoint, the client is likely to counter with reasons why the anger was appropriate and justified — and will be justified in the future — and why there is little reason for change. Clients can easily become rigid and get their "back up against the wall." Rather than increasing the conviction that the anger is best reduced, the client becomes further entrenched in his or her original position. So, how can practitioners present a convincing case, without increasing client resistance?

We believe the answer lies in the *method of presentation*. Resistance occurs in response to an unacceptably strong, one-sided message from the practitioner that mandates change. The remedy is to present the message in an acceptable way that encourages the client to consider both sides of the situation in a non-confrontational dialogue. In such an environment, clients can resolve ambivalence and move toward a commitment to change (Miller & Rollnick, 1991).

To do so, remember that although the client is likely to respect the practitioner's base of knowledge, he or she also wants *freedom* and *choice*. Thus, the practitioner might couch the message in a way which encourages talk about the negative side of anger, but never directly tells the client to give up the anger. For example,

Practitioner initial probe:	*"Sounds like the argument between you and your girlfriend was pretty serious. Tell me more about it."*
Practitioner follow up:	*"How do you think this is going to affect your relationship?"*
Practitioner follow-up:	*"Even though you think you were right, were there any downsides to yelling?"*
Practitioner follow-up:	*"Do you think that your girlfriend is starting to see you differently?"*
Practitioner follow-up:	*"Do you think your relationship is going to last?"*

Another example,

Practitioner initial probe:	*"Martha, it sounds like you are angry about how your boss treated you. Tell me about it."*
Practitioner follow-up:	*"Do you think about it a lot?"*
Practitioner follow-up:	*"How has it affected your productivity at work?"*
Practitioner follow-up:	*"Given your anger, what do you see as your long-term job prospects?"*

Remember, the goal is to move the client to the action stage of readiness to change. These messages, in and of themselves, are not intended to produce change. Rather, the goal is to subtly increase awareness of the negative costs of anger while not increasing client resistance. As Miller and Rollnick (1991; 1995) have noted in their *motivational interviewing* approach, *the more arguments the client can see about the value of change, and the cost of not changing, the more likely the client is to consider change.*

Finally, some clients will respond better to approaches labeled as *joining the resistance* or *paradoxical intention*. As noted by Reibel (1985), these techniques have been a part of almost every therapeutic model. In paradox, the practitioner prescribes the symptom and takes the position that anger is good — and, perhaps, that the client actually does not feel enough anger. Thus, a practitioner might say,

"I hear that you fume when you think of how you were mistreated in the repair shop. But, actually you may not be fuming enough. I think you could work at feeling even more angry, becoming red faced, and getting yourself really juiced up. After all, it *was* unfair! So, you should ruminate even more about what happened. Why forget what happened months ago? Think of it every hour of every day! Never stop!"

The goal is to have the client see how silly some parts of anger are, and to take the position that it actually might be better to be less angry. Often, if done correctly, clients will laugh as they begin to understand what the practitioner is doing.

Paradox is a technique to be used with caution. It is important that the practitioner prescribe ongoing, excessive, *experiential* anger to the client — *not* retaliatory aggression or hostility. The anger prescription is to be for more self-perceived feelings, more physiological responses such as sweating, and more pervasive ruminative thoughts about the anger event. Do not have clients imagine revenge or an aggressive response. Joining the resistance is an alternative to direct persuasion, and motivational interviewing, and may be considered when these approaches fail to persuade the client about the costs of anger.

In summary, four suggestions have been made to help move clients to a stage of readiness to act and change:

1) give angry clients the facts about frequent, intense, and persistent anger experiences;
2) teach angry clients to discriminate short-term from long-term outcomes;
3) teach angry clients that continued venting of anger is likely to increase personal and interpersonal distress; and
4) decrease client resistance by developing a less direct, or perhaps paradoxical, presentation style.

A client information sheet titled, "Can I Benefit from an Anger Reduction Program?" appears on the next page. Used in conjunction with other materials, it may also help clients to come to the awareness that their anger is a problem to be resolved.

Client Information Sheet

Can I Benefit From an Anger Reduction Program?

You may wonder if your anger is a true problem. To answer this, consider your responses to the following questions. There are no right or wrong answers. However, your honest responses will provide you with guidance about whether you can profit from an anger reduction program.

1. I have experienced episodes of anger for 6 months or longer:
   Yes _____   No _____

2. I become angry:
   ___ More often than   ___Less often than   ___As often as
   most other people   most other people   most other people

3. When I become angry, my anger is experienced at a level of intensity or strength that is:
   ___More intense than   ___Less intense than   ___The same level of
   most other people   most other people   intensity as most other
                                           people

4. When I become angry, my anger seems to last:
   ___Longer than that of   ___Shorter than that of   ___The same
   most other people   most other people   length as most
                                           other people

5. As a result of my anger, I have experienced the negative consequences listed below:
   ___ Damage to personal relationships (e.g., with spouse, children, friends, etc.)
   ___ Difficulties at work (e.g., with colleagues, bosses, people who work for you, etc.)
   ___ Reduced ability to handle difficult situations
   ___ Experiences with the criminal justice system (e.g., traffic tickets, incarceration, etc)
   ___ Physical health problems (e.g., heart palpitations, sweating, sleep disturbance, etc).
   ___ Personal and emotional distress (e.g., worry, dwelling on problems, shame, etc.)

6. There have been times where my anger has blocked me from achieving important life goals:
   Yes _____   No _____

7. I would probably be more successful in my life if I had better control over my anger:
   Yes _____   No _____

[Howard Kassinove, Ph.D. and Raymond Chip Tafrate, Ph.D. *Anger Management: The Complete Treatment Guidebook for Practitioners* © 2002]

6

PREPARING FOR CHANGE

Developing a Strong Therapeutic Alliance

It is probably not love that makes the world go around, but rather those mutually supportive alliances through which partners recognize their dependence on each other for the achievement of shared and private goals.

— Fred Allen

In the quest to reduce anger, working on client *motivation* and therapeutic *technique* are both important. In fact, these are probably the two most important factors which lead to client change. After all, many motivated people change their behaviors without ever consulting a professional. Instead, they eagerly read books and newspapers, watch television news reports, go to public lectures, read the Bible or the Koran, or listen to religious sermons. Then, they select a technique they believe would be helpful and use it to change their behavior — all in the absence of a professional helper.

A personal example illustrates this point. More than 35 years ago, one of the authors of this guidebook decided that it would be good to stop smoking. After reading the psychological literature, a form of over-practice or stimulus satiation was selected and used. On the day that was to be the last day of smoking, five packs of cigarettes were consumed in what seemed to be a constant stream of smoke. The goal was to produce nausea, and an end to the smoking habit. It worked and the habit was completely eliminated! The important point is that no professional therapist was involved. Change was produced by a strong desire to modify the behavior (i.e., motivation) and self-selection of a procedure thought likely to help.

Help, nevertheless, often occurs within the structure of a formal practitioner-client relationship in mental health centers, schools, hospitals, prisons, independent practice, etc. Thus, it is important that we consider the role of the *therapeutic relationship* (also known as the *therapeutic alliance,* the *helping alliance,* or the *therapeutic bond*) in producing an increase in motivation and a change in behavior.

Figure 6-1.

The therapeutic relationship.

Debate continues as to what are the active ingredients in the counseling or psychotherapy process. Indeed, consideration of the influence of the practitioner-client relationship on the outcome of psychotherapy is one of the oldest themes in psychotherapy research. In the very early 1900's, Freud explored differences between the neurotic (or *transference*) aspects of the client's attachment to the practitioner and the normal, friendly and positive feelings that clients often have toward their psychotherapists. Although major focus has been placed in the literature on the distorted aspects of the transference, Freud thought that the positive and reality-based component of the relationship provided for a useful therapeutic partnership, helpful against the client's/patient's neurosis (Freud, 1912; 1913; 1958). It was actually within the psychoanalytic literature base that the term "working alliance" was first used. Greenson (1967) saw positive collaboration and feelings between client and practitioner as one of the essential components for success, and labeled it as a *therapeutic alliance.*

As time progressed, however, many different forms of intervention aside from psychoanalysis were developed and found to be helpful for a variety of human problems. Thus, the search for *common factors* leading to psychotherapeutic success emerged.

The most common factors which seemed to lead to change were found to be the collaborative and affective bonds which develop between practitioners and clients. This line of thinking continued with the work of Carl Rogers (1957), whose client centered or non-directive psychotherapy gave credence to the relationship between the client and practitioner. Rogers focused on the roles of *empathy* and *unconditional positive regard,* which he saw as necessary and sufficient for change to occur. According to his proposal, unless the *relationship* between the client and practitioner is positive, achievement of therapeutic goals (e.g., anger reduction) is unlikely. The stronger the bond, the greater the likelihood of a successful outcome.

The alliance, however, is a changing force. It can be strong at some points, can rupture at others, and can later be repaired. Since proponents of the importance of the therapeutic bond see it as a central force in change, they believe that weak or ruptured bonds will interfere with compliance regarding the tasks of an anger reduction program.

Unfortunately, no studies have examined the effects of the *strength* of the therapeutic bond on the success of anger reduction programs. However, at least two meta-analytic reviews have supported the overall importance of the therapeutic alliance. Horvath and Symonds (1991) examined the results of 24 working alliance studies in which patients received from 10 to more than 50 sessions of treatment. They found a, "moderate but reliable association" (p. 139) between the client-practitioner alliance and positive treatment outcome. In addition, they noted that the importance of the therapeutic bond was not a function of the type of therapy practiced, the length of treatment, or whether the study was published or unpublished. Rather, the bond was an independent factor which predicted psychotherapy success. In 2000, Martin, Garske, and Davis reviewed data from 79 studies in a second meta-analysis. Their results again indicated that the overall relationship of the therapeutic alliance to treatment outcome is, "moderate, but consistent, regardless of many of the variables that have been posited to influence this relationship" (p. 438). As found earlier, the positive relationship of the alliance to outcome appeared to be independent and not influenced by other moderator variables such as the type of treatment provided, the publication status of the study, the type of outcome measure used, the type of outcome or alliance rater, or the time of alliance assessment.

Research interest in the practitioner-client alliance has increased in the past 25 years. This has been partially driven by an inability of researchers to find consistent differences in the effectiveness of psychotherapy across orientations. Some have concluded that psychotherapies are generally equal in effectiveness (e.g., Lambert & Bergin, 1994; Smith, Glass, & Miller, 1980; Stiles, Shapiro, & Elliot, 1986) and believe that common factors such as the therapeutic bond can explain therapeutic outcomes. According to Martin and his associates (2000), "Some have even begun to argue that the quality of the alliance is more important than the type of treatment in predicting positive therapeutic outcomes (e.g., Safran & Muran, 1995)." And, many contemporary theories of behavior change now emphasize the importance of the practitioner-client alliance (Wolfe & Goldfried, 1988, p. 449).

This is a difficult, yet important issue for practitioners who work in the field of anger reduction. It certainly is true that many different forms of intervention are helpful. It is also true that many clients report being helped by practitioners who we, ourselves, may view as unpleasant, ineffective or even incompetent. Thus, practitioners often get cases in which the client reports something such as, "I really liked my previous therapist at the clinic. He/she (who may have been older or younger, black or white, fat or thin, psychodynamic or behavioristic) taught me a lot." Such reports argue on behalf of the importance of common factors such as the client's perception of the therapeutic alliance.

Unfortunately, many angry clients will be seen under circumstances or in settings that tend to work against the development of a working relationship. For example, individuals mandated to anger management programs through the criminal justice system or by employee assistance counselors may be less willing to engage in a collaborative relationship with any practitioner. Alliance issues need careful attention when clients are in treatment due to external coercion. Certain environments, such as correctional institutions, pose serious alliance challenges. Since custody and security are the main missions of most prisons, treatment issues often take a back seat. Inmates are likely to be distrustful of anyone who is viewed as part of the institutional staff. Even when an alliance is established in prison settings, custody issues may interfere with treatment. For example, sessions may be interrupted or cancelled due to security concerns in a particular area or building. Inmates may be moved from one institution to another with little notice or consideration given to their relationship with a given practitioner. Similar concerns may emerge in schools where adolescents, in particular, may be distrustful of practitioners. School psychologists, counselors and social workers work for the school and cannot guarantee confidentiality, which can further disrupt trust. When anger management programs are conducted in correctional, school or similar settings, extra time may have to be devoted to alliance building.

Although the alliance does seem to be important, successful treatment can still be conducted even when the environment is not conducive to establishing a collaborative relationship. The alliance may be important but, according to the latest research, it is not *critically* important. In the largest meta-analysis available, Martin, Garske, and Davis (2000) found that, "The overall weighted alliance-outcome correlation was .22" (p. 445). This represents only a small-to-moderate relationship between the two variables. The authors then reanalyzed the data, recognizing that the relationship they found is low. They then concluded that their new analysis, "indicates that the overall alliance-outcome correlation of .22 is not an overly conservative estimate and therefore adequately depicts the relation of the alliance and outcome" (p. 446).

Finally, we return to our initial comment that many people change in the total absence of a relationship, after reading books, the Bible, watching television programs. In this modern age, they *may* even change after home study courses — on anxiety, or anger, or child rearing techniques, or smoking. They may have purchased the course on videotape or a computer CD, or signed up for an online class. We can only conclude that the therapeutic alliance is *an important factor to consider* when working with anger-disordered clients. However, a good alliance is probably neither necessary nor sufficient for change to occur. Rather, some combination of high client motivation and effective technique, combined with a good relationship between the client and the practitioner, is most likely to lead to successful anger reduction.

❖ *Enhancing the Therapeutic Relationship*

To this point, we have referred to the alliance as though it were a single construct. Bordin (1979) and Luborsky (1976), however, noted that the alliance is actually based on multiple elements. Although there are differences among alliance conceptualizations, most include the collaborative nature of the relationship between client and practitioner in which (a) treatment goals and (b) methods are agreed upon, and (c) there is a positive affective bond between client and practitioner (Bordin, 1979; Gaston, 1990; Horvath & Symonds, 1991; Saunders, Howard, & Orlinsky, 1989).

Defining elements. For a strong alliance to develop it is important, first, that there be *agreement on the goals of the intervention program.* What is to be achieved? Has the client agreed that it is he or she who is to be changed? Or, as is often the case, does the client want to change another person who is perceived to be the cause of the anger? All too often we have had clients/patients come to our offices blaming others, labeling "them" as instigators of anger in the relationship. These clients are either seeking skills to change other people or are looking for verification that other people are, indeed, evil or malicious. They often say, "If only my wife (mother, husband, son, partner) would stop doing that, then I wouldn't be getting so pissed off."

In order to achieve some degree of progress, practitioners have to show these clients that although what they are reporting may indeed be true, it is unlikely that others will change much since the other person has not come for help. In fact, these clients have to learn that others in their life *will* often continue to act poorly (according to the client's desires), *will* neglect them although they may profess to like or love the client, *will* act slowly when they are looking for fast action, *will* fail to act in their best interests. That is reality! And, it happens to all of us. The client may not *like* the behavior of others and, over time, may even be able to effect some little degree of change in others. However, it is critical that the client and practitioner agree that the *primary goal of an anger intervention program is client change.* That is, to reduce angry reactions *in the client* – no matter what others do.

We certainly agree that it is useful to give others feedback about their behavior, and to gently try to produce some change. After all, if we can change some of the aversive behaviors of our children (e.g., belching at the dinner table), or spouse (e.g., cutting us off when we talk), or our friends (e.g., failing to keep their promises), that would be desirable. At the same time, we encourage clients to *accept reality* and to recognize that they would be wise to try to adjust to an imperfect world (e.g., to sloppy spouses, to colleagues who don't work as hard as they do, to misbehaving children.). So, the *goal* to be agreed upon is *self-change*, perhaps in addition to other-change.

Consider the case of Ray, an owner of a small hardware store. At age 52, Ray has had a long history of anger outbursts at work and at home. He often thinks his efforts at running a successful business are unappreciated by his employees and he has a history of taking out his frustrations at home with anger outbursts at his wife and children. Ray is overweight, has high blood pressure, and both of his parents died young of heart disease. He has been having arguments with his wife, who he perceives as unwilling to listen to his stories about his personnel problems in the business. After much coaxing by his wife, Ray applied for help at the local mental health center.

Practitioner: *"Hi, Ray. It's good to meet you. I understand you are seeking some help for anger."*

Ray: *"Yeah. It does seem to be getting worse. But, it's not really my fault. I'm trying so hard to keep my hardware store afloat. But, no one seems to appreciate how hard I work and how much competition there is from those big guys, like Home Dome. It's really getting to me. I seem to fly off the handle almost every day and I just feel so tense inside. It just seems as if I'm always agitated. And, I think my wife is disgusted. I try to tell her about the problems but she just won't listen anymore. I get pretty pissed at her sometimes also."*

Practitioner: *"Tell me more. I'd like to understand how you see what is happening."*

Ray: *"Well, like I said, I own a small hardware store. And, it's getting harder to stay in business with the competition from the bigger stores. They have lots of money to keep a large inventory. And, they can stay open from 7:00 a.m. to midnight because they have so many employees. Me, I have just three guys who work for me and no one ever wants to work late, or early for that matter. They just don't understand the trouble we are in. A small store like mine survives by providing personal service to our customers. We have to be in early and stay late. We have to give the customer attentive advice. We have to listen patiently to their stories when they break items and them try to return them to us. That's the only way to survive."*

Practitioner: *"I think I understand. Indeed, these* are *difficult times for small retail stores. But, tell me Ray, how can I help you* with your *anger."*

Ray: *"Well, these guys who work for me really piss me off. They whine and moan about short lunch hours, few breaks, complaining customers, and not being able to take vacations during Christmas week or Easter week. I want to learn how to handle them. You know, how to react when they mouth off at me. I've just got to get them to understand what the story is."*

Practitioner: *"OK, so I hear you telling me that you're seeking some skills to change your employees to make them realize the seriousness of the situation. I can certainly review your conversations with them, and we can try to work on ways to communicate more effectively. But, what about you? What would you like to change in* you*?"*

Ray: *"I don't understand."*

Practitioner: *"Well, it seems that you get angry quite often. It would probably be better if you could learn to react less strongly to them — even if they keep acting as they do."*

Ray: *"I'm still not getting it."* (Appears uncomfortable)

Practitioner: *"Ray, I'd like to develop an anger intervention program for you that has two parts. One part would consist of reviewing your procedures for giving feedback to employees, setting work rules, things like that. We can discuss what you do, and we can role play typical scenes. As you know, there are some better and some poorer styles of communication, and I can be helpful in that regard. But, I'd also like us to agree that another goal is to change how strongly you react to your staff."*

"Let's assume, for example, that one man asks to take off three days during Christmas week. That's a busy week for you, right?"

Ray: *"You got that right!"*

Practitioner: *"OK. Now, let's assume that you have already said no to his request. But, now he asks again. That's the kind of*

> *situation in which you usually either explode or silently stew. Right?"*

Ray: *"Right again."*

Practitioner: *"Well, let's assume he knows the answer. He knows you can't give him off during Christmas week. But he asks for a second time anyway. You could react with great anger, and tell him "no" in a loud and offensive way. Or, you could react with minimal anger, and tell him "no" in an assertive way."*

"As one goal of our program, I would like to help you react with less anger — no matter what he asks for and no matter how many times he asks. I'd like to give you some power, *some* control over your own reactions *no matter what others do.*

"I'd like us to agree *that* you can change you, *that you are in charge of your life, and that we will work to give you that power and emotional freedom. What do you think?"*

Ray: *"Worth a try."*

Second, it is important to *agree on the methods* that will be used in the intervention program. This can be problematic if the client has strong ideas about what to do to change. These ideas may have come from early learning (e.g., "Like my parents taught me, I bring up my children according to the rule of 'Spare the rod and spoil the child'"), from TV, from observations of how friends have acted, etc. For example, if the client expects the practitioner to encourage catharsis by beating a pillow or taking boxing lessons or screaming in the woods, and if the practitioner knows that catharsis is unlikely to decrease anger, then not much progress will be made.

We suggest that a specific, *written intervention plan* be developed for each client, and that it be shared openly with the client. Talk briefly about the benefits of relaxation, skill development, and working collaboratively and safely in the office on new behaviors before seeking generalization in the real world. Open preparatory discussions about the methods to be employed, and a written document which can be given to the client, will increase confidence in the practitioner. A sample is provided at the end of this chapter.

Particular issues that lead to a modification of the plan may be discovered as treatment progresses. For example, the client may have already tried assertiveness training and found that it was very helpful or, perhaps, that it didn't work. The treatment plan can then be modified accordingly.

Let's again consider Ray.

Practitioner: *"OK, Ray. I think I really understand the problem now. I suggest that our anger reduction plan for you have two parts. First, we can develop skills to help you become less reactive. Second, we can develop skills to help you give feedback to your employees in the clearest way possible. I'd like us to put the plan in writing so that we both know what we are aiming for. OK with you?"*

Ray: *"Sounds good to me. I appreciate how clear you're making this whole thing."*

Practitioner: *"Thanks. To help reduce your reactivity to the behavior of your employees, and your wife and children, I suggest that we use techniques to help you appraise situations as realistically as possible, to predict the most reasonable outcomes of what you say and do, and to become a bit more accepting and forgiving of the behavior of your employees and your wife."*

Ray: *"Wow! I don't know. Actually, that only sounds partly OK to me. I can understand the part about seeing problems realistically and even accepting the stupid behavior of my employees. But, why should I forgive them? What's that about? They have a job to do. I pay them well. Why should I forgive them when they act stupidly?"*

At this point the practitioner might explain the differences among some of these terms discussed. Depending upon Ray's reactions, all or only some might be included in the final written treatment plan. It seems that Ray is having a strong reaction to the word, or the concept, "forgiveness." Since there is little reason to pursue the topic at this early phase of treatment, it would probably not be mentioned for a while. Treatment plans, naturally, are flexible. More often than not, they are modified as treatment progresses.

Third, it is important to develop a *personal and positive affective bond* with clients, to increase *trust* and the *likelihood of behavioral compliance* with the tasks agreed upon. Although agreement on goals and tasks also increases compliance, when the going gets tough it is the affective and trusting bond that allows for greater compliance with assigned tasks. Clients are more likely to improve and follow the treatment plan if they perceive the practitioner as similar to them in some meaningful way. Similarity increases the likelihood of a positive bond. Of course, we understand that this is hard to do in some environments — as in correctional institutions. We also understand that it is hard in "unequal" relationships as when a 45-year-old school counselor works with a 15-year-old student. And, we know that some clients feel more comfortable with practitioners who are male or female, black or brown or white, older or younger. Some practitioner characteristics obviously cannot be changed.

At the same time, if the practitioner and the client are both religious, or of the same religion, then simply mentioning this may strengthen the bond. Or, both may be interested in current events, literature, karate, etc. Telling clients that the practitioner has been working on his or her own anger, and still is, is also likely to lead to a better bond. Research indicates that *coping models* (i.e., practitioners who admit that they have modified their own personality in positive ways, but are still working on improvements) achieve more change in their clients than do *mastery models* (i.e., practitioners who give the impression that they have already solved all of their personal/anger problems and can now pass along their perfected wisdom). So, we recommend that practitioners be humble and admit their own struggles.

Another way to enhance the affective bond is for practitioners to show accurate empathy with angry clients. That is, to demonstrate an understanding of the problem from the client's perspective. This is not necessarily easy, especially given the harsh treatment that angry clients sometimes inflict on others. And, it is certainly not necessary for practitioners to agree with the client's interpretations or actions. Instead, the goal is to convey that the practitioner can see a situation from the client's point of view by understanding the client's stress level, motivation, and goals.

Figure 6-2.

The importance of trust.

In addition, after working with hundreds of angry participants in various projects, we have found that many are surprisingly amenable to trying different intervention strategies — as long as we take the time to explain the rationale. In fact, compliance will be greatly increased if careful attention is paid to making sure that participants fully understand the types of activities they will be expected to perform and why these might be beneficial. Most anger-disordered adults seem to appreciate this straightforward and honest approach.

It may be hard or impossible to generate some of the behaviors and personal characteristics (e.g., gender, skin color, and ethnicity) that *increase* the affective bond. And, as noted above, we cannot even be sure of the range and effectiveness of factors that positively affect outcome. Nevertheless, some behaviors are certainly to be avoided. Ackerman and Hilsenroth (2001) reviewed a series of therapist characteristics and techniques that have been shown to *weaken* the therapeutic alliance. A negative effect on the client-practitioner bond was found when practitioners are rigid, uncertain, critical, distant, tense, and distracted. A negative effect on the client-practitioner bond was also found when certain techniques — such as over-structuring the therapy, inappropriate self-disclosure, unyielding use of transference interpretation, and inappropriate use of silence — were employed. These behaviors can be minimized and this research suggests the importance of reviewing one's own therapy tapes, or obtaining supervision, to bring them to a minimal level.

Anger is omnipresent and we all seem to work throughout our lives to bring anger reactions under control. A *collaborative partnership*, in which the goals and methods of intervention are agreed upon and the partners enjoy good feelings and mutual respect, is likely to increase the working relationship and the client's motivation to work on change with the practitioner. Change will then emerge as the client exhibits greater compliance with the planned strategies for anger reduction.

Collaborative Treatment Plan

Name_____ Date_____

Brief history [Describe common anger triggers, how anger is experienced, and how anger is expressed]:

_____

_____

_____

What are some typical negative outcomes of your anger?

_____

_____

Goals of the anger treatment plan [short-term and long term]:

_____

_____

Specific behaviors targeted for change:

_____

_____

_____

Intervention Strategies   Discussed and agreed

____ Relaxation skill development   _____

____ Behavioral life skill development   _____

____ Interpersonal problem solving
     skill enhancement   _____

____ The art of avoidance or escape   _____

____ Exposure to anger triggers   _____

____ Cognitive restructuring of reality   _____

____ Acceptance and Forgiveness   _____

____ Other _____   _____

[Howard Kassinove, Ph.D. and Raymond Chip Tafrate, Ph.D. *Anger Management: The Complete Treatment Guidebook for Practitioners* © 2002]

7

Increasing Awareness of Anger

The ultimate value of life depends upon awareness, and the power of contemplation rather than upon mere survival.

—Aristotle

It may seem strange to devote a chapter to increasing client awareness of anger. After all, we have defined anger in terms of the personal experience of angry thoughts, physical sensations, and expressive behaviors. The expression of anger is a public event which is easy to see even by clients themselves. However, the actual picture is not as clear as this line of reasoning might predict.

Much of what we do in life is actually done on "autopilot." For example, when we first learn to drive a car we *think* about adjusting the side-view and rear-view mirrors before leaving the parking spot. We *think* about where the parking brake is, and whether it is on. We consciously *tell ourselves* to check the gas gauge to see if there is enough to get us to our destination. However, once

Figure 7-1.

Well practiced behaviors are completed automatically.

driving becomes part of our system of habits we don't think about any of these issues. We seem to know *automatically* what to do. We operate on autopilot. When we drive the same route to work each day, we don't count the exits on the parkway or say to ourselves, "three more to go — two more to go — next one." Instead, we just get off at the correct exit — automatically. We rarely run out of gas, even though most of us don't consciously check the gauge every 50 miles. And, in spite of the urging of the manual that came with the car, we don't "systematically

111

and regularly" check the air in our tires, or tell ourselves "remember to lock the car." For tasks that are repetitive, our typical autopilot operation works well.

We humans function successfully on some kind of compartmentalized automatic process. This compartmentalization allows us to engage in multiple tasks at the same time, while focusing on only one of them. While driving, many people listen to the radio, talk on the cell phone, smoke, talk to passengers, eat, brush their hair, and more. Whatever safety hazards these activities may present (and the hazards are real), we generally don't miss the exit on the parkway, or stop lights, or traffic signs, or needed gas stations, because of these activities.

The same process operates in other motor activities, such as learning to dance or type. In the beginning, much conscious attention is required to count the dance steps or recall the location of the various keys. After a great deal of repetition, however, dancers can talk about personal matters and never lose a step; professional typists can keystroke hundreds of pages and never remember a word they "read." Of course, as noted in chapter 1, where we discussed the Yerkes-Dodson Law, complex activities can be disrupted by unwanted, aversive thoughts. However, those aversive thoughts have to be relatively strong and, even then, the motor activity may still be carried out — simply not as well. The fact is that most of the time multiple tasks can be carried out successfully. While focus is on one task (e.g., thinking about an argument with a spouse) the other task (e.g., dancing) is carried out automatically.

The same automatic process operates in anger reactions. Much of our anger reactivity appears as a function of automatic processing. We just *become* angry, before we *know* it. We are not particularly *aware* of how or why we respond with anger, and we don't think about the other skills we may already possess to respond differently. Anger experiences and anger expressions seem to *just happen,* and we may be quite unaware of what we have said or done. When angry behavior has been practiced over and over again, it becomes like driving, typing, or dancing. That is, it occurs automatically.

For this reason, it is important to teach clients to become aware of their *automatic anger response tendencies.* As this awareness develops, they will become able to *anticipate* their typical anger reactions and *interrupt* them. In addition, they will become able to initiate alternative cognitive, emotional, and/or behavioral responses.

This, of course, is a simplified outline and the process actually takes some time. Nevertheless, it is important for clients to learn that they probably become angry more often than they know, and that they do not consciously choose to become angry. Anger happens as a function of habits built up over the years, and it occurs without thinking about it or its consequences. The job of the practitioner is to break this chain of automatic responding.

❖ *Techniques for Increasing Awareness*

A number of techniques are available for use by practitioners. Each of these procedures can help increase client awareness of the various elements of anger episodes.

Self-monitoring. Clients can be asked to keep logs or journals about their anger experiences. In chapter 3, we provided a self-monitoring *Anger Episode Record* that can be used to increase awareness of individual episodes of anger. Asking clients to fill out this kind of form helps them attend to the (1) triggers of their anger, (2) associated cognitive, behavioral, and physiological experiences, (3) reactions of others, and (4) consequences. Responses to the form can be discussed in session with the practitioner. This builds awareness about the automatic chain of events that is part of the anger as well as highlighting the clear interpersonal reactions and potential negative outcomes.

Awareness can also be developed by encouraging clients to *monitor their bodily reactions.* This will be rather easy if they have already been taught relaxation skills, since they will have learned a significant amount of self-monitoring during relaxation training (see chapter 9). If not, it will be wise to focus on bodily reactivity during the relaxation training that will later be done as part of the overall anger management program. In either case, practitioners can ask for reports of bodily sensations as clients think about potential anger triggers. Over time, an increased awareness of their heart rate, sweating, muscle tension, and gastro-intestinal symptoms in potentially anger-evoking situations will develop.

Clinical interviews about past anger episodes. Simple discussions about past anger episodes builds awareness, and if handled skillfully, can also allow for some degree of extinction of angry arousal to occur. After all, much anger is reinforced by outcomes such as the inflammatory verbal attention it provides to the client. This kind of interchange can be seen almost every day on television shows where people reveal emotionally charged secrets and are "helped" by the hosts. Consider the following dialog which is typical of what occurs.

John: *"I'm furious. I just discovered that my girlfriend has been sleeping with my best friend Peter. It's been going on for two months!"*

TV host: *"Wow! That's really terrible. How can you stand what she did to you? She sounds like a real jerk. And what about*

Peter? Is he really your friend? They both made a fool out of you and you should do something right away!" (Said loudly and quickly.)

In contrast, practitioner responses are likely to be different in timing, tone, amplitude and content.

John: *"I'm furious! I just discovered that my girlfriend has been sleeping with my best friend Peter. It's been going on for two months!*

Practitioner: *"It must have been surprising and difficult to learn about that. The situation among the three of you seems to be complex and confusing. I bet there are a lot of difficult feelings all around. Perhaps we can talk more and consider some options for you at this point."* (Said calmly and at a moderate conversational volume.)

Clinical interviews provide opportunities to discuss aversive, anger-engendering events in a calm way. The practitioner *models* a reasoned reaction to the trigger and begins to build an awareness that there are alternate ways to construct the problem (e.g., "It must seem confusing," rather than, "They really made you look like a fool"), and to suggest alternate responses that might be made. Awareness of options is a powerful way to help clients feel or regain a sense of control. Assisting them with discussion of their anger situations while reinforcing a calm and rational perspective is discussed in more detail in chapter 12, which addresses the topic of exposure.

Role-plays of anger episodes. Clients frequently report anger episodes that have occurred since the previous session. A role-play allows the practitioner to act in the role of the anger trigger with the advantage that the behavior of the trigger can be replayed many times, the manner can be varied, and the action can be stopped. For example, a mother may report that her son was disrespectful. When the practitioner plays the role of the son, it can be played in various ways. The practitioner can be terse, verbally critical, and/or loud. The practitioner (role-playing as the trigger) can give reasons for the disrespect (e.g., "You treated me like a jerk yesterday. So, why should I care about your feelings!") or can omit them (e.g., "You deserve it!"). The use of role-plays assists in creating awareness of anger reactions and allows the practitioner to better assess how the client actually acts in provocative situations. Role-plays also help the practitioner determine the skill level of the client in handling interpersonal difficulties.

Role reversal. A useful variant of simple role plays occurs when the client plays the role of the instigating trigger and the practitioner plays the role of the client. It allows the client to see the episode from a different perspective and may increase awareness of the motivation of the person viewed as the trigger. In addition to building greater awareness, another benefit of the role-reversal is that it allows the practitioner to model a number of potential alternative responses when confronted with the same trigger.

Simulations of common anger-engendering interactions. We recommend that practitioners develop common anger-evoking scenarios which are relevant to the client's life. Such scenarios, of course, will vary as a function of the client's age, sex, marital status, and lifestyle. However, there are many common triggers that involve unfairness, demands by others, disrespect, and social neglect, which can be used as topics of discussion and for role plays. Such role plays, again, allow for practicing alternative responses and for understanding the motivations of others. Of importance, clients can often learn more from these kinds of "generic" role plays since they are not immediately salient to the client's life. In contrast, clients can be quite passionate about their personal anger episodes, which diminishes their ability to discuss and learn from them.

Consider the following parking lot scenario (from Pinto, 2000). In this exercise, the client is asked to sit quietly and respond at multiple points, identifying thoughts, bodily reactions, desires, etc. The goal is to build self-awareness of the clients' reactions and consideration of response options.

Sit back in your chair and close your eyes. Imagine that you are driving your car to the mall to do some shopping. You are alone. You come to a red light, at the entrance to the parking lot, and pull up behind another car. You want to make a right turn to enter the parking lot.

The light turns green, but the car in front of you does not move for a long time, holding you up. You honk your horn but the driver still does not go. The light turns red, again, and his car finally goes. But you miss the light. [Get client response]

It is very crowded as you enter the parking lot. There are no parking spaces. You drive further and further away from the mall looking for a space. Then, you come up to an older man who is pulling his car into a spot. He is very slow in parking, going back and forth many times to get into the spot. There is no room for you to go around him. You have to sit and wait. [Get client response]

As you continue looking for a parking space you come up behind some people walking in the middle of the lot. They block your way and you can't go around them. Even though they turn around and see you behind them they continue to talk to each other and walk slowly. You follow them for a long time. [Get client response]

You continue looking for a place to park. You come to a four-way stop sign. You stop, but see no other cars. As you begin to go through the intersection you see a car coming from the road to your right. The woman driving the car goes through her stop sign without slowing down and almost hits your car. You slam on your brakes to avoid getting hit. [Get client response]

As you slam on your brakes to avoid getting hit by the other car, another car behind you stops short to avoid hitting you. You look in your rearview mirror and see the teenager driving the car behind you is very angry, making obscene gestures. He begins to drive around your car. The driver honks his horn, stops and yells 'Asshole!' Then he speeds away. [Get client response]

You are driving along the rows of cars looking for a space to park. Suddenly, a man backs his car out of a parking space without looking. His car almost hits yours. You slam on your brakes to avoid an accident. [Get client response]

Once the car pulls away from the parking space, you put your signal on and begin to pull into the spot. Suddenly, a man who appears to be "foreign" drives his car quickly into the parking space from the other side of the parked cars. You roll down your window and tell him you were waiting for the space. With a heavy accent, he says 'Tough' and walks towards the mall. [Get client response]

Since the other driver took the parking space you were waiting for, and think you deserved, you drive away quickly, looking for another space. A few seconds later you get pulled over by a police officer. He gives you a ticket for speeding through the parking lot. [Get client response]

These kinds of imagined scenarios and role plays can be very instructive. They build client awareness in a way that cannot be achieved by simple discussion. Imagination, we believe, is a great asset to the practitioner. Consider some cognitive options to be discussed in the scenario presented above. Why was the other driver slow at the light? Was that driver drunk, in a drug induced stupor, mentally slow, preoccupied with a personal medical problem, having a stroke or epileptic attack? Why does the woman miss the stop sign? Are women just bad drivers? Was she preoccupied with her cell phone? What about the teenage driver? Are all teenagers hyper and prone to be disrespectful? Why did the other driver take the parking spot? Did he make an honest mistake and not see you? Did he have to use the restroom with such urgency that he acted in a way that was unusual for him? Are "foreigners" less respectful? And, why did the police officer issue the summons? Does he have a quota to fill? Were you honestly at fault?

This one scene gives many opportunities to build awareness. The characters are purposefully portrayed as men, women, teenagers, seniors, foreigners. Scenes such as this provide an opportunity to assess attitudes, bodily reactions, thoughts, and desires. For practitioners who work in specialized settings such as correctional institutions or schools, scenes can be developed that target challenges faced by clients in those environments.

Imagery recall of past anger events. A variant of working with common anger-engendering scenarios or simply interviewing clients about past anger events, is to have them imagine problematic past events in detail. Recalling events through imagery also allows for discussion, for some degree of extinction of angry affect, and consideration of events and response opportunities from other points of view. However, when imagery is added to simple verbal discussion the experience becomes far more real for the client and more opportunity exists for the elicitation and reduction of the angry feelings.

Naturally occurring experiences of anger during the session. Clients periodically experience anger in session, in response to practitioner comments or behaviors. One of the most common events is when a client says, "You don't understand!" or "These sessions are not helping me!" In addition, in group therapy there may also be opportunities for acknowledging client's anger in reference to other group members. In-session anger can be discussed and defused. It provides an opportunity for clients/patients to observe the components of their anger responses, to practice alternate responses under the guidance of the practitioner and the group members, and to obtain feedback about new responses as they are being developed.

Standardized anger questionnaires, such as the *State-Trait Anger Expression Inventory* (discussed in chapter 3). These paper and pencil instruments can also be used to build awareness of the prevalence of anger in everyday life. Completing questionnaires not only helps the practitioner to understand the level and mode of anger expression, it also provides feedback to clients regarding their level of anger in reference to other groups of people. Providing feedback about where they score in comparison to "most" other people can be an important awareness enhancer.

As they engage in activities that increase awareness of all elements of their anger episodes, the likelihood of eventually interrupting the automatic process and initiating alternative cognitive, emotional, and/or behavioral responding is increased. Below, several additional forms are provided that can assist practitioners in increasing client awareness of anger *(Client Self-Monitoring Form; Life Experiences Survey).*

Self-Monitoring Form for Anger

Describe a recent time when you become angry.
Answer each question in the space provided.

Trigger: What began the anger episode?
_____
_____

Your *internal* experience: What was the anger like for you? Describe
what you *thought,* what you *felt* in your body, and what you *wanted to do.*
I thought _____
In my body I felt _____
I wanted to _____

Your *external* expression: How did you show your anger? What signs
of your anger were seen by others?
_____
_____

Reactions of others: How did other people react to your anger? What
did you they say or do? What do you think was going on inside of
them? What were they telling themselves about you?
I observed _____
I think that inside, the other person(s) _____
Other people were saying to themselves _____

Outcome: When the anger episode was over, what happened? What
is your relationship like with the other person(s) now? How was the
anger helpful? How was your anger harmful?
_____
_____
_____

[Howard Kassinove, Ph.D. and Raymond Chip Tafrate, Ph.D. *Anger Management: The Complete Treatment Guidebook for Practitioners* © 2002]

Life Experiences Questionnaire – Page 1

We would like to learn about some of your life experiences. There are no right or wrong answers to the questions, so please answer them according to your own *personal* experiences.

1. I can tell the difference between those times when I feel **annoyed,** those times when I feel **furious,** and those times when I feel **angry**
       __Always __Usually __Sometimes __Rarely __Never

2. I would say that I usually become **angry:**
___ once a day, or more ___ a few days a week ___ once a week
___ once a month   ___ rarely, if ever   ___ never

3. Describe an *experience* you had when you became **annoyed.**

_____

_____

_____

Think back to that *experience of* **annoyance.** Rate the *strength* of the emotional arousal you felt;

0..........!..........!..........!..........!..........!..........!..........!..........!..........!..........100

No emotional   The maximum emotional arousal
arousal   I have ever experienced

How long did the annoyance last?
___ 5 minutes or less   ___5 to 30 minutes   ___30 to 60 minutes
___one hour to half a day ___half a day to a full day ___more than a full day

4. Describe an *experience* you had when you became **furious.**

_____

_____

_____

Think back to that *experience* when you became **furious.** Rate the *strength* of the emotional arousal you felt;

0..........!..........!..........!..........!..........!..........!..........!..........!..........!..........100

No emotional   The maximum emotional arousal
arousal   I have ever experienced

How long did the furious feeling last?
___ 5 minutes or less   ___5 to 30 minutes   ___30 to 60 minutes
___one hour to half a day ___half a day to a full day ___more than a full day

[Howard Kassinove, Ph.D. and Raymond Chip Tafrate, Ph.D. *Anger Management: The Complete Treatment Guidebook for Practitioners* © 2002]

Life Experiences Questionnaire – *Page 2*

5. Now, describe an *experience* you had when you became **angry**.

_____

_____

_____

THE FOLLOWING QUESTIONS ARE ONLY ABOUT
THE ANGER INCIDENT DESCRIBED ABOVE IN QUESTION #5

a) Think back to that **anger** experience. Rate the strength of the emotional arousal you felt;

0.........!.........!.........!.........!.........!.........!.........!.........!.........!..........100

No emotional   The maximum emotional arousal
arousal   I have ever experienced

b) What *physical symptoms* did you have during or right after the anger experience? (Check as many as apply)

___ Upset stomach	___ Tight muscles
___ Headache	___ Nausea
___ Diarrhea	___ Surge of positive energy
___ Indigestion	___ Flushing of the face
___ Sweating	___ Fatigue and loss of energy
___ Rapid heart rate	___ Tingling sensations
Heart is pounding	___ Hunger
___ Dizziness	___ Thirst

c) *How long* did the anger last?

___ 5 minutes or less   ___5 to 30 minutes   ___30 to 60 minutes
___one hour to half a day ___half a day to a full day ___more than a full day

d) *Where* were you when you experienced this *anger*? _____

e) When did the anger experience *begin*?

___ Early morning	___ Late morning	___ Early afternoon
___ Late afternoon	___ Early evening	___ Late evening
___ Just prior to bed	___ Middle of the night	

(___ can't remember)

f) Now, *what* or *who* was the *cause* of your anger? _____

[Howard Kassinove, Ph.D. and Raymond Chip Tafrate, Ph.D. *Anger Management: The Complete Treatment Guidebook for Practitioners* © 2002]

Life Experiences Questionnaire – Page 3

g) Would you say the *cause* of your anger was;

___ something that *you* did (or didn't do)

___ something that *someone else* did (or didn't do)

___ *unrelated* to you or anyone else

___ Unclear to me. I can't seem to figure it out

h) Which would be most true about the *cause* of the anger?
(Make *three* checks)

1. The *cause* of my anger was:

___ something I *expected* to happen

___ something I *didn't expect* to happen

2. The *cause* of my anger was:

___ something that *could* have been controlled/prevented

___ something that *could not* have been controlled/prevented

3. The *cause* of my anger was:

___ something done *intentionally/on purpose*

___ something done *unintentionally/not on purpose*

i) During that *time* when you became *angry,* who/what caused the
anger? (Check more than one, if appropriate)

___ family member or live-in partner

___ someone who I know well, and like

___ someone who I know well, but dislike

___ someone I love

___ myself

___ an acquaintance

___ a stranger

___ an animal

___ an object (examples: a car, a computer, the TV, etc.)

___ an institution (examples: government, businesses, etc.)

[Howard Kassinove, Ph.D. and Raymond Chip Tafrate, Ph.D. *Anger Management:
The Complete Treatment Guidebook for Practitioners* © 2002]

Life Experiences Questionnaire – Page 4

j) When you became **angry**, check ALL of the things that you *wanted* to do, and/or *actually* did.)

I WANTED TO   I ACTUALLY DID

I WANTED TO	I ACTUALLY DID	
_____	_____	Fight, hit, push, or shove someone
_____	_____	Hit, break, or destroy something
_____	_____	Yell and argue
_____	_____	Make nasty, sarcastic, or verbally abusive remarks
_____	_____	Exercise, play a sport, or do some physical work.
_____	_____	Glare, frown, or give a stern and icy look that could kill.
_____	_____	Make bodily expressions (roll my eyes, shake my head, cross my arms, etc.)
_____	_____	Control my anger and temper, and not show it to anyone.
_____	_____	Get rid of it (e.g., by talking it over or distracting myself).
_____	_____	Think and get my head together, before I acted.
_____	_____	Compromise, discuss the problem and find a solution.
_____	_____	Take time out, relax, and cool down
_____	_____	Just be quiet, harbor my grudges, and not tell anyone
_____	_____	Keep things in, boil inside, and withdraw.
_____	_____	Resolve the problem
_____	_____	Drink coffee or tea
_____	_____	Drink beer or alcohol
_____	_____	Take aspirin, Tylenol, Valium, etc.
_____	_____	Take a drug (marijuana, LSD, cocaine, etc.)
_____	_____	Eat something
_____	_____	Do nothing
_____	_____	Try to think about the positive aspects of the situation.

Life Experiences Questionnaire – Page 5

k) Considering that *incident,* how did you feel **after the anger passed**? (Check more than one, if appropriate)
___ Irritated or annoyed ___ Disgusted ___ Joyous ___ Foolish
___ Guilty or ashamed ___ Concerned ___ Happy ___ Depressed
___ Satisfied ___ Triumphant ___ Sad ___ Anxious
___ Relieved ___ No reaction or Can't identify my reaction

l) What **results** or **changes** followed your *anger episode?*
(Make *six* checks, one in each category)
___ I realized some of my own *faults.* Example _____
___ I realized some of my own *strengths.* Example _____
___ Unsure

___ My relationship with the person or institution became *stronger.*
___ My relationship with the person or institution became *weaker.*
___ Unsure

___ I *gained* respect for the person or institution.
___ I *lost* respect for the person or institution.
___ Unsure

___ I did something that was *good for the person* I was angry at.
___ I did something that was *bad for the person* I was angry at.
___ Unsure
Describe what you did _____

___ I did something that was *good for me.*
___ I did something that was *bad for me.*
___ Unsure
Describe what you did _____

___ I *continue to interact* with the source of my anger.
___ I *no longer interact* with the source of my anger.
___ Unsure

m) In terms of **the *final and overall outcome*** of the anger episode, I believe that:
___ The overall outcome was generally positive
___ The overall outcome was neutral
___ The overall outcome had both positive and negative features
___ The overall outcome was generally negative

Describe why you have rated the outcome in this way.

_____
_____
_____

[Howard Kassinove, Ph.D. and Raymond Chip Tafrate, Ph.D. *Anger Management: The Complete Treatment Guidebook for Practitioners* © 2002]

CHANGING

Avoidance and Escape

Avoid dishonest people and ill-gotten gains.

— Chinese proverb

In some instances there is little benefit to *immediately* facing a conflict or problematic situation and keeping a "stiff upper lip." Sometimes, encouraging clients simply to *avoid* their anger triggers is the best medicine! And, if already in a state of anger then *leaving* the situation may be just fine! If clients can avoid or escape, and function for a while with less anger, they may then be able to generate better solutions to their problems and implement them at a later time.

Avoidance and escape, of course, are not permanent solutions. These strategies do not enhance the coping skills necessary to deal more effectively with anger triggers. And, since avoidance and escape reduce tension, they are reinforcing activities that may easily become overused "crutches" when dealing with problems. Indeed, for many clients avoidance is already problematic in many life areas so it may seem frivolous to even entertain these options. Nevertheless, some clients do believe that they must face all of life's challenges, every time, and never give themselves the opportunity to "sit this one out." This can lead to needless anger.

As illustrated in the case example below, *thoughtful* avoidance and escape maneuvers may be especially critical for clients who are at risk for harming others, or at risk for suffering some type of loss such as a relationship or a job. The immediate goal in these situations is to prevent further damage. We hope that practitioners working with angry clients will, at least, give consideration to the judicious use of these strategies.

❖ The Case of the Feuding Foreman

Brandon, a 36-year-old married machine shop foreman, was recently sent to work the night shift at Remington Tools. He was referred for treatment after ongoing problems with the day shift foreman. Apparently Brandon and the day shift foreman disagreed about how best to handle the production of certain hand tools. Brandon believed that he was far more skilled about production issues and was frequently angered when the other foreman ignored his advice about how projects should be handled. During a typical work week, the two foremen would meet during shift changes to discuss the status of ongoing projects. Since they rarely agreed on how to proceed, these meetings were a source of great tension for Brandon. Angry, heated arguments were frequent and they included many demeaning and threatening remarks. On several occasions, just prior to entering treatment, Brandon and the other foreman had to be physically restrained from each other. Brandon was told by the management of his company that any additional anger episodes would result in him being fired.

Obviously, a primary concern for any therapist working with Brandon would be to help him keep his job. Since even one lapse may be costly, it is important to provide him with strategies that can be implemented immediately following the first session. Although, the longer-term goal is to teach Brandon a number of anger reduction skills, the first objective is to prevent any further damage to his career. Thus, in some ways avoidance and escape procedures can be viewed as *temporary emergency anger control measures*. Several of the interventions described below will be related to Brandon's specific case.

❖ Avoidance = Stimulus Control

A formal name for avoidance is *stimulus control*, since the goal is to control the presence of anger-producing triggers by the selection of environments where such triggers do not exist. Obviously, anger can be lowered by avoiding those situations or people most associated with anger. Sometimes, of course, the avoidance will produce some degree of worry or guilt, as when an adult child decides to avoid visiting an elderly or sick parent because of an anticipated argument. The anger is, nevertheless, temporarily avoided.

Fortunately, much anger occurs in response to repetitive and predictable triggers, allowing for a healthy, but only occasional, degree of avoidance to occur. For example, a client's anger may occur in response to seeing a child repeatedly resist doing homework, or talking excessively on the phone, or when a spouse asks the same accusatory question repeatedly. So, if the client can be taught to be absent from the situation there is a decreased chance that the anger will be elicited. In this way, the anger cycle at home, work, or play can be broken, and the problem can be dealt with at a later time.

This kind of avoidance strategy will not produce long-lasting results. And, it may exacerbate problems if the avoidance is not explained in some way to people directly involved with the client. However, *temporary avoidance may lower overall arousal* to common repetitive triggers and will provide clients/patients with an opportunity to develop other coping strategies, such as those described in the following chapters. This is similar to what might be recommended by a physician for a patient with an allergy. If the patient is reactive to cat dander or peanuts or dust, that patient is told to avoid these allergens as much as possible. The physician instructs the person to not have cats in the house, to avoid eating peanuts, and to keep the home as dust free as is reasonable. Of course, a dust-free home and the total avoidance of certain contaminants found in the environment may be almost impossible. What the physician is really doing is *prescribing total avoidance* in the hope that *reduced exposure* will occur. In the interim, other techniques can be tried, such as desensitization injections and medications that provide longer-term help. In the same way, it is important for the practitioner who is dealing with an angry client to occasionally suggest total or partial avoidance of a specific anger trigger. This is especially helpful in the beginning of an intervention package, before other coping strategies have been learned.

Sometimes, you may be thinking, avoidance is impossible. We agree! Nevertheless, some thoughtfulness on the part of the practitioner may go a long way. Consider some of the following possibilities:

• *Planned Avoidance*
In this strategy the individual identifies in advance a situation that has previously led to anger, and avoids it. For example, in some jobs it is possible to adjust employment hours or to work at home, thus avoiding the potential anger trigger of rush-hour traffic. University professors, as another example, can teach their classes but can avoid going to the department office where they might encounter a particularly annoying colleague. Prison personnel may be able to ask for a temporary change of assignment to a different location or shift. If a client is angry upon seeing children's toys scattered around the house, it may be possible to agree with the spouse to arrive home later, after there has been time to clean up.

Consider the case of Charlotte and Frank, a young newly wedded couple, both brought up in New York City. Charlotte worked in a law office in Manhattan and Frank was a high school teacher in Queens. This is where the problem begins. Charlotte's parents were caring but somewhat intrusive, "old-fashioned," types. In addition, her father was ill, having had two minor heart attacks during the past five years. Thus, her mother and father believed it would be "nice" if Charlotte and Frank lived "nearby" so they could have dinner together every Wednesday evening. This concerned the young couple, as there had been many angry discussions in the past about when they would have children, what type of religious training the children would receive, how to decide on names for the planned children, what kind of house to buy, how to plan for their financial future, and other marital issues. Charlotte and Frank, admittedly, were unclear about these matters but wanted to resolve them independently from her parents. Thus, they decided to buy a small condominium in New Jersey. This location was close enough to be near their parents so they could visit on every holiday and would be near enough in case some type of emergency arose. However, it was far enough so they could not easily visit every Wednesday evening. This planned avoidance strategy, they decided, was the best solution.

Charlotte and Frank's approach was to generate a long term solution, in contrast to Brandon's case (the "feuding foreman"). Brandon decided in the first session that he would try to reschedule his hours — temporarily — so as to avoid any direct contact with the day foreman. This was viewed as an early strategy that would be altered once he developed skills to handle the situation differently.

• *Avoidance by Time Delays.*
In this technique, the client is taught to request a *time delay* before responding. For example, if asked to work on a Saturday, when family plans have already been made, the client might be taught to respond with, "Can I tell you tomorrow if I can make it this Saturday?" This delay will enable the client to regain composure, consider more options, and to initiate calmer and more reasonable and cooperative behavior. University professors, high school teachers and others often use this technique with challenging students. When students ask questions to which the answer is unknown, or when the student is unwilling to back away from a strongly held position, the teacher may say, "Let me think about what you are saying until tomorrow. I'll get back to you then." The simple delay until the next day often defuses the situation.

For Brandon to continue to meet his responsibilities, he was still required to have at least limited communication with workers from the day shift, even though he was to avoid the other foreman completely. Again, in the first session, Brandon and his counselor agreed that if he was asked to respond to a request, he would not react immediately.

Rather, he would tell the person that he wanted to "thoughtfully evaluate" the issues and would give his response "shortly," thus allowing time to generate a non-angry reaction.

• *Avoidance by Seeking an Alternative Method of Responding.*

All too often clients believe that they *have* to respond verbally to an anger trigger. Thus, they wind up yelling at their spouse, child, employee, or co-worker. What alternatives exist? Actually, quite a few. For example, one of the authors of this book found, when his children were growing up, that it was often preferable to have his wife express dissatisfaction to them rather than expressing it himself. His own arousal led to ineffective communication. However, as the messenger of parental dissatisfaction, his wife was typically less emotionally aroused by the same triggers and she did a better job of dealing constructively with the children.

As another example, it may be possible to avoid a direct interaction with a co-worker in which anger is likely to emerge by responding with an e-mail, or memo or letter, rather than in person. This may yield a beneficial time delay and the client may be able to express thoughts about the problem in a less angry way. This is also possible when the anger is triggered by a spouse. A written note may work much better than direct verbal confrontation.

During Brandon's second session, he and the practitioner came up with an alternative method for communicating with the other foreman. Through discussions about his job, it became clear that Brandon's primary responsibility was to oversee his workers and to make sure that the machines on the line operated well. Although it had become convention, it was not a major part of his job description to have meetings with day shift employees. Brandon decided to appoint one of his subordinates, someone who had a calm and relaxed nature, as the "shift liaison." It would be the responsibility of this person to be the representative of the workers on the night shift. This new structure was presented to Brandon's managers and they found it acceptable. He, thus, quickly eliminated the major source of his anger.

Practitioners can often help clients by creatively coming up with ways to avoid specific ongoing anger triggers. We do not promote stimulus control as a panacea. Rather, we simply encourage that it be considered, especially when the situation calls for a short-term intervention, since the temporary avoidance or removal of the anger trigger will give the client time to rethink the whole situation and, hopefully, handle it better.

❖ *Escape = Leaving the Field*

While stimulus control is an *avoidance* procedure, the disruption of anger responses is an *escape* strategy. Escape strategies are important because it is sometimes impossible to avoid situations in which conflict and anger emerge. Thus, it is useful to give clients escape strategies to help them leave a situation when anger is imminent, or has already developed. As social psychologists noted years ago, people want to escape from situations in which there are only aversive choices (Lewin, 1935; 1948).

Figure 8-1.

Escape from aversive stimuli.

Removing oneself from an anger situation is simple, from a motor point of view. Just do it! However, it is a little like the drug use prevention strategy of "Just say no!" Some people find it easy to do. Most, however, find it to be difficult and benefit from knowing a specific strategy. The following are some client options.

• *Time Outs*

When management and union leaders negotiate, they often reach temporary impasses and they take a break (i.e., they avoid each other for a time). In a similar manner, clients can "take a break" by telling a spouse, "I'm upset now. So, I'd like us to talk about something else (or go out to eat, or watch TV) for a while. We can try to talk about this later." If the anger trigger is a colleague at work who is making problematic remarks at a meeting, it is OK to excuse oneself to go to the bathroom for a few minutes to escape a problematic discussion. The world will not end, even though your client may think it will. "Time outs" can be used spontaneously by clients whenever they start to feel themselves becoming angry.

• *Planned Escape*

From a social compliance standpoint, it may be difficult to leave certain situations in which the client's presence is expected. However, if the client knows in advance that a particular meeting with somebody is likely to be unpleasant, it might make sense to limit the amount of time to be spent in that interaction. Angry clients often spend too much time and energy engaged in dialogues that are not productive.

In some cases, clients can actively plan to schedule only brief periods of time for such meetings and to let others know that they have previous obligations that limit their availability. Another possibility is to plan to have a colleague or friend or family member assist in removing the client from an unpleasant situation, as when an executive asks a secretary to interrupt a meeting after 30 minutes, feigning a prior but forgotten engagement on the calendar. Obviously, in order to utilize this type of escape strategy clients must anticipate situations where they are most likely to have difficulties managing their anger and have a plan in place to escape.

• *Distraction*

Since rumination is likely to increase anger, and does not usually produce effective solutions to difficult problems, practitioners may consider suggesting assignments that allow clients to become absorbed in non-anger related and enjoyable, exciting activities. For example, clients could be asked to make time to go to a bowling alley, a baseball game, out to dinner with a family member, or to have a phone conversation with an old friend. Of course, an important stipulation is that the anger-related situation is not discussed during any of the prescribed activities. Also, if anger-related thoughts intrude during involvement in a recreational activity, the client is instructed simply to let them pass and bring mental focus back to the activity at hand (see chapter 9 for discussion of "mindfulness"). Another possibility is to have the client escape to a very noisy restaurant or similar environment, where it would be hard to talk about the anger episode. The goal in distraction is to break the rumination cycle, through competing thoughts and activities, in order to allow clients to step back from their anger triggers and experience pleasure for a time.

Brandon was instructed to plan one enjoyable activity following each shift. Since he was often tired from his work, these did not involve a great deal of effort and were kept simple. For example, Brandon made phone calls to friends, rented videotapes, and read action novels. These activities were in contrast to his usual pattern of going out after work with a friendly co-worker and complaining about his job.

Again, we recommend that escape and avoidance be used as short-term interventions in the *early* stages of anger management, *before there is an opportunity to develop new skills* and when the client is *at risk for suffering serious loss* due to his or her anger episodes. As we have noted, there are obvious drawbacks to any attempt to implement these approaches as long-term strategies. Although escape and avoidance of anger triggers may prevent further anger development, they do not allow for continued personal growth. In Brandon's case, if avoidance and escape were the only methods he used to deal with the problem, he would not have learned alternative ways to interact with people who might disagree with him. Also, avoidance and escape do not serve to reduce the client's arousal level since this approach takes away any need to deal with the anger triggers. Again, in Brandon's case, it is likely that he would continue to experience high levels of anger when he again encountered the day-shift foreman. Long term functional change is unlikely when there is no opportunity to adapt to, or change, the anger trigger.

We trust it is clear, then, that we promote avoidance and escape as *early* and *temporary* aids to adjustment. Ultimately, we want to teach people new skills to manage their anger and to function more effectively. The next seven chapters are designed to help you do just that.

9

Managing Physical Arousal

He that can take rest is greater than he that can take cities.
— Benjamin Franklin

W hen aversive triggers appear in our lives, we *automatically* have cognitive, behavioral, and physiological reactions. These reactions are often very strong and gather together to produce the well-known "fight or flight response" (Darwin, 1872/1965; Cannon, 1915/1963).

❖ Fight or Flight

Originally designed to protect us from predators, the fight or flight response is well developed, historically assisting humans to adapt to a hostile world and assuring our *physical* survival. This response can be observed readily among other mammals as well. When an animal flees from a stronger opponent, for example, it may first put up an angry show of bravado. Before taking the path of retreat, the animal may first hiss, change color, stand erect, paw the air, or puff itself up. Such threatening gestures hopefully scare off the opponent. One can easily see the equivalent in an angry person who shouts, becomes red in the face, stands up and leans forward, points at the target of the anger, and says something such as, "You had better be damned careful!"

When *physical survival* is threatened, this is an incredibly important response system. The fight or flight response leads to a surge of adrenaline and other stress hormones. Breathing, oxygen consumption, and vigilance increase, and the organism feels powerful. We gain strength and courage that may, or may not, lead to wise behavioral actions. For example, when faced on a dark evening with a robber who might cause great physical harm, potential victims experience this highly charged cognitive-behavioral, physiological reaction designed to help determine an appropriate response. But, for modern day humans the

133

appropriate response may be neither fight nor flight! Most law enforcement authorities recommend that you simply hand over your money and save yourself from harm.

The fight or flight response may also be activated when we observe that others' physical survival is being threatened. For example, in times of war the fight or flight response can lead to heroism, as when we protect and defend lives and family or community standards to which we attach value. It may, however, also lead to personal destruction in an effort to protect the larger group, such as when a person risks his or her own safety to intervene in a mugging or robbery.

Nevertheless, the fight or flight response is generally a vestige of past needs. Most of the aversive triggers we face today are not a threat to physical survival. Although crimes against people do occur, clients seen by most practitioners typically face triggers that threaten only *social* survival (i.e., social relationships, status, or reputation). As noted in chapter 2, these are triggers such as having a verbal argument, being the recipient of teasing, being asked to move from a preferred seat in a theater, being the recipient of a "spit ball" from another middle school child, and observing other drivers, friends, colleagues or family members act inappropriately. *Only rarely do modern triggers threaten our physical well-being and only rarely do we actually have to invoke a strong fight (or flight) response.* We note, parenthetically, that practitioners in certain settings such as prisons, battered women's shelters, or those who work with police officers, will likely come across proportionately more cases of physical threat than will other practitioners. Nevertheless, the overwhelming majority of aversive triggers are verbal and social, and this contrasts sharply with the original need for the survival-oriented fight or flight reaction.

Unfortunately, modern day triggers such as verbal insults or being ignored at a party commonly activate a strong fight or flight reaction, just as if physical survival was threatened. Clients and, indeed, many of us, react very strongly to such social triggers. Many angry clients "rant and rave" about social misfortune as if survival itself depended upon events going as planned. Consider Beatrice, an upper middle class woman who decided to move from her present location to a small apartment in New York City. When she returned to the realtor for a second look at the apartment, she discovered that it had already been rented to someone else. Beatrice became furious, claiming that what happened was awful and intolerable, and that she was going to sue the realtor. Her heart raced and her breathing increased, and she become highly agitated; "I just wanted to let the air out of that realtor's tires!" Of course, such things happen every day in major cities and since Beatrice already had a place to live, there was no physical threat to her survival. Nevertheless, her evaluative thoughts, behavioral desires, and physiological reactions were needlessly very strong.

Since this kind of anger and desire to retaliate aggressively occurs with great frequency in angry clients, they are constantly subjected to the effects of toxic stress hormones that are secreted in response to triggers that pose no actual threat to physical survival. And, there is a *cumulative danger* from the buildup of these fight or flight stress hormones, including the long-term negative medical outcomes presented in chapter 2, such as persistent headache, high blood pressure, susceptibility to infection, cancer, and heart disease.

In addition to the negative effects on the client's body that result from the physiological arousal, it is useful to teach clients that *in modern society the fight or flight reaction is usually counterproductive to long-term problem solution.* In fact, we can neither fight against, nor flee from, many everyday triggers. When faced with aversive bosses, colleagues, neighbors, or children, we actually have little choice but to control our reactions and find solutions that do not involve fighting or fleeing. To hit or run away will, in most cases, cause greater trouble. For example, to become angry, controlling, and aggressive against one's spouse and/or children shows the same lack of ability to deal effectively with challenges and problems as does abandoning them. And, it is clearly best to learn to control our reactions as we sit in traffic jams, where fleeing is impossible and becoming angry by horn-honking or driving on the sidewalk or grass will only increase the likelihood of trouble. Similarly, it is best to learn to control one's tendency to react angrily while waiting for a service technician to fix a broken stove that was "dead on arrival" from the supplier. Becoming angry with the technician may lead to slower or deficient service, with corresponding increases in delay and expense. On the other hand, "flight" (e.g., not staying home all day to wait for the repair person) will also be self-defeating.

In angry clients, the aversive triggers of modern society still lead to full activation of the fight or flight response, and cause anger, argumentativeness, aggression, hypervigilance, hormone secretions, muscular tension, and heightened reactivity. This, in turn, leads to behavioral reactions that are often counter-productive to problem solution. Consider the following two cases. Dr. Max Salmon, a 40-year-old university professor, frequently reacts with intense anger to such triggers as not being consulted about department and student issues. He often thinks that his input is devalued or ignored altogether. When he reacts with a strong anger (fight) response, he pushes his colleagues further away; they have no urge to interact with an angry colleague. However, if he does nothing (flight), his ideas will not be heard. Neither fight nor flight responses are helpful. And, in any event, his strong and almost daily physiological arousal in response to the situation bodes poorly for his own health. There is no physical threat and his strong anger-oriented, fight-or-flight reaction is certainly unwarranted. Instead, anger control and reduction, coupled with assertive discussions with his peers, is the most likely path to a solution for Dr. Salmon.

Another case involved Sarah Sommers, a relatively well-paid computer programmer working in a market where jobs are becoming scarce. At age 48, Sarah was told that, along with several other employees, she had two choices: reduce from full-time to half-time employment without health care benefits, or take a 35% salary cut and maintain her full-time job with benefits. Certainly, it would be counterproductive to scream and punch the boss (the angry fight response) and without a doubt it would be counterproductive to stay at home and not return to work (the flight response). Objectively, Sarah is in a difficult situation. However, her automatically engaged fight or flight reaction elicits self-defeating behaviors which work against finding a solution. It is surprising how often clients will choose options at one or the other extreme.

Along with angry cognitions/verbalizations (e.g., "I am really pissed and just want to scream!") and behavioral expressions (e.g., throwing a pad of paper onto the floor), clients with excessive anger commonly report such symptoms of physical arousal as muscle tension, increases in heart rate, respiration, sweating, and hypervigilance. (Blood pressure and oxygen consumption also increase, however, clients do not typically report these symptoms as they are not consciously perceived.) *Although angry arousal and agitation are natural, they are often excessive, more harmful than helpful, and contribute to the negative short-term interpersonal and long-term medical outcomes that often exist in angry clients.* Importantly, angry arousal prevents the client from developing appropriate options to the social-interpersonal trigger. As noted in chapter 1, such arousal not only inhibits successful motor behavior (such as playing basketball or a piano at a high level of competence), it also inhibits clear thinking. Indeed, no one wants to be the patient of an angry, agitated, highly aroused dentist or surgeon. Nor would we want a highly agitated angry president to negotiate international treaties on our behalf. Motor skills and judgment are both affected by anger.

Thus, to solve most modern day social problems (which do not affect physical survival) clients can be taught to reduce their anger-oriented, maladaptive thoughts and reactive behaviors and to replace them with thoughts and attitudes less likely to lead to anger. This, however, is not an easy task when the body is highly aroused, filled with fight or flight hormones, the muscles are tense, and/or respiration is excessive. It is always difficult for clients to implement new strategies, and especially so when physical arousal is high. Thus, a first step in anger reduction is to teach clients how to physically relax in the face of adversity.

❖ *Relaxation As an Alternative Response*

Much research has supported the general benefits of relaxation training and the specific effects of relaxation as part of an anger management program (Benson, 2000; Deffenbacher and colleagues, 1992, 1995, 1996; Jacobson 1977, 1987; and Wolpe, 1958, 1973). Knowing and practicing relaxation skills is beneficial for the client and has almost no risks, increases the credibility of the practitioner, and often leads to significant anger reduction as well as improvement in other areas of cognitive and motor functioning. As but one example, consider the findings of Benson and colleagues (2000) regarding school achievement. They followed up middle school students who had been taught to relax by their teachers. Their finding showed that students who had more exposure to a relaxation training curriculum showed greater improvement in academic scores over a two-year period. These youngsters had higher grade point averages, better work habits, and were more cooperative. In short, arousal management helped them to solve problems more effectively.

Relaxation is a hard-wired or "built in" physiological response. In theory, it can exist in all humans and, thus, can be applied in almost all cases and settings. When relaxation is triggered, neurochemicals released by the brain counteract the activation of the fight or flight response. Clients begin to breathe slower, there is less need for oxygen, blood pressure and heart rate decrease, and hypervigilance diminishes. Since it is a hard-wired reaction of the body, the practitioner does not have to "convince" clients that such a response is possible. Rather, practitioners simply have to work with clients to foster an already existing reaction.

Relaxation is like many other physiological responses. There are many ways to elicit it. Just as an increase in heart rate can be caused by exercise, the sight of an approaching aggressive dog, a viral infection, or a dentist saying that the procedure will involve "deep drilling" on the tooth, there are various ways to elicit relaxation. Then, once relaxation is achieved, the stage is set for developing an improved set of cognitive and behavioral reactions to aversive triggers. Relaxation helps the client become less impulsive and reactive to problems, and able to make more positive choices regarding his or her life. Thus, learning relaxation techniques to remain calm in the face of provocation is important in interrupting the anger cycle.

❖ *Development of the Relaxation Response*

The most common, quickest, and easiest technique to use in a practitioner's office is *progressive muscle relaxation training (PMR)*. This is a voluntary, conscious, self-control strategy which provides significant benefit by teaching clients to relax by tensing and letting go of various muscle groups. Relaxation can be first learned and practiced in isolation, then in imagined stressful situations, and then in the presence of real-life anger triggers. However, the benefits of learning to relax are important in their own right, as relaxation provides an improved capacity to deal with a variety of life problems and the lowered reactivity of the body has long-term positive health consequences.

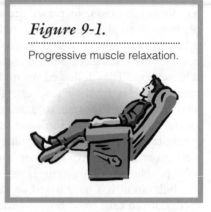

Figure 9-1.
Progressive muscle relaxation.

PMR involves the tensing and releasing of different muscle groups (e.g., starting with the arm muscles, then moving to the legs, stomach, chest, shoulders, neck and face). Using a low-pitched and slow voice, begin by giving instructions to *tense* a muscle group for about five seconds and ask clients to *focus on the discomfort* being created. This, they are told, is what happens when they feel angry. After tensing, the client is told to *stop clenching the muscle*, to release the pressure, and to *focus on the warm, heavy, and relaxed feelings* that naturally develop. Clients are asked to tense only one specific muscle group during the tension part of the exercise, while leaving the other parts of the body relaxed. One goal is to teach an awareness of the difference between tensed and relaxed muscle groups.

During the procedure it is common for a variety of thoughts to emerge and sometimes clients want to talk. We instruct them to gently bring their focus back to the sensations in their muscles. It is also important to remain awake during the procedure! It is not uncommon for some clients (approximately 10%) to fall asleep. Although it can be pleasant to drift off to sleep while relaxing, this will not help in the voluntary development of relaxation in the face of aversive triggers.

Practitioners can use PMR with clients by following the instructions below. We recommend *creation of an audiotape recording for clients* so they can practice at home, and associate the practitioner's voice with relaxation. However, if the practitioner happens to have a high-pitched voice, or desires a well-practiced professional presentation, an audiotape can be purchased directly from a number of sources.*

❖ *Taping Instructions for Progressive Muscle Relaxation*
——

If you elect to make a personalized relaxation tape for your client, do not go too quickly through the following procedure. Allow for the time indicated (in parenthesis) for each exercise. Once the tape is made, recommend that the client play it back while in a comfortable and quiet place, allowing for plenty of time without worry that the phone will ring or that another distraction will occur. The tape can be used by angry clients while sitting up in a comfortable chair or lying down on a bed, couch, or on the floor. Clients will find it useful to remove eyeglasses and ties, to open the top shirt button, and/or to loosen other tight clothing.

— — — — —

START recording here.
Close your eyes, sit quietly for a few seconds, and focus on smooth breathing. (Pause 10 seconds.) Notice that you are in control. You can regulate yourself to breathe slowly, smoothly, and deeply. (Pause 5 seconds.) Good, you are doing very well.

[1.] Now, make fists with both of your hands and feel the tension building in your lower arms, hands, and fingers. Focus on that tension and silently describe the uncomfortable pulling sensations to yourself. That's what happens when you are angry. OK, hold the tension. (Pause 5 seconds.) Now, release the tension and let your hands and arms relax. Focus on the warm, heavy, relaxed feelings in your hands and notice the contrast with the tension. Just focus for a while on your relaxed hands and continue to breathe slowly, smoothly, and deeply. (Pause 10 seconds.)

[2.] Now, bend your arms and press both of your elbows firmly into your sides. While pressing your elbows inward, also flex your arm muscles. Notice the tension building up throughout your arms, shoulders, and back. Hold that tension. (Pause 5 seconds.) OK, now release your arms and let them fall heavily to your sides. Focus on the heavy, warm, and relaxed feelings in your arms, and continue to breathe slowly, smoothly, and deeply. (Pause 10 seconds.)

---

* We often recommend "Learning to Relax," spoken by Arnold Lazarus, Ph.D. On this 37-minute tape, clients listen to the very pleasant voice of Dr. Lazarus as he teaches the whole set of tension-relaxation contrasts. It does not contain any imagery and thus, unlike some similar products, is suited to a general audience. The tape can be purchased from the Albert Ellis Institute in New York City [e-mail to orders@REBT.org or call 212-535-0822].

[3.] Moving to your lower legs, flex your feet by trying to point your toes toward your nose. Notice the tension spreading through your feet, ankles, and calves. Hold the tension. (Pause 5 seconds.) OK, now release the tension in your lower legs and focus on your sense of comfort as your lower legs become more relaxed. Continue to breathe slowly, smoothly, and deeply. (Pause 10 seconds.) You are doing very well.

[4.] Next, build tension in your upper legs by pressing both your knees together and lifting your legs off the bed or chair. Focus on the tension in your thighs and the pulling sensations in your hips. Describe those uncomfortable feelings to yourself. (Pause 5 seconds.) Now, release the tension, and let your legs fall slowly and heavily onto the bed or chair. Focus on letting go of all the tension in your legs, arms, and shoulders. Just let go. Breathe slowly, smoothly, and deeply. (Pause 10 seconds.)

[5.] Next, pull your stomach in toward your spine. Notice the tension in your stomach. (Pause 5 seconds.) Now, voluntarily let your stomach relax. Breathe slowly, smoothly, and deeply, and focus on the relaxation you can produce in your stomach, in your legs, and in your arms and shoulders. (Pause 10 seconds.)

[6.] Now, take in a very deep breath and hold it. (Pause 15 seconds, until some discomfort is likely.) Notice the tension in your expanded chest. Now, slowly let the air out and feel the tension gradually disappear. Notice that you can voluntarily relax your body, and you can breathe slowly, rhythmically, and deeply. And, with each breath that you take you can allow yourself to relax even more. Focus on relaxing and just letting go of all of your tension. (Pause 10 seconds.)

[7.] Now, imagine that your shoulders are on strings and are being pulled up toward your ears. Feel the tension building in your shoulders, your upper back, and neck. Hold that tension. (Pause 5 seconds.) OK, now just let the tension go. Allow your shoulders to droop down. Let them droop down as far as they can go. Notice the difference between the feelings of tension and relaxation. (Pause 10 seconds.)

[8.] Pull your chin down and try to touch your chest with it. Notice the pulling and tension in the back of your neck. (Pause 5 seconds.) Now relax. Let go of the tension in your neck. Focus on letting your neck muscles relax. Let your arms and legs relax. Breathe slowly, rhythmically, and deeply. (Pause 10 seconds.)

[9.] Now, clench your teeth together and focus on the tension in your jaw. Feel the tight pulling sensation. (Pause 5 seconds.) OK, release. Allow your mouth to drop open and relax all of the muscles around your face and jaw. (Pause 10 seconds.) Very good.

[10.] Build up the tension in your forehead by forcing yourself to frown. Try to pull your eyebrows toward each other. Focus on the tension in your forehead. (Pause 5 seconds.) Now release. Smooth out all of the wrinkles and let your forehead relax. (Pause 10 seconds.)

[11.] At this point allow your whole body to feel relaxed and heavy. Breathe deeply and rhythmically and voluntarily relax your arms, legs, stomach, shoulder, and facial muscles. You are in control. Every time you breathe out, silently say the word "relax" to yourself, and imagine that you are breathing out all of the tension in your body.

Breathe in and out deeply five times, say the word "relax" to yourself, and voluntarily let all of the tension disappear. Just let go and relax. I am going to stop talking for a while, and allow you to enjoy the pleasant relaxing feelings you can let yourself have.

STOP the recording here.

— — — — —

From the very beginning most clients respond to relaxation training quite positively. They readily follow the instructions and show signs of relaxation, such as spontaneous sighing. Nevertheless, we hope that you will not become discouraged if a particular client does not feel relaxed after the first session. It may take a few repetitions to get the desired effect. The best results are often achieved if clients receive the instructions in the office for two or three sessions to produce relaxation, and are then given the tape with instructions to rehearse the procedure two times per day for two weeks. We suggest that at least 30 minutes be set aside, at a time when no distractions are likely. Unfortunately, experience shows that many clients will only practice once a day. Regular practice will help clients get to the point where they can ultimately use the procedure without the assistance of the tape.

Cue-controlled relaxation will also help patients to relax, without going through the whole tension-relaxation sequence. In this technique, tension and relaxation muscle contrasts are taught as described above. However, some extra focus is placed on the cycle of breathing in and out. As exhalation and the release of muscle tension occur, the client is taught to quietly say a cue word or phrase such as "relax," "be mellow," "stay calm," or "this too shall pass." This helps to associate the cue word with a state of relaxation, so that eventually the cue word alone elicits a relaxed state.

❖ *Alternatives to Progressive Muscle Relaxation*

For some clients, progressive muscle relaxation training can be replaced with, or supplemented by, other strategies. Sometimes, the name given to the procedure is also important. For example, some clients are eager to be "hypnotized" and if the procedure is labeled as hypnosis it may help. However, in our experience most clients want to remain in control. Thus, labeling the procedure as a self-produced form of relaxation works best in most cases.

The advantage to PMR is that it is taught in the office, allowing practitioners to observe progress. In addition, PMR can be paired with exposure to aversive triggers in the office in order to reduce angry arousal (discussed further in chapter 12). Nevertheless, practitioners can consider some of the following formal or informal alternates to PMR as a means of producing relaxation.

1. Some clients find it helpful to choose a calming word (e.g., "calm" or "mellow") to say or think during a *repetitive exercise* such as walking, swimming, or running. The word is repeated in cadence with the steps or strokes and is reported to bring on relaxation, perhaps by pairing the calming word with the physiological "high" caused by the exercise.

2. Some clients like to practice *yoga* and report that it elicits a feeling of relaxation. This may be due to its focus on body position and breathing, rather than continued rumination about the anger trigger.

3. Some reports suggest that slow, *deep diaphragmatic breathing* exercises lead to relaxation. Since breathing during anger episodes tends to be rapid and shallow, the client is practicing a response that is opposite to what characteristically occurs during anger and is typical of breathing during relaxed states.

4. Almost any form of *repetitive prayer* seems to elicit relaxation. Indeed, for more than 30 years Benson (1996, 2000) has conducted studies on prayer and meditation. He concluded that all forms of repetitive prayer evoke a relaxation response that reduces stress and body arousal. According to Benson, it is the repetition of sounds or words that is most important. Praying that requires verbal or motor repetitions brings about relaxation since it typically requires deep rhythmic breathing connected with a sound or word or phrase. A single prayer is not enough, as it is the repetitive nature of the experience that elicits relaxation.

Repetitive prayer and the associated relaxation response are part of the history and tradition of many religions and cultures. For example, Jews engage in a form of prayer called "davening." This consists of reciting text in a soft droning manner while bowing or rocking back and forth. This goes on, repetitively, with the goal of abandoning outside distractions. In Christianity, the relaxation response is produced by repeating the "Jesus Prayer" or the prayer of the heart that consists of many repetitions of the phrase "Lord Jesus Christ, Son of God, have mercy on me, a sinner." The prayer may be compressed into "Lord Jesus Christ have mercy on me" or to the one word "Jesus." In use for nearly 2,000 years, it is recommended that this prayer be repeated endlessly. Some people repeat it up to 6,000 times a day and track the number of repetitions using a prayer rope. Since people often synchronize the prayer with breathing there is ample opportunity for the relaxation response to emerge. In Catholicism, the "Rosary," which is in itself a repetitive prayer, can be repeated for 54 days as a novena. In many forms of Protestantism, and in Catholicism, use of a "centering" prayer is often promoted. This prayer involves choosing and repeating a sacred word while sitting comfortably with the eyes closed. When awareness develops of external thoughts, the person is instructed to gently return to the sacred word. At the end of the prayer period, the person is instructed to remain in silence with eyes closed for a few minutes. Similar practices exist in Islam, Buddhism, Confucianism, Shintoism, and Taoism.

Religion is a touchy issue for practitioners and clients, except for those who work in religious organizations, such as Christian counseling centers and religious-affiliated colleges. We are not suggesting intrusion on the personal beliefs of clients, nor are we promoting any particular religious position. Rather, we note that the data on the benefit of *repetitive* prayer can be explained to clients and some may increase their prayer activities to bring out more moments of relaxation.

5. *Mindfulness meditation,* a technique that comes from Buddhist practice, also seems to elicit relaxation (Kabat-Zinn, 1990). This type of meditation involves learning to simply "observe" or "notice" without reacting to worldly surroundings. For example, we might say, "I am cooking. I am putting oil into the frying pan. Now I put in broccoli and carrots. A carrot fell on the floor. It looks quite orange against the white floor. I am covering the pan. I feel hot. I am opening the window." The goal is to simply notice one's behavior and experiences, and to name or describe them, *without evaluation.* No judgments of good, bad, right, wrong, lazy, weak, strong, kind, or mean, are made.

The key in mindfulness is to simply notice the external world and our internal states. Emotional mindfulness might sound like: "I am feeling angry. My face is becoming tense. I remember when John ignored my question at the office. I kept trying, but he ignored me. I was annoyed and withdrew. My stomach is upset. I have a headache." Notice there is only the simple acknowledgement, recognition and naming of the event and the early and current feelings. There are no judgments in the monologue. If judgments about feelings emerge (e.g., "I shouldn't feel angry. It's a sign that something is wrong with me.") they are to be recognized as such and the individual is encouraged to return to the status of observer. The goal would be to return focus to the simple observation or naming of emotions or bodily sensations. Relaxation increases as judgments decrease.

6) Clients may be able to achieve relaxation by taking a walk on a sandy beach and listening to the crashing waves, or going near a field or

forest in the early evening where there is nothing but the sound of crickets (if such locations are available). Thus, spending time in nature may be relaxing for some clients and quiet outdoor experiences could be assigned on a weekly basis.

7) Water, in many forms, has often been associated with relaxation. Clients can take a warm bath, walk by a creek, listen to running water, or visualize a quiet lake. Consider that it is hard to be angry after spending only five minutes in a bubbling hot tub at 102 degrees F.

9) *Singing or chanting* a rhythmic but mellow song or short poem can elicit relaxation.

10) Local bookstores carry a wide range of relaxation-related materials such as audio-tapes, videotapes, and books.

Oftentimes, it is useful for clients to experiment with different methods of bringing about relaxation. The important point to share with angry clients is that they will be better prepared to make decisions about the aversive triggers of life if they practice evoking the relaxation response whenever possible. In effect, it is useful to teach angry clients that *thoughtful cognitive and motor functioning follows a quieting of the body*. In contrast, angry bodily arousal often leads to a false sense of optimism and bravado that can easily backfire.

Of course, learning a formal relaxation technique is best done when things are calm. We tell our clients that just as we don't learn how to swim in a stormy ocean we are unlikely to learn the relaxation response in the midst of an anger episode. We learn these skills (swimming and relaxing) best when things are calm. Then, when aversive triggers appear, we can utilize the previously learned techniques.

We believe that it is useful to learn relaxation techniques simply because they help patients to navigate the rough waters of life. Relaxation leads to lowered responsiveness to anger triggers and, thus, raises the anger threshold. At the same time, practitioners will have developed the foundation for other powerful tools once relaxation has been learned. Relaxation is the foundation for systematic desensitization and, as described in chapter 12, exposure in imagination or in-vivo to anger triggers. Thus, there are multiple benefits to teaching relaxation.

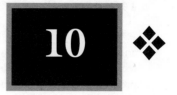

CHANGING

Building Life Skills

The skill of acknowledgment applies to feelings — not to misbehavior. When a child is using the living-room wall as a mural for his Magic Markers, empathy is not in order — clear limits are. This is not the time to say, "You wish you could use Magic Marker on the walls." This is the time to state firmly, "Markers are to be used only on paper."

— Nancy Samalin, author and parent educator.

Many anger problems can be reduced by skill development. There is less likelihood of conflict, or thoughts of personal inadequacy, or feelings of guilt, when well-developed skills exist. Consider, for example, parents who read books, talk to friends, and attend workshops, on "Parenting the elementary school child." They emerge from such experiences with skills to encourage studying and the completion of homework in their children. They learn about the importance of a clean, well-lit place to work, minimizing noisy and visual distractions, discussion and planning between parent and child about how long to work and, of course, the significant role of supportive statements ("You're super!) and, perhaps, the promise of a reward ("After you complete those ten problems, we can check them over and then go for some ice cream"). Parents with these skills are more likely to have anger-free interactions with their children than those who simply say "Go do your homework!" Good skills make life easier, more successful, and more enjoyable.

We consider three types of skills in this chapter: *social interaction skills, assertiveness skills*, and *specialized motor skills*. The first two enhance communication between clients and the people with whom they interact. *Social interaction skills* minimize conflicts during daily interactions with supervisors, employees, bank tellers, clerks, doctors, etc., and also improve more intimate relationships with significant others, close friends, and family. *Assertiveness skills,* which involve the communication of feeling and personal desires, are especially important to minimize problems when we interact with persons close to us. Some authors place these skills in the same category. For example, Alberti and Emmons (2001) write that, "assertive behavior promotes equality in human relationships, enabling us to act in our own best interests, to stand up for ourselves without undue anxiety, to express honest feelings comfortably, to exercise personal rights without denying the rights of others" (p.6). Although this is a very acceptable position, we believe it is useful in the beginning to work with clients on the expression of feelings separately from the development of social interaction skills.

The third type are *specialized motor skills,* which include learning to ride a bicycle, use a computer, master the kata of Tae Kwon Do, repair an automobile, work with paint, set up fish tanks, etc. These are also important for life success and enjoyment. Consider, for example, that a neat and clean painter will have far fewer complaints from customers than will a sloppy painter. Fewer complaints translate into fewer episodes of annoyance and anger. However, mental health practitioners typically do not have the ability to teach such skills and, in any event, they are usually outside of the approved scope of practice. We note, nevertheless, that if a client does not know how to successfully complete tasks which are important for daily functioning (e.g., how to run a computer, manage personal and family finances, be a quality parent, study and obtain good grades, read a newspaper, etc.), then there are likely to be many truly frustrating experiences. And, if the same situation in which the client lacks skills reappears with regularity (e.g., tests in school, monthly checkbook statements, etc.) then frustration will be frequent. In cases of skill deficit, frustration and inappropriate, inflammatory appraisals of daily triggers will be common, leading to a pattern of angry, aggressive, or other dysfunctional patterns (e.g., procrastination).

Consider the case of Angela Lewis, Ph.D. Dr. Lewis arrived at her new job as assistant professor of biology at a small college where teaching excellence was highly valued. Although Dr. Lewis was well trained as a researcher, she had never had full charge of a class of 50 college students, and her teaching skills were still at an early stage of development. Her students had become triggers for almost daily anger. When they came to see her, and said she talked too fast in class for them to understand the materials, she became annoyed and defensive. After a short while, Dr. Lewis had developed a standard answer for them: "Students are expected to be able to follow the materials! Study harder to prepare for class!" Her unspoken appraisals, however, included, "It's their fault. They are so stupid." At the end of the first semester, her student ratings were poor and her job was in jeopardy. In addition to anger, Dr. Lewis felt ashamed and had thoughts of personal inadequacy. Quietly, she questioned her career choice. The major problem, it turned out, was a skill deficit and, in this case, Dr. Lewis was lucky. An older professor began to meet with her. This mentor showed her how to plan lectures, encouraged her to supplement the lectures with films and slides, asked her to include student discussions and presentations as part of the class, and observed her in the classroom. Dr. Lewis was respectful of this person and thankful for the help. Her teaching improved and the students began to like her. Some even chose her as an advisor, thus increasing her sense of competence even more. Dr. Lewis continued to improve her teaching skills as each semester passed and this was accompanied by less anger.

In skill building, the practitioner helps the client identify the behaviors required to negotiate life with *more actual competence*. As competence increases, less frustration and anger are likely to emerge. The goal is to give the client an increased repertoire of effective job, family, and life skills to increase success and reduce failure. In this sense, we believe that *skill building can be a true crisis prevention strategy*. At the same time, we note that an important cognitive skill is knowing when other skills are absent, so that temporary avoidance of, or escape from conflict-laden situations is the proper response (see chapter 8). For example, sometimes a tutor is better than a parent to help a child learn.

Social skills are the expected verbal and motor behaviors that we learn as we develop in order to interact appropriately with others. We learn these skills in our families, in schools, in religious training, through interactions with friends, by reading, and through observational learning (e.g., on television). Some social skills are very basic. These include motor behaviors such as arriving on time, dressing appropriately, using deodorant, bringing coffee to colleagues, and waiting on lines. Other skills, which may be novel, are required only in specific situations and are learned on the job, or in the military, or in prisons, or in other unique settings. Social skills (and deficits) can be identified at any time of life, although we typically expect them to develop in childhood. Nevertheless, in adulthood, new skills are required as we take on new roles, such as parent, teacher, mentor, or supervisor. Many social skills are primarily verbal and involve communications between people that enhance giving, receiving, and interpreting messages. In addition to content, these skills almost always include nonverbal behaviors such as posture, use of eyes, tone of voice, and facial expressions. Of course, the definition of appropriate and acceptable may change based on the client's family background, religion, or culture. Some of these allow for more direct verbal feedback (e.g., Italian) while others (e.g., Japanese) require indirect verbal behaviors. Be sure to take these factors into consideration.

❖ Common Social Skills

Some skills are important in almost all work, play, or family interactions. Others are specific to certain individuals, as when a practitioner interacts with an elderly client with a hearing loss or vision problems. Or, the skills may be required in limited environments, such as dealing with customers, raising children, working on military bases, or appearing in court. When performed successfully, social skills increase the "connection" between people.

Central components of many social skills that are taught to clients include the following (Alberti & Emmons, 2001):

- *Eye contact. If the interaction occurs in person, look directly at the other person.* The reader may recall interactions where other individuals failed to make direct eye contact. What messages are sent when this occurs? How do people typically feel when someone does not look at them? Although this is a very basic skill, some clients (and practitioners) need to start with the fundamentals in terms of improving interpersonal functioning. Usually, direct eye contact (without staring) leads to the best outcome.

- *Distance. If the interaction occurs in person, stand not too far, nor too close to the other person.* Has anyone ever shouted out a request to you from another room? Usually, this is not as powerful a message. At the other extreme, if two people are too close it can also lead to discomfort.

- *Posture. If the interaction occurs in person, turn the whole body toward the listener.* Facing directly toward the other person is usually best to increase connectedness.

- *Physical contact. Many business interactions begin and end with a handshake. Psychotherapists and other practitioners are taught to never go beyond this level of contact with their clients.* Nevertheless, touch is a central component of normal social skills and, for example, parents learn when and how to touch their children to provide comfort. In fact, when family members and friends do not touch they may be seen as cold and distant. Knowing how and when to touch another person can enhance or discourage the bond between people.

- *Gesturing.* According to Alberti & Emmons (2001), "Accentuating your message with appropriate gestures can add emphasis, openness and warmth" (p. 58). We agree that such gesturing is important when interacting face-to-face with others. At the same time, this is a good place to note that *all of the central elements of social skills have a cultural component* of which practitioners must be aware. As but one example, consider that

"Bob Alberti traces his enthusiastic use of gestures in conversations to his Italian heritage" (p. 58). Many clinical reports and scholarly studies have noted the differences among persons from European, Asian, African, South American, and other backgrounds. It is wise to be aware, therefore, that "proper" distance, tone, gestures, facial expression, posture, and other non-verbal behaviors will differ among clients.

- *Listening. Central to good social skills is letting the other person know that the message has been heard.* This can be accomplished by *summarizing* what the person has said, *paraphrasing* what has been heard, or *asking a question* based on what has been heard (Ivey, 1999). At the very least, it is usually important to respond with, "OK" or "I hear you," or " Yes."
- *Tone, inflection, and volume. Responding in an appropriate manner adds much to the actual content of messages.* Whispers and shouts are usually less preferred than is a well-modulated spoken message of moderate volume that does not seem to hide other attitudes or feelings.
- *Reception.* It is easy to say, "I'm listening." *However, a central social skill involves truly being open and receptive to the message or response of the other person.*

Although there are central elements to be learned by clients, there are also many specific life situations that may require some discussion.

Greeting others. This is one of the most basic of social skills. Yet, many clients have never thought about their initial meeting with others and have never questioned whether or not they are accomplishing the goal of putting their "best foot forward." Greetings and introductions are critical, since judgments are made about people in the first moments of meeting. Although we may say little more than "hello," when asked people will say, "She seems nice" or, "He seemed like a good person." Being viewed positively in the beginning of a relationship can do much to offset anger. In business, focus is often placed on how to greet others on the telephone or when they first appear in the office. Decisions are to be made about whether to shake hands, offer a soft drink or coffee, or ask personal questions. In addition to the central components listed above, consideration is to be placed on the appropriate words for the situation ("Hi..." "Hello..." "Glad to meet you..." "J & R Enterprises, Good Morning."). Attention is also paid to smiling, the appropriateness of a handshake, introducing yourself by name, saying, "It was very nice to meet you."

Giving and accepting compliments. It is interesting to discover that many clients have difficulty giving compliments to others. And, they may have even greater difficulty accepting them. Andrew Salter observed this rather fundamental skill deficit in many clients over a half-century ago (Salter, 1949). Compliments pave the way for smooth interpersonal relationships. If clients have difficulty giving them, they may be seen by others as cold and ungrateful employers, lovers, partners, co-workers, neighbors, or teachers. If clients have difficulty accepting compliments, they also may be seen as ungrateful and disconnected. In addition to the central components, when teaching clients to give compliments, it is important to stress that the compliment is best delivered with a smile and is to be clearly focused on the behavior of the other person. For example, "Your work with those children has been excellent. I really appreciate the extra time you took to teach John how to use the disk drive. Thanks so much." Some of this occurs in industry as part of employee recognition programs. Compliments and recognition go a long way to reduce anger in future interactions.

Of course, compliments work best when they are accepted appropriately. Unfortunately, many clients respond to compliments with statements such as, "No big deal. It was nothing." However, a direct accepting statement is much better. A client can be taught to say, "Thanks. I tried hard to teach John to tie his shoes. It actually took about six days of practice. I really appreciate the fact that you noticed it. Thanks again."

Following instructions. As part of socialization we all learn to comply with instructions given by others. Legitimate instructions may be given by supervisors, teachers, parents, family members, partners, coaches, religious leaders, military superiors, judges, probation officers, civil authorities, and perhaps others. Compliance with these instructions has clear benefits. For example, if followed, instructions from supervisors may lead to an improved sales record and a promotion. Instructions from a shop teacher may lead to improved safety, and following the instructions of a spouse can increase marital happiness. In addition to the central components noted above, carrying out the instruction as soon as possible and checking back with the person who made the request enhances the relationship between the two people.

Making a request. Surprisingly, what the client thinks is a *request*, may be considered by others as a *demand*, due to the manner — especially the non-verbal cues — in which it is presented. Learning to properly make requests can be surprisingly difficult for some clients. It is best to begin with "please," and then to express what is wanted in a direct manner, with careful attention to non-verbal elements of the communication.

Refusing to comply with requests. There are many legitimate times when compliance with the requests of others is not in the best interest of clients. These include requests to cover up inappropriate business practices, to act illegally, to do something that a client strongly does not want to do, or to demean others. Refusal skills are important for ethical functioning and for being true to oneself. In addition to the central components, refusal is best done in a polite but firm manner. Statements such as, "No, I don't want to" are direct and honest. It is important for clients to learn not to blame the person who makes the request and to explain the reason for the refusal. Even if the other person is acting illegally, blame will only lead to an angry interaction. Often, it is best to leave the situation after the refusal and the explanation are given.

Accepting criticism. No client is successful in every arena. Poor performance as a salesperson, flight attendant, teacher, or friend often leads to negative feedback by supervisors or peers. Such feedback, of course, is a common trigger for defensiveness, anger, and blame. Thus, learning to accept criticism is an important social skill. Considering the feedback of others promotes growth and change.

Giving criticism. Just as clients learn to accept criticism, they sometimes require training in how to give it. It is usually best to try to find some positive behavior to note first, then to express the criticism in a clear, unembellished manner — and to listen to the response.

Accepting no for an answer. Life is rarely totally fulfilling, nor totally fair. Many of our requests, no matter how reasonable, are denied. Hard-working employees may be denied a raise (hopefully, only temporarily), students may work hard and produce an excellent paper but receive only a "B" and not an "A," and marital partners may deny each other's requests. Thus, learning to accept negative responses is an important skill so that positive relationships will be maintained and requests may be granted in the future.

Disagreeing and contradicting. It is easy to say, "You're wrong!" Such direct challenges, however, have pitfalls unless they are paired with other verbal and non-verbal messages. Thus, learning to disagree appropriately is central to success in family life, business, and education. In addition to the central components, it is best to deliver the disagreement in a clear but not demeaning manner, to give a brief reason for the position taken, and to listen openly to the other person's response.

Apologizing. Let's face it. All of us are sometimes wrong. At that point an apology can do much to thwart the development of anger. Indicating sorrow or regret for an offensive action is helpful; excuse-making is less effective. Instead, it is helpful for the client to indicate how the behavior will be improved next time.

There are, of course, many other social skills that enhance interpersonal communication. For example, clients can be taught to ask for help, to approach strangers at a party or business gathering, to show respect for the opinions or behaviors of others, to change the subject without offending others, to un-offensively break into small group conversations, to ask others to make less noise, to return food in a restaurant, or merchandise in a retail store. In clinical work, an assessment of client skills and a shared agreement to work on developing specific social skills to help clients better achieve their goals is incorporated into programmatic intervention.

❖ *Social Skills Training Methods*

First, conduct a *collaborative assessment* to identify the verbal and motor behaviors that are lacking and to generate *possibilities for improvement*. Does the client have difficulty on the job, at home, at school? Is it agreed that the problems are related to initially meeting others, or disagreeing, or accepting negative feedback? Might private tutoring be helpful to bring a child's skill in Spanish up to the level of her peers? Would extra private swimming lessons give the sense of competence required to jump in the pool with others? Would a public speaking course in an adult education program in the local high school help the client speak up and express ideas at work? Are videos available to teach money management skills to a father who is struggling to make ends meet? What books are available to teach a middle-aged daughter about caring for an elderly parent? Does the local high school offer courses in self-defense, self-management of diabetes or asthma, art history, reading improvement? Consider which skills can appropriately be developed within the practitioner-client relationship, and which require outside resources.

After the assessment is made, and it is determined that the practitioner can help, the steps consist of *discussion, warm-up exercises, role plays and practice, modeling appropriate behaviors, homework,* and *reinforcing client progress* as enhanced skills are developed. Many of these techniques also work well in group settings.

- *Discussion.* Clients are taught about different behaviors in detail. The use and importance of specific behaviors in differing social situations is then discussed and evaluated. This step is particularly important for clients from different cultures who may misinterpret behaviors of individuals from the new culture or who may be unaware of how their actions are viewed by members of the new culture. Discussion allows the practitioner to tailor the program to be maximally helpful to the client.
- *Warm-up exercises.* These are designed to allow clients to practice the different aspects of behaviors to be trained in the session, but they do not usually include real-life situations in which the client has major difficulty. For example, clients and practitioners might practice greeting each other, making small talk, or giving

compliments. Discussion might center around the importance of looking at the other person, using a pleasant voice, asking questions, giving information about yourself, and allowing the other person to talk.

- *Role-playing.* After discussion and verbal instruction, brief real-life situations are acted out. Often role reversal is useful, wherein the practitioner plays the role of the client and the client serves as the anger trigger. For example, if receiving negative feedback has been a source of anger, the client would give the kind of feedback usually received and the practitioner would offer a response. Thus, the practitioner models an appropriate way to receive the feedback. Roles are then reversed and the client practices responding in a similar manner to the criticism. That is, with good eye contact, without defensiveness, and with a statement such as, "OK, I will certainly think about that." It is always important to remember to reinforce the client for "trying" (i.e., for successive approximations). This technique is particularly useful in groups, so that the practitioner can observe carefully and give effective feedback. Videotape is also a highly useful tool here, as the client can see clearly how he is coming across, and the feedback and behavior-shaping process is even more powerful.

- *Modeling.* The practitioner, in the role-playing example above, serves as a "model" demonstrating appropriate behavior. In another case example, a client who was working as a receptionist in a small office had major difficulty greeting people she did not already know. When they tried to be friendly, or ask questions, she would become annoyed and say, "Please sit down! Mr. Super will be out to see you as soon as he can!" Her tone and vague message turned many people off, as they viewed her as hostile. In this case, the practitioner and client went into the natural environments of a local shopping mall. As strangers appeared, the practitioner would say, "Good morning. It's really nice out today. Have a good day." Although the client found this to be almost shocking at first, she was encouraged to do the same, while walking with the practitioner. After a short time, she became quite comfortable with such interactions and spontaneously changed her behavior at work to be more verbal and pleasant with customers.

- *Homework assignments.* At some point, clients have to practice the new social skill in the real world. They try out the newly learned behavior in real-life situations, monitor and report the results, and gradually begin to experience more positive experiences with others.

- *Reinforcement.* Skills that are learned through verbal instruction and modeling are then shaped through reinforcement: positive feedback from the professional; strokes from the group; pleasant feelings from a videotape of success; *in vivo* goal achievement.

For example, consider a client who has difficulty and becomes angry when dealing with aloof salespeople in stores. Methods of getting the salesperson's attention could be practiced in the office, and the client then could go to the store with the practitioner. The practitioner observes as the client tries to get the attention of a busy or aloof or inattentive salesperson. The client may express a complaint and/or ask a silly question, without becoming angry at the salesperson (as previously practiced in the office). The practitioner observes the interaction and gives feedback later.

In the office, behaviors can be rehearsed under differing provocative situations to maximize transfer to the real world. Thus, the role-played salesperson might announce she is "on a break," or become angry herself, or she might refuse to take an item back, or she might "threaten" to call the store manager or the security guard. Each of these outcomes could be rehearsed in the office. Over time, it might be possible for the client to develop general principles and strategies which would be available in novel situations. The probability of transfer of skills can be enhanced by use of client self-monitoring, repetition of in-vivo rehearsal, and contracted between-session homework assignments to be completed in the natural environment.

❖ *Assertiveness*

Assertiveness is defined as the *appropriate expression of feelings* (Wolpe, 1990). Specifically, "Assertiveness training is indicated when a person finds it difficult to express his feelings in social contexts because anxiety inhibits him" (p. 135). Thus, when teaching a client to be assertive, you are teaching a particular kind of expression. In fact, many assertive responses to others begin with, "I feel . . . "

Thus, as commonly practiced, assertiveness training involves techniques for teaching the *direct, honest,* and *appropriate expression of feelings* (along with associated beliefs, desires, opinions, and preferences). *Direct* means to the right person, usually the anger trigger. Unfortunately, it is common for clients to tell many others about their angry feelings, including the practitioner, but they don't tell the anger *source* directly. In the end, of course, unless anger is directly expressed there is little likelihood of change. *Honest* means no hiding. If the client is high on anger expression/in or anger expression/control (see chapter

2), anger festers and the client ruminates, or verbally denies, and little or nothing will be resolved. *Appropriate* refers to the frequency, intensity, and duration of the expression of the anger. Unfortunately, some clients go on and on about their anger triggers and for others it is more frequent and intense than is warranted (see chapter 7 for *Self-Monitoring* and *Life Experience Forms*). The goal is for the expression to be of reasonable frequency (perhaps once or twice), intensity (strong enough to be "heard," but not overpowering), and of reasonable duration (see chapter 15 for a discussion of forgiveness interventions). The reader will recall that in chapter 1 we stressed the importance of developing a clear emotional vocabulary. Assertiveness training expands on this, by developing skills to express emotions in interpersonal interactions.

Historically, specific training in assertive self-expression began with Salter's 1949 book, *Conditioned Reflex Therapy*. Moreno's (1971) *psychodrama* and Kelly's (1955) *fixed role psychotherapy* both advanced procedures which contributed — if indirectly — to assertiveness training. Wolpe and Lazarus (1966) were first to outline a modern version of "assertion training," in their text *Techniques of Behavior Therapy*. There is great similarity among the recommendations of these authors. In 1970, Alberti and Emmons (2001) synthesized these ideas and spelled out in detail the basics of modern "assertiveness training" in the first edition of their text, *Your Perfect Right*.

Salter recommended six "excitatory" assertive exercises for his clients. Four are particularly useful in the treatment of anger. These are:

1. *Feeling Talk: Clients are encouraged to develop an emotional vocabulary and practice the expression of their feelings.* We recommend that when feeling talk is practiced in the office, it is best done in the "when. . . then" format.

Examples of *correct* feeling talk:

> *When you become silent, I feel quite angry.*
> *When you spilled the coffee, I felt really annoyed.*
> *When you didn't show up for that appointment, and I waited for 45 minutes, I felt furious.*

Comment: *These expressions are direct, with no extra baggage, and are clearly linked to a trigger.*

Example of *incorrect* feeling talk:

> *When you come home late, I think you are out with other women. I begin to feel angry and bitter, and thoughts of revenge come into my mind. You are such a jerk. Why don't you just call me? I just don't understand you. You must know what is going to happen. What's wrong with you.*

Comment: *This is incorrect because it gives too much, goes on for too long, and blames.*

2. *Facial Talk. Clients are encouraged to develop a facial expression of anger.* Have clients work with a mirror, video camera, or digital camera (see chapter 3). Practice facial expressions, without talking, to represent fury, anger, annoyance, calmness, and happiness. If necessary, practice other emotions such as anxiety, shame, guilt, and depression (as well as happiness) in order to differentiate feelings. Teach clients to use different facial expressions for different intensities of anger. The pictures below show this woman's beginning attempts to express annoyance and anger.

Figure 10-1.

Facial talk: beginning attempts at annoyance and anger.

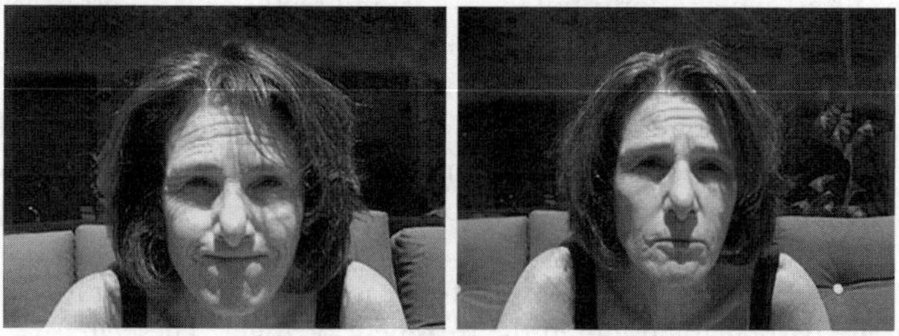

3. *Contradiction.* Many clients, even though they disagree with others, and feel strongly about what they hear, do not express their opinions. It is useful to have these clients practice contradictions, without anger and without demeaning the other person. It is useful to begin with simple, but clearly untrue statements. For example:

Practitioner: *The New York Mets are a singing group.*
Client: *I disagree. I think the New York Mets are a baseball team.*
Practitioner: *Well, OK, I guess they are. I think Babe Ruth played for them, right?*
Client: *I don't think so. Again, I disagree. I think Babe Ruth played before the Mets existed as a team.*

Then, slowly progress to problematic statements.
Practitioner: *Pornography is good for our country.*
Client: *I disagree. But, tell me more so that I can understand what you are saying.*
or

Practitioner: *Hitler, actually, had some rather good ideas.*
Client: *I strongly disagree. Hitler was evil. But, tell me more about your position. Perhaps I don't understand exactly what you are saying.*

The goal is to help the client recognize that there is often much to disagree about and that disagreement is acceptable. It is the manner in which the disagreement is made that is the more important issue. Direct, honest, and appropriate disagreement can be reinforced by the practitioner in sessions. In contrast, discuss and extinguish disparaging disagreements such as, "I don't understand how you could even say that!! Hitler was scum and to just utter those words make me really question who you are."

4. *"I" language.* All too often, clients try to achieve solutions by appealing to logic, or rules, rather than by simply expressing their personal desires. Although there is little wrong with logic, it is important that clients be able to express their ideas without justifications. Consider these two comments:

Client 1:   *I would like to talk about our problem now.*
Client 2:   *It makes sense to talk about our problem now because if we put it off I will forget what I want to say and some things that I'd like to say will be lost.*

Although the longer, justified request of Client 2 may be true, the request of Client 1 is direct and more to the point.

Differentiating assertiveness from other responses. Clients, and others, are often confused about the important differences among assertive responding, verbally aversive responding, aggressive responding, and unassertive non-responding. So, teaching the difference among these responses is also part of the life skills treatment package.

Assertiveness involves the expression of feelings and thoughts in *appropriate* ways, which don't violate the rights of others. The goal is to convey simple messages about thinking, feeling, and desires, without embellishments, and with respect for the other person. Here are some examples.

This is what I think:
Assertive: *I believe that my boss doesn't like me.*
Embellished: *My boss, the asshole, doesn't like me.*

This is what I feel:
Assertive: *When I remember what you did to me, I feel angry.*

Embellished: *When I remember what you did to me, I feel really pissed off and I remember what a jerk you really are. I could never forgive you for this, you bastard!*

This is what I want:

Assertive: *I want to talk with you about what happened. I'd like to do it now.*

Embellished: *We better talk about our problem right now! By tomorrow you will probably not think it was so important!*

Assertiveness is not a way for the client to get what she wants. The *goal of assertiveness is appropriate expression and improved opportunity for communication.* Because of situational factors (e.g., a financially strapped company) or personality factors (an obstinate boss), an assertion may not lead the client to attain desired goals (e.g., a raise in salary). In those cases, the various modes of adaptation and adjustment presented in chapters 13, 14, and 15 are very helpful. However, assertiveness greatly increases the probability of success in many interpersonal interactions.

Verbally aversive responding, in contrast to assertiveness, is considered to be the *expression* of feelings and thoughts at the *expense of others.* This type of outward verbal response is usually motivated by anger and is aimed at increasing power. It often involves dishonesty, neglect and a demeaning attitude. When a client responds in this way, the message typically leads to a decrease in successful interpersonal relations. The other person is given no credit for having a different opinion. Here are some illustrations of ineffective angry interactions.

Angry husband speaking to his wife:

> *I think you are really stupid about money. There is nothing wrong about having six credit cards, as long as you keep track of what you are doing. Since you don't work, I'm sure you can do that, can't you?*

Angry mother speaking to her son:

> *Why can't you learn that? Is something wrong with you or are you just plain stupid? I want you to do it now, and don't talk back!*

The general message given is: "My thoughts and feelings count and yours don't matter. This is what you better do! I don't care what you want."

Aggressive responding, as noted in chapter 1, consists of motor behavior such as pushing, shoving, slapping, punching and kicking. When extreme, it also consists of the use of weapons such as knives, guns, and ropes. Aggressive responding is *almost always* inappropriate, as the goal is to cause physical harm to others. Aggressive responding has no place in most interpersonal relationships. The exception relates to situations when one's physical well-being or life is in danger. Thus, in times of war or when faced with a would-be rapist or physically abusive spouse, defensive aggression is usually considered to be appropriate. However, even in those situations, "optimal" aggression is proportional to the threat and stops when the threat is alleviated. Thus, the aggression which has been documented in some prisoner of war camps is inappropriate because the prisoners pose little threat to their captors. And, once an aggressive spouse or rapist is deterred, defensive aggression is to be stopped. With these exceptions, in cases seen by mental health practitioners, it is fair to note again that aggressive responding is almost always inappropriate.

Unassertive responding might be better labeled *unassertive non-responding*. Unassertive angry clients may not express themselves at all. They violate their own rights and do not express feelings and thoughts or, when they are expressive, it is done apologetically. Unassertive responding is a negative, but not physically destructive alternate. Consider these unassertive interactions.

Unassertive client and her mother:

> *I understand you want me to visit you more often. Maybe I can reduce my hours at work, or give up going to the gym on Tuesdays and Thursdays. Then, I can see you and take you places.*

Unassertive client and girlfriend:

> *I guess I was wrong to become annoyed when we went to your parents' house for dinner. Your interpretation of what your father said about my job was probably correct. Even if I disagree, in the future I'll keep my mouth shut.*

When clients behave unassertively, the goal is to avoid conflict at all costs. This, of course, is silly, and virtually impossible. Conflict is part of life.

In order to develop assertive (not verbally aversive) responding, in addition to what has been mentioned above, discussion can help clients define their personal rights and the rights of others, help them to reduce blocks to acting assertively (e.g., believing that it is wrong to disagree with a boss), and develop assertive behaviors through active practice. Role-play, behavior rehearsal, and modeling are the techniques to be used. And, as always, repeated practice in the office is critical to success. Begin with the assertive responding practice sheet on the next page. Discuss the client's responses to each scenario, and give corrective feedback and reinforcement as appropriate.

Practicing Assertive Responding

Assertiveness involves the direct, honest, and appropriate verbal expression of feelings and desires. Assertive responding to others often helps you to achieve your goals. Verbally aversive responses, in contrast, represent a forceful attempt to get your own way — no matter what — at the expense of others. In the long run, angry and verbally aversive responding leads to poor relationships with others.

The situations described below each have the potential for conflict with others. Consider each problem and write down an angry response and an assertive response for each one.

1. In the past, you have told your friends that you do not like to wear sweaters. Yesterday, your good friend Charles bought a sweater for you for your birthday. You can tell it was expensive and Charles seemed very proud of the gift. He said he spent a lot of time picking it out. However, you really dislike it. In fact, you don't want a sweater and would like to exchange it for something else.

Charles says, "Here's your birthday present. I love it and hope you like it. Also, I hope you will wear it to my party next week."

Your *verbally aversive* response

_____

_____

Your *assertive* response

_____

_____

2. You have been watching an enjoyable movie on TV for the past 45 minutes. Your spouse/roommate walks in, changes the TV channel, and says, "Let's watch the news. I want to hear the sports results."

Your *verbally aversive* response

_____

_____

Your *assertive* response

_____

_____

3. You been having a rather tough time at work. The company is having economic problems and your supervisor is often stressed. Today, the supervisor says, "Listen up. I want you to work until 10 PM on Thursday and Friday nights. We can't give you any more money, but we need you to do this. Things are bad in our industry, and you have to work harder!"

Your *verbally aversive* response

_____

_____

Your *assertive* response

_____

_____

4. You went to dinner with family members, including your 70-year-old mother. After dinner, your sister-in law privately makes a number of disparaging remarks about your mother. She says, "Wow, your mother is really getting bad. She doesn't remember names and she said some really stupid things."

Your *verbally aversive* response

_____

_____

Your *assertive* response

_____

_____

CHANGING

Social Problem-Solving

Everything that is in agreement with our personal desires seems true. Everything that is not puts us in a rage.

— Andre Maurois

C lients with anger problems fail to see the difficulties and challenges of life as problems to be solved. Instead, they react with a narrow and persistent pattern of rumination about perceived unfairness and injustice, complain and whine about both everyday and complex frustrations, contemplate revenge, pout, or shout, and/or engage in avoidance activities, such as excessive gambling or substance use. Obviously, such reactions are not likely to lead to successful resolution of problems.

Angry clients are also prone to react impulsively, without forethought, to aversive and unwanted triggers, and they fail to consider the immediate and long-term consequences of their actions. In addition, they rarely take into account the full range of alternative responses available to them when confronted with an unpleasant situation. For these reasons, it is useful to teach these clients about the value of approaching difficulties from a social problem-solving perspective and to present a problem-solving strategy that can be used in their everyday lives.

Psychologists have developed a number of different problem-solving approaches to help children and adults cope with problems ranging from the reduction of negative emotions to the increase in health-enhancing behaviors in cardiac patients (Bruene-Butler, et al., 1997; Ewart, 1990; Nezu & D'Zurilla, 1989). The fundamental premise is that anger is more likely to be triggered — and intensified — when clients are faced with stressors and do not have adequate coping behaviors or solution possibilities. The four-step model we recommend in this chapter is adapted from the work of D'Zurilla and Goldfried (1971).

As with many other intervention strategies presented in this manual, we believe that it is best when practitioners and clients engage

163

in a collaborative effort to learn new skills. Thus, in the "spirit" of problem solving, the practitioner refrains from directly telling the client what to do. Rather, the *practitioner's role is limited to helping the client generate alternatives and choose the best course of action for a particular ongoing problem.* "Telling" angry clients how to act is likely to backfire, as they may perceive such a direct approach as an attack on their personal freedom.

The four steps of the problem-solving model are presented in detail below. The goal of the problem-solving approach — to assist clients in finding the most effective of many solutions to a specific personal problem — is to be clearly communicated. Since the client and practitioner are usually in agreement regarding goals of the intervention, the problem-solving approach, when done correctly, usually does not create resistance but actually enhances the therapeutic alliance. Of course, a secondary — but nonetheless important — goal is to teach a model that clients can apply in the future as new anger triggers emerge.

❖ *Steps of the Problem-Solving Model*

1. Clearly identify the situation and generate potential solutions.

An ongoing interpersonal situation that is challenging or difficult for the client is first identified in a collaborative manner. This single situation becomes the focus of the session and it is crucial to maintain focus on the identified trigger. If the client brings in other issues (as often happens) they can be worked on after a resolution is obtained for the first problem.

Identify the problem trigger(s) in a clear, objective fashion. Typically, this is done in a "when-then" format. For example,

> *John, you said that **when** you come home late from work, your wife is **(then)** angry and the interaction **(then)** usually escalates into a serious fight. Do I understand it correctly?*

By using the "when-then" format there is less probability of excess "descriptive baggage," such as casting blame or magnifying the situation out of proportion.

Once the trigger is clearly identified, multiple solutions are generated. The practitioner might say,

> *Let's come up with some things that you could do the next time you come home late, so that an argument is avoided.*

Write down each alternative that the client presents. This is not to help you remember them but, rather, to model organized thinking, behaving, and problem solving for your client. Remember, angry clients are often not able to conceptualize their problems clearly. One of the goals of this technique is to teach the problem-solving process, so it is important that practitioners be highly structured and organized throughout the session.

Clients often present ineffective or extreme "solutions" to their problems. This may be because they are not able to conceptualize alternatives clearly or they may be trying to be provocative and see how the practitioner reacts (see example below). No matter what the client suggests, record *all* of the alternatives generated, no matter how effective or ineffective, simplistic or outlandish, they might be. Do not comment on, or criticize, the client's suggestions or react strongly to an extreme thought. Just write down what is said.

Occasionally, the client may come up with one or two bad alternative courses of action and will then stop making suggestions. In this case, gently urge the client to think of other possibilities. For example,

> *John, you said that **when** you come home late and your wife gets angry at you, you **then** could: (1) tell her that she's stupid and should shut up, or you could (2) ignore her and just go to bed. Are there other things that you could say or do?*

With persistence, most clients will eventually come up with several constructive alternatives. Notice, in this example, the two options the client proposed represent extremes. One represents direct *confrontation* and the other *avoidance*. Angry clients frequently have difficulty conceptualizing "middle ground" alternatives such as explaining, discussing, and developing a mutually agreed upon plan for how to behave when a late arrival occurs. You can gently help with suggestions, such as, "Do you have any ideas about ways to help solve the problem if it happens again?"

Once a list is developed, which includes a full range of ineffective to effective actions, read them back to the client to make sure they were all accurately recorded. Then, move to the next step. A *Problem Solving Worksheet*, along with a sample to show to clients, appears on the next two pages.

Sample Problem Solving Worksheet

1. Description of the problem (use a "when-then" format). And, include *actions*, *thoughts*, and *verbalizations* in both parts.

(When)   Sometimes we get really busy at work.

I come home late, but I don't call my wife to tell her I'll be late.

(Then)   I appear at the door. She has a frown on her face, and is obviously pissed.

I think she doesn't understand, and I tell her so!

We go back and forth until I finally tell her to shut up. I go to the basement and watch TV.

2. Now, list at least five alternative responses and the predicted short-term and long-term outcomes to each alternative.

Alternative Responses	*Short-term reaction*	*Long-term reaction*
1. Smack her and tell her to make dinner.	She makes dinner and we are silent.	Lack of communication. Bitterness.
2. Stop and get her flowers.	She is both angry and happy.	Greater understanding on her part.
3. Stay out very late. Go drinking.	She is angry, then worried.	Bad.
4. Apologize. Ask her what to do.	Some forgiveness.	We could develop a plan, as to what to do when this happens again.
5. Tell her she is just like her mother!	Anger.	Anger.

[Howard Kassinove, Ph.D. and Raymond Chip Tafrate, Ph.D. *Anger Management: The Complete Treatment Guidebook for Practitioners* © 2002]

Problem Solving Worksheet

1. Description of the problem (use a "when - then" format). And, include *actions*, *thoughts*, and *verbalizations* in both parts.

When _____

Then _____

2. Now, please list at least five alternative responses and the predicted short-term and long-term outcomes to each alternative.

Alternative Responses	*Short-term reaction*	*Long term reaction*
_____	_____	_____
_____	_____	_____
_____	_____	_____
_____	_____	_____
_____	_____	_____

[Howard Kassinove, Ph.D. and Raymond Chip Tafrate, Ph.D. *Anger Management:The Complete Treatment Guidebook for Practitioners* © 2002]

2. Assess the probable consequences of each alternative.

Each response is then evaluated in terms of the likely consequences that it would produce. The client is asked to think about what would actually happen, both in the short-term and long-term in each case. For example,

> *OK, one of the things you said that you might do **when** your mother criticizes your parenting is to **(then)** point out to her all the things that she did wrong when she was a mother. What do you think would be her immediate reaction if you responded to her in this way? How would she react? In the long term, what would it do to your relationship with her?*

Your job is to ask questions in order to encourage the client to think more carefully about the consequences related to each specific action.

Once the client responds, write down the probable consequences. As you go through the list, try not to judge any of the particular alternatives at this point. Do not rule any actions in or out until you have gone through the entire list. Most clients are able to accurately assess the likely consequences when they are focused in this manner. However, it is also appropriate to discuss and debate the consequences if you believe that the client is not viewing them accurately. For example,

> *Alan, you said that if you tell your colleague directly that he should mind his own business and stay out of your department, that it would result in him interfering less. What else might happen if you approach the problem this way?*

The goal is to *collaboratively* agree on the most likely scenario.

Once you have agreement, explore the next listed alternative. For example,

> *Marge, you also said that you could react to your mother by choosing not to spend any time with her. What would happen if you did this? How would it affect your life in the long run to not have a relationship with her? What affect would it have on your extended family?*

Once the consequences for each of the alternatives have been identified, read them back to the client. This is done under the guise of checking with the client to make sure the list is correct. Actually, a more important reason to read the list is that it allows the client to see that there are, indeed, a whole range of alternatives available — each of which is likely to produce a different outcome. The client, hopefully, will identify which responses are extreme and which are moderate.

3. Select the best alternative and put it into practice.

Once you and your client agree on the list, the next step is to choose the alternative perceived to be best. Again, it is not up to the practitioner to decide, but rather to ask questions to allow the client to make an informed decision. One way to begin is to eliminate those choices that would be unlikely to lead to a desirable outcome for the client. For example,

John, which of these choices will create more conflict between you and your wife, and which would help strengthen the relationship?

Usually, there are two or three choices that might produce a positive outcome and the real task is picking among those options.

Another issue to keep in mind as you and your client work toward selecting the "best" solution is the client's level of interpersonal skill. A common mistake that practitioners make is to select the alternative that is likely to be associated with the most positive outcome but one that the client cannot execute properly. For example, when working with a client who is unhappy in his job, assertively asking for a raise and more responsibility at work may seem like the best option. However, the strategy would be risky if the client does not possess the skills necessary to respond to potential criticisms and reasons why the raise might not be granted. In this type of situation, the client and practitioner have two choices. The first is to pick an alternative that the client can implement successfully at his or her current skill level. A second possibility is to work with the client to build the skills necessary to successfully implement the most desirable option, as presented in chapter 10.

4. Implement and evaluate the effectiveness of the new response.

Once a course of action has been agreed upon, and it has been determined that the client has the skills necessary to use the identified alternative, the final steps are implementation and evaluation. The client is asked to engage in the agreed-upon behavior, and told that the effectiveness of the new response will be reviewed in a later session. This can be done in a number of ways. Clients' reports are certainly acceptable, and they represent a primary source of information for practitioners. However, as noted in chapter 3, it may also be desirable if client stories are confirmed by a report from an informant (e.g., husband, wife, child, friend, co-worker) who can come to a session. Alternatively, it *may* be possible for the practitioner to directly observe some client responses. For example, direct observation in a school, on the job, in a correctional institution, or in a home setting, is occasionally possible. Such direct observation gives the practitioner an opportunity to provide reinforcement of the newly acquired skill. Once the client experiences success with one interpersonal problem the model can then be applied to others.

❖ *A Sample Problem-Solving Session*

Rick, a 17-year-old adolescent, had been in and out of juvenile correctional facilities for the past three years. He had a history of impulsive anger outbursts that often resulted in verbal arguments. However, on several occasions these arguments escalated into physical altercations. Rick had recently been released on probation. One of the stipulations of his probation agreement was that he successfully maintain a part-time job for four weeks. If he could not keep the job, or if he got into a fight, he would be sent back to the correctional facility. However, during the first week on the job (a stock room at a large supermarket), Rick was already having difficulty.

The session takes place in an outpatient, prison-affiliated (alternative to incarceration) counseling facility.

Practitioner: *OK Rick, I hear that you are having some difficulty at your new job.*

Client: *Yeah, I am. You people sent me to work at this job with a guy who acts like an a**h*** and doesn't know how to treat people with respect. You set me up to fail! Nobody could work with this guy. I'm pissed off at you and this entire place!*

Obviously, Rick becomes angry when he thinks about, or talks about, his current situation. It would be easy for the practitioner to become the target of Rick's anger and for the session to be unproductive. Notice how the practitioner attempts to bring focus back to Rick's goals. When problem solving, the practitioner almost always attempts to align himself with the goals of the client.

Practitioner: *Well, it seems we've sent you to a tough place to work. It's probably not the best place for you, since you are trying to get back on your feet and want to avoid coming back to the facility.*

Client: *Yeah, it is a shitty place for me right now. I don't know how I am supposed to manage this job and stay out of prison.*

Practitioner: *How long do you have to keep this job?*

Client: *I have to keep it for four weeks. Then, I can move on to something else.*

Practitioner: *So you really are in a bind here. You don't want to be at this job but, on the other hand, you want to succeed and move on, and not come back.*

Client: *Yeah.*

Practitioner: *Which part of that is more important for you right now, getting away from this job or staying out of prison?*

Client:	*You know. Staying out of prison.*
Practitioner:	*So, do you want to work on hanging in there for four weeks?*
Client:	*Yeah, I guess I do.*

Once Rick's goal has been clearly identified, the practitioner obtains more detail about the interpersonal conflict.

Practitioner:	*Rick, you said that your new boss doesn't treat you well. What kinds of things does he do?*
Client:	*For starters, he orders me around. He tells me what to do and then he just walks away. He doesn't look at me when he talks to me. He knows I'm from the prison program and he acts like I'm a piece of garbage.*
Practitioner:	*So, he just kind of tells you what to do by barking out orders, like in the military?*
Client:	*No, it's worse than that. At least in the military they look at you. He just barks out orders into the air, and then he walks away.*
Practitioner:	*And that's upsetting to you?*
Client:	*Yeah. Wouldn't you be pissed off it people treated you that way?*
Practitioner:	*Well, it sure sounds like a difficult situation. Yet, you really do want to hang in there and keep this job so you'll stay out.*

The practitioner continues to: (1) remind Rick of his goal and (2) to position himself as being on Rick's side. It is important to avoid arguments.

| Practitioner: | *Rick, could you show me how he talks to you? For example, pretend that I am you and that you are your boss for a minute. Show me how he talks.* |
| Client: | *OK. "Hey, bring up those boxes by the steps downstairs. When you are through with that come back and sweep out the store room."* [Said in a loud tone of voice, while not looking at the practitioner.] |

The practitioner now guides Rick through the first problem-solving step.

| Practitioner: | *So, Rick, given that you want to keep your job, how could you respond to your boss **when** he barks out orders to you like that? I'd like to generate some possibilities and we will write them down on this* Problem Solving Worksheet. |
| Client: | *Well, I could take one of the cans off the shelves and whip it at his head.* |

The practitioner doesn't react or judge this statement, but just writes it down.

| Practitioner: | *What else could you do when he talks to you that way?* |

Client:	*I suppose I could just take a break. Just walk outside and smoke a cigarette.*
Practitioner:	*And, what else could you do?*
Client:	*I could tell him to go to hell and walk out.*

The practitioner keeps going until some better alternatives are generated. Also, Rick is reminded of his goal.

Practitioner:	*OK, Rick. So far you said that you could throw a can at his head, take a break and smoke a cigarette, or tell him to go to hell. How else might you react to achieve your goal of holding the job for four weeks so you won't have to come back to prison.*
Client:	*Oh, to keep the job. Well, I guess I could try to not react to him at all. You know. Just keep quiet.*
Practitioner:	*You mean just do your job and not take it personally — maybe to just see it as his unpleasant style?*
Client:	*Yeah.*
Practitioner:	*What else could you do to keep the job for four weeks?*
Client:	*My sister thinks I should talk to him and tell him not to treat me this way.*
Practitioner:	*So, you could tell him how you feel when he talks that way, and ask him to change the way he talks to you.*
Client:	*Yeah.*

Now the practitioner moves to the second step of assessing the consequences of each alternative.

Practitioner:	*OK, so I've written down five ways you might respond to your boss when he talks to you: (1) throw a can at his head, (2) take a break and smoke a cigarette, (3) tell him to go to hell, (4) just focus on doing your job and not take it personally, (5) talk to him about your feelings and ask him to change. Did I get them right?*
Client:	*Yes.*
Practitioner:	*Remember, your goal is to keep your job. So, let's look at each of these possibilities. What do you think would happen if you threw the can at his head?*
Practitioner:	*I would feel good for a moment, but I would lose my job and get locked up again. I'd probably get more time.*
Practitioner:	*So, that doesn't help you achieve your goal. What would happen if you just took a break and went and smoked a cigarette?*
Client:	*I'm not sure. On the one hand, I would cool down. But I think he'd get mad that I was taking a break without permission. He'd probably fire me.*

Practitioner: *So, if you took breaks every time he asked you to do something, because you were feeling angry, he would probably fire you. Then what would happen?*

Client: *I'd have to go back to prison.*

Practitioner: *So, that one doesn't work for you either. What about telling him to go to hell?*

Client: *Well, again, I'd probably get fired and have to go back to prison.*

Practitioner: *What about just doing your job and not taking it personally. Understanding that barking out orders is just his style. And, understanding that it is unpleasant but believing you can handle it.*

Client: *Well I wouldn't like it. But, if I could just stay focused on doing my job I could move on in four weeks.*

Practitioner: *So, not saying anything back to him would get you to your goal.*

Client: *Yeah.*

Practitioner: *What about the last choice, trying to talk to him. What do you think would happen if you did that?*

Client: *Well, my sister says that I shouldn't let him treat me this way and that I should tell him what I think.*

Practitioner: *OK, what do you think would happen if you did that?*

Client: *He might change and realize that he has to treat me with more respect.*

Practitioner: *You don't sound that sure. What else might happen if you told him to treat you better?*

Client: *He might tell me to get lost and fire me.*

Practitioner: *So this option is more risky. And, it might mean returning to prison.*

Client: *Yeah*

Practitioner: *Rick, give me a sense of what you might say to him if you decided to have that discussion.*

At this point, the practitioner briefly steps out of the problem-solving model to assess Rick's skill level. A determination is to be made about Rick's assertiveness skills. Is it likely that a conversation with the boss would lead to an argument or could Rick express himself without blaming the boss or infuriating him in some other way?

Client: *I would tell him that he shouldn't treat people like they are garbage. That I have been in prison and that I am tougher than most of the other people that he has around here. He should make it easier for me and try to understand my problems. I'd try to make him see that he's wrong.*

Based on Rick's response, the practitioner thinks that he currently lacks the skills required to have a productive conversation with his new boss.

Practitioner: *OK, Rick, you said that if you tried to talk to him he might change his attitude. But, he also might tell you to get lost. And, you've described your boss as being pretty tough to deal with. So, how do you think he would react?*

Client: *I don't know. He might change. Or, he could fire me.*

Practitioner: *So, it's unclear what would happen. Sounds like that choice could be very risky. In considering all of your options, which one is most likely to help you hang in there for four weeks?*

Client: *I guess just keeping cool — focusing on my job and not reacting.*

It may seem to some practitioners that it would be more desirable in the *long run* to teach Rick how to talk assertively with his boss. We agree. However, given the seriousness of the situation, the lack of time to teach Rick such skills, and the dearth of information about his supervisor, it seems that the best choice is for Rick not to respond to his new boss and wait out the four weeks.

The practitioner next moves to step three.

Practitioner: *So, it seems like the surest way to achieve your goal of not losing the job and staying out of prison is just to stay focused on the work and not to take his comments seriously. Do you think you can do it?*

Client: *Yeah. I can definitely just ignore him. I know I can.*

Practitioner: *OK, maybe you can show me. Let's practice having you not react to his statements the next time you are at work...*

Practitioner and client role-play the likely scenes Rick will face with his boss.

Practitioner: *Good! Let's schedule a session immediately after work, perhaps in three days, to see how it went and talk about it.*

At this point, the incorporation of other techniques such as *rational self-statements* to help Rick not respond would be useful, along with *exposure* and *relaxation*. The goal would be to prepare Rick to handle the negative statements from his boss and not react with anger. Although practice of such techniques would be helpful, we are also aware that the reality of time may affect what happens next.

In terms of the outcome for this particular case, Rick was able to successfully ignore his supervisor during his next scheduled workday. Even though he still did not like his supervisor's actions, he remained focused on his own goals and felt a sense of accomplishment at not reacting.

During the next session, the practitioner focused on additional exposure practice (chapter 12). The practitioner played the role of the gruff and critical boss while Rick practiced not responding to a variety of graded provocative statements. This strategy was used in several subsequent sessions. The practitioner and Rick also addressed the issue of beginning to search for a new job once the four-week probationary restriction was lifted. Rick managed to control his anger outbursts for the four weeks. Unfortunately, as is common in many criminal justice related facilities, Rick was considered a short-term case. Thus, after four weeks he had no further contact with the practitioner.

Social problem solving was clearly helpful for Rick, although he certainly had more work to do to manage his anger effectively. Nevertheless, the problem-solving model proved a useful and practical intervention given the time restrictions and the possibility of serious negative consequences. In addition, the problem-solving approach allowed the practitioner to establish an alliance quickly, by connecting with Rick's goal to stay out of prison, thus side-stepping Rick's potential anger at anyone who was connected with the criminal justice system.

Social problem solving is designed to give clients thoughtful planned options to deal with life's problems. In the universe of anger management procedures, it is among the most practical because of its applicability in a wide variety of circumstances. If the practitioner can teach the client the principles of this very effective four-step model, the client may be able to apply it to a range of situations to help deal with anger and improve interpersonal relationships.

CHANGING

Exposure

There is no alleviation for the sufferings of mankind except veracity of thought and of action, and the resolute facing of the world...

— Thomas Henry Huxley

As noted in chapter 8, strategies that promote avoidance or escape from interpersonal challenges and stressors are sometimes quite useful. However, in the long run they limit opportunities for growth. Avoidance and escape maneuvers may further reinforce dysfunctional behaviors and anger patterns while strengthening the belief that coping and problem resolution are impossible. Eventually, change is likely to require that clients voluntarily face what is challenging and difficult, that they remain in those situations, and that they learn new skills to deal with aversive people and circumstances. This model has led to the successful treatment of many human problems, especially anxiety disorders. For example, clients who suffer from panic attacks benefit from experiencing uncomfortable sensations through physical exercise, social phobics improve by repeatedly placing themselves in evaluative situations, and clients with obsessive-compulsive disorder can reduce their symptoms by repeatedly imagining uncomfortable images. If they are not allowed to escape from the discomfort, structured and repeated exposure to feared stimuli often leads to symptom reduction.

When it comes to managing anger, practitioners have largely ignored these exposure-based methods. Given their success in the management of anxiety, why have mental health practitioners neglected to include exposure as a component of anger treatment programs? One common concern is that clients will resist because they do not understand why they are being asked to re-experience their anger-provoking triggers and the resultant angry feelings. Clients are quite used to avoidance and may, initially, be unwilling to participate in exposure sessions. Their resistance may take the form of statements such as, "I just want to forget about it. Wouldn't you?" Recognizing such resistance, practitioners may worry that the client will terminate treatment prematurely. Another practitioner concern is that while doing exposure exercises, clients will become angry and uncontrollable, and may lash out or destroy property. This, of course, would be quite problematic for both the practitioner and client. Yet another concern is that facing ongoing anger triggers could lead to persistent increases in anger or exacerbate other existing emotional problems.

Although it is important to be aware of the potential adverse affects of any procedure, we have used exposure techniques in research and clinical settings, and found these concerns to be unwarranted. In fact, we found that carefully planned exposure techniques promote less angry responses, decrease anger associated physical arousal, and are safe for both clients and practitioners. The key is to work collaboratively with the client, to explain what is likely to happen, and to decide jointly that exposure is a treatment of choice. If the planned exercises are discussed in advance, in the context of a strong therapeutic relationship, the probability of a successful outcome is increased.

In this chapter we present exposure-based strategies that are useful to help clients face their anger triggers. Four specific techniques are presented: trigger review, verbal exposure, combining imaginal exposure with other interventions, and *in vivo* exposure. Guidelines for determining if exposure may be useful for a particular client are provided, along with potential contraindications. Suggestions for implementing exposure in group therapy settings are also offered. However, we first provide some detail on how exposure works to decrease anger. This analysis can be presented, perhaps in simplified form, to clients so that their knowledge base and expectations will be shared with those of the practitioner.

❖ How Exposure Works

Clients frequently report that their anger emerges automatically in particular situations or in the presence of specific individuals. They say it "just comes" over them and they give reports such as, "I don't know. I just can't help myself. Whenever I talk to her I seem to get into an argument and feel really pissed!" The trigger repeatedly, and seemingly automatically, leads to angry experiences and expressive behaviors. In truth, their reactions are mostly a function of conditioning which has occurred out of their awareness.

Let's examine the case of Stephen, a 34-year-old teacher. He had a history of difficulties controlling his temper with his wife of three years, Jill. Stephen often exploded in response to minor incidents and disagreements. When questioned, he recognized that his anger reactions were excessive and that they had a negative effect on his marriage. Yet, his anger seemed to occur instantaneously. He said, "She just gets under my skin... I can't seem to help myself... The same damn thing happens in me over and over again."

After monitoring his anger episodes, it became clear that Stephen happened to get angry during almost *any* disagreement with Jill, no matter how small or large the problem was from an objective perspective. For example, the daily log he kept showed that anger was evoked by a newspaper Jill had misplaced, by some vegetables she served which he disliked, and by her preference that he wear a particular tie. Because of the constant anger, their relationship had deteriorated markedly. He said, "Yeah, I love her. But, sometimes *when I just see her* I become angry."

Certain characteristics of Jill's body language, and her level and tone of voice, were enough for his anger to emerge. He would often verbally attack her to a degree that was way out of proportion to the problem. And, sometimes there was no problem! He just felt angry while sitting together at the dinner table or when watching TV and commenting on the programs.

Stephen described a typical interaction. He and Jill were talking about their bills and were disagreeing about how much money to pay to various creditors. Jill's "attitude was sarcastic," and he thought she blamed him for their financial predicament. He particularly focused on her sarcastic tone and the way she put her hands on her hips and pointed her finger when they discussed payment of his student loan. Although she denied it, Stephen has always thought that Jill blames their poor financial state on his choice of careers.

Following her comments Stephen thought, "It's unfair for her to blame me.... She should be contributing more.... I can't tolerate her when she gets this way.... Man, she can be a real bitch.... Sometimes, I'd like to just belt her one!" Physically, he recalled that his hands trembled during this interaction and that he felt hot flashes in his face. Expressively, as her criticisms continued, he finally "had enough" and started to swear at her, stomp around the house, and slam doors.

Figure 12-1.

The sight of Jill as an anger trigger.

Stephen's automatic anger reaction has been learned over time, and is diagrammed below. Note that, in addition to the actual critical content of her verbalizations, a "sarcastic tone," hands placed on her hips and a pointed finger, accompanied Jill's criticisms. Because these episodes were repeated over and over again, the stage was set for conditioning to occur. Of course, no one enjoys criticism so Jill's verbalizations legitimately represented a negative trigger. However, Stephen appraised her criticisms as unduly harsh, untrue and unfair, leading to his anger.

In the early phase of their relationship it took a few seconds of interaction for Stephen to interpret and appraise what Jill was saying, and to feel himself become angry. However, over the course of time, Jill's voice and body posture *alone* became triggers for his anger. His angry reactions were swift and strong, irrespective of the actual content of what she said. Stephen's anger took on an automatic quality. Because Jill's comments were always associated with her postural cues, he had almost the same angry reaction to a minor or major disagreement. A connection had been conditioned to Jill's pointed finger, hands on hips, and voice. In order for the anger to emerge it was no longer required that he even perceive what she was saying. His reaction was automatic.

To make matters worse, this pattern was activated in other situations. For example, Stephen reported exaggerated anger in response to women at work who he perceived had spoken to him in a critical and condescending tone. On one occasion, he yelled at a clerk at the motor vehicle department because she refused to process his car registration when he didn't bring the proper paperwork. He thought that the clerk had treated him with an "attitude." Once an anger reaction like Stephen's is conditioned, it can easily generalize to other situations that have similar features. Since these conditioned reactions often occur out of conscious awareness, they may be a source of confusion and embarrassment for clients who realize, after the fact, that they behaved out of proportion to the precipitating event.

Connections are strengthened by a number of reinforcing processes. Stephen eventually reacted by yelling and arguing to the stimuli of a "sarcastic tone" and Jill's body posture. As noted in chapter 2, although Stephen's anger was self-defeating in the long run, it had short-term benefits that reinforced the trigger-anger connection. These included self-perceived tension reduction. Bushman, Baumeister, and Phillips (2001) have shown that people who *believe* in the value of expressing anger outwardly are more likely to do so to regulate their anger. The reinforcement is more of a perception than an actuality, but works nevertheless to keep the anger going. Another short-term benefit for Stephen was that his verbal attacks usually prevented Jill, or any other person, from delivering further criticism (e.g., Jill would stop talking when Stephen's anger escalated). A third short-term outcome was social compliance. In angry interactions, the less dominant person often goes along with the demands of the other, albeit with some resentment. When Stephen yelled at Jill about the bills, it usually wound up that she listened to him about which bill to pay. In the short run, at least, his anger seemed to work. Also, recall Stosny's explanation (chapter 2) that anger causes the brain to release both epinephrine and norepinephrine, which are both reinforcing. And, finally, the entire episode leads to a perception on Stephen's part that he is right, that she is wrong, and that he does not have to consider his own shortcomings.

In conceptualizing Stephen's situation, it is important to remember that reinforcement is critical in strengthening the trigger-anger bond. As presented below, Stephen's angry reaction to Jill was strengthened by a combination of negative and positive reinforcement. And across other situations that had stimuli related to criticism, verbally arguing and yelling became automatic for Stephen.

Figure 12-2. Stephen's anger development sequence.

DEVELOPMENT OF ANGER FOR STEPHEN

Associated Stimuli	*Trigger*	*Trigger Appraisal*	Anger (*Experience & Expression*)
Jill's tone of voice Jill's pointed finger Jill's hands on hips	Verbal criticism	"What she is saying is wrong, unfair, and harsh. I can't take her any more! She's a bitch."	Physical activation, angry thoughts, angry images, yelling, pouting, and slamming objects.

Reinforcing Outcomes
Tension reduction
No more criticism
Behavioral compliance by Jill
Does not have to consider his own shortcomings.

So, how does exposure work? Exposure techniques break these automatic, reinforced and bonded reactions. By repeatedly exposing clients to a specific trigger, under controlled conditions, and not allowing the usual anger responses and reinforcements to occur (response prevention), the bond extinguishes through habituation.

To use these principles with Stephen, we would expose him to a series of critical and even condescending statements, delivered with a critical tone of voice, forward-leaning body posture, and pointed finger. The practitioner and Stephen might collaboratively agree that statements around money problems would be on target since they have historically been associated with his anger reactions. An exposure statement would be developed such as the following: *"Stephen, it was* your *bad choices that have created this financial mess that we now have to deal with."* After discussing the procedure with Stephen, the practitioner would then deliver the statement repeatedly, making sure that Stephen did not engage in his usual verbal counterattack. (See dialog in next section for a more detailed description of how to implement *verbal barb exposure.*)

At first, this would be uncomfortable for Stephen. He would feel some physical arousal and have a number of negative thoughts. Of course, this arousal would not be of the same magnitude that he usually experienced with Jill because the interaction is simulated. But, nonetheless, he would feel some physical activation and negative thoughts. After hearing the statement repeated a number of times his reactions would diminish. In fact, following 50 or so repetitions of the statement we would expect that Stephen would have almost no reaction. This repeated exposure process interrupts the automatic-like responses to this specific trigger.

Something else would also happen during the process of being exposed to the negative statement, with the associated condescending tone of voice and body posture. Stephen would find that it was not so terrible to hear and absorb negative feedback. In fact, he would realize that he can actually handle it quite well and even learn from it. Thus, with practice his tolerance for critical feedback would increase. Another benefit is that, since his physical arousal is likely to decrease with repeated exposure, he will become better able to consider alternative and more effective ways of dealing with the problem.

Many conditioned anger response patterns can be modified through the use of exposure. Of course, anger problems take on many different forms and treatment has to be tailored to the client and environment in which the practitioner works. In fact, some practitioners prefer to use exposure only in the latter phases of treatment. We would agree. Teaching clients relaxation, life and problem-solving skills, and awareness of when to use avoidance and escape are all part of the early phase of intervention. Nevertheless, the point here is that it is important for the client eventually to become less reactive when facing the anger trigger.

❖ *Trigger Review*

Although it may not be used until later in the treatment program, an opportunity to *introduce* exposure and response prevention to angry clients often presents itself early. It is common to ask clients to describe recent events where anger was experienced. They are often eager to give detailed accounts of, for example, how they were mistreated by others. As these anger situations are described, it is common for them to re-experience anger. This can be observed easily from their tone of voice, muscle tension in face and hands, body posture, and flushing of the face. We have had some clients get out of their chairs and pace angrily around the room while describing an anger episode.

When this type of client behavior occurs, practitioners have a choice as to how to handle it. One possibility is to allow the client to vent while describing past anger episodes. This, according to older notions, allows the client to engage in a sort of cathartic expression of anger while in the session. Proponents of this approach use terms such as "letting the anger out." We have never understood this phrase. Out of what? Does anger reside in the pancreas or small intestine? Catharsis is actually *practicing* the social role of anger and, since "practice makes better," it is likely to further reinforce the connection between the trigger and the angry thoughts and actions (chapter 2; Bushman, Baumeister, & Stack, 1999; Bushman, Baumeister, & Phillips, 2001; Geen & Quanty, 1977; Kassinove 1995). By *not* stopping the client who retells stories in an angry manner, the practitioner has indirectly endorsed the idea that the client *must* feel and express anger when thinking about the trigger.

Another drawback of allowing clients to vent angrily while describing past episodes is that it sends the message that the practitioner may not be in control of the session. Ultimately, the practitioner will be less likely to be of help when strong emotions emerge. We believe that allowing clients to vent while describing their anger experiences gets therapy off on the wrong track and undermines practitioner credibility. This approach may be of even greater concern for those who work in correctional or other types of settings with dangerous clients. A lack of therapist control and structure can foster an environment where aggressive physical outbursts, based on a hostile aggression model, are more likely to take place.

A better option is to work on shaping clients to describe anger triggers while remaining calm and in control. Although this may initially be difficult, it becomes easier with practice. It may be appropriate to interrupt a client by saying something such as this:

> *You know, Stephen, it is really important for me to understand what happened between you and Jill. This was obviously an important event for you and you seem to be getting angry while describing it right now. Your voice is raised and you're talking fast. Unfortunately, although I'm listening, I'm having difficulty following what happened. Can you start again and tell me from the beginning what happened? Try to keep your anger in check. Please speak slowly, and in a normal voice, so I fully understand you.*

By not expressing anger as they usually do, clients begin the process of response prevention and "chip away" at their automatic patterns. This approach reinforces control in the face of anger triggers.

Of course, even after intervening to get clients to describe situations in a calm manner, it is not unusual for them to quickly revert back to venting. It may take several reminders to get them to describe the situation with less anger. When a calmer description is given, reinforcement is very important. For example,

> *You did a much better job of telling me what happened with Jill the other day. I would like you to go back over it one more time; this time I want you to do it in an even calmer tone of voice. OK?*

With some persistence most clients can eventually get to this point.

When employing this strategy in individual treatment sessions, you can emphasize that in order to understand the client best it is helpful to hear the events described in a calm manner. Also, in order to learn new and better ways of dealing with difficulties, the client can benefit from learning to stay calm even when thinking about aversive situations. Being able to discuss difficult situations calmly is the first step in that process.

In a group treatment format, it can be useful to emphasize that one goal is to strengthen each member's emotional and behavioral control. Therefore, a group rule is instituted that the person describing anger triggers will try to remain calm. In fact, if other group members see the person becoming angry, they are asked to point it out and describe the way in which the person is showing anger. The speaker is then asked to describe the situation again while showing less anger. This helps to create a group culture that emphasizes exposure and prevention of the angry response. Having clients vent anger in a group format can be particularly unproductive. It contributes to a group that is unfocused and that may be hard to control later.

Let us be clear once more about the difference between angry *feelings* and angry *expression.* We are not advocating that clients be taught to "swallow" their angry feelings, but are pointing out that simple "venting" is not psychologically sound. It is certainly important that angry feelings be recognized and acknowledged. When it is appropriate to express them, a calm and reasoned approach is healthiest.

❖ Verbal Exposure

Most, but not all, anger situations, are social in nature, in that they involve some sort of interaction with other persons. Therefore, verbal statements perceived to be aversive are common triggers to which clients have developed conditioned reactions.

The first step in using verbal exposure is to conduct a careful assessment of a client's anger episodes. The *Anger Episode Record* (chapter 3), *Self-Monitoring Form,* and *Life Experiences Questionnaire* (chapter 7) are useful for these assessments. Identify the triggers that precede the very first moments when the client starts to feel anger build. Assist the client in identifying specific statements, vocal tones, facial expressions, and body language from others that lead to the anger reactions. Then, identify the manner in which clients typically respond to these triggers (e.g., pouting, yelling, throwing, and withdrawing).

The next step is to collaboratively develop specific exposure statements, otherwise known as "verbal barbs." *Barbs are aversive, negative words or statements designed to simulate anger triggers that occur naturally in the client's life.* For example, with Stephen, statements that were critical of his career choice and difficulty earning money were common anger triggers. And, as noted above, it is always important to provide a rationale for the use of verbal barb exposure that is easily understood by the client. A common base of knowledge with the client will further enhance treatment compliance.

A sample dialog between a practitioner and Stephen is presented below, addressing some of the reasons it is helpful to practice hearing negative statements. Also, in this dialog the practitioner and Stephen identify a specific barb statement that is relevant for his ongoing anger problem.

Practitioner: *Stephen, based on the diary you kept during the past week, we've identified several important triggers for your anger. What is it that jumps out for you as most important?*

(Notice that instead of lecturing Stephen, the practitioner uses a Socratic — questioning — style to bring out information.)

Stephen:	*I guess I get pretty burned up when Jill gets critical of me. She does it way too much.*
Practitioner:	*I understand. What else precedes your anger? Before Jill even says anything that's critical of you?*
Stephen:	*Like it's her tone of voice and when she puts her hand on her hips. And, when she points her finger at me. That really gets my goat.*
Practitioner:	*Yes, that seems to be important to you. Do you think that you respond almost automatically to that kind of criticism, or tone of voice or finger pointing?*
Stephen:	*Oh yeah. I even respond to other people when they act that way or when they treat me with an "attitude."*
Practitioner:	*OK, so you seem to be conditioned to react pretty quickly to a certain tone of voice, to body posture, and to critical statements. How might we work on that, so that you wouldn't react so quickly to that sort of thing?*
Stephen:	*I'm not sure. I guess talking about it helps.*
Practitioner:	*Certainly talking about it helps you become more aware of the pattern, and I'm happy that we are doing that. But, uh, how could you learn to react less quickly to a condescending body posture, tone of voice, a pointed finger, and criticism?*
Stephen:	*I'm not sure what you are getting at.*
Practitioner:	*Well, after all, criticism is a part of life for all of us. And, of course, I wish that when someone is critical of something I've done, that it be done gently. But, sometimes I'm criticized in a manner I don't like. For example, I have a neighbor who has been critical of the color I painted my house. He's a nice guy, but he needles me quite often – with the same kind of sarcastic tone you describe.*
Stephen:	*Uh, huh. So, what do we do?*
Practitioner:	*What do you think would happen if we practiced having you deal with the body language, tone of voice and critical statements right now, in the session? I could act like Jill and you could practice not getting angry.*
Stephen:	*I dunno. That might help.*

(Most angry clients quickly understand the rationale for exposure interventions. Unlike anxiety-disordered clients, persons with anger problems are more readily agreeable to facing their anger triggers.)

| Practitioner: | *I think it is important to be able to deal with critical statements and attitudes from others with minimal anger. After all, we will both probably face lots of criticism, as well as getting lots of praise, in the rest of our lives. The best way to* |

help you is to practice having you hear the critical statements while not reacting to them.

Stephen: *You mean you will say stuff that is negative and I'm supposed to not react to it?*

Practitioner: *Yes, that is exactly what I mean.*

Stephen: *But, you're not Jill and I'll know that it's not real.*

Practitioner: *Even though the situation will be somewhat artificial, we will be practicing with the types of statements that are challenging for you. What do you think would happen if you could learn to keep your cool here in the office, after hearing critical statements over and over again?*

Stephen: *I guess I might be able to do it at home and in other situations. Maybe.*

Practitioner: *Good! Why don't we try to come up with some statements that would be difficult for you to deal with if Jill said them to you? Can you give me some examples?*

Stephen: *That's easy. When she blames me for our money problems.*

Practitioner: *I'd like to write down the exact words she would say. Could you give me a specific sentence?*

Stephen: *How about: "OK, genius boy, you made these choices and now we both have to live with your student loans."*

Practitioner: *Would that be tough to hear?*

Stephen: *Yeah, especially if she pointed at me, and said it with that tone in her voice and her hands on her hips. Even when she says, "Stephen," I can hear the sarcastic crap that's coming next.*

Practitioner: *Could you actually show me how she might say it? I want to get a sense of how it would actually sound.*

Stephen: *Yeah.*

(Stephen gets up and puts his hands on his hips and says the statement in a sarcastic, biting tone. In this way, the practitioner gets a clear understanding of the anger trigger.)

Practitioner: *Good. Now, how do you typically respond when Jill says the statement in that manner?*

Stephen: *I get pretty angry. Then, I tell her that she doesn't contribute that much anyhow and all the pressure seems to be on me.*

Practitioner: *Do you say it in a calm manner, or in another way?*

Stephen: *You know. I yell and scream. Then, maybe slam the door and walk away or something.*

Practitioner: *What I would like to do now, is to practice saying that statement to you the way Jill might say it. But, uh, when I say it, I want you to just hear the statement but not to react. Just sit there.*

Stephen: *Okay.*
Practitioner: *Can you do it?*

(It is important not to surprise clients and to make sure that they understand what is going to happen. Also, it is a good idea to check with clients to make sure they think they can maintain control and not react. We always ask before we proceed. Occasionally, clients indicate they might not be able to stay in control. If that happens, we move to something easier. In this case, for example, it might be just Jill staring at Stephen with her hands on her hips.)

Stephen: *Sure.*
Practitioner: *OK Stephen, I'm going to say the statement now. "You made these choices, genius, and now we both have to live with your student loans." How was that?*

(The barb is delivered slowly the first time, in a flat monotone voice, to gauge Stephen's reaction.)

Stephen: *Not bad. I felt a little something, but not much.*
Practitioner: *No problems staying in control and not reacting?*
Stephen: *No.*
Practitioners: *How much anger did you feel on a zero to ten-point scale, where zero represents no anger and ten is the most anger you ever felt?*

(It is important to get some phenomenological measure of how clients are responding to the barbs in order to detect decreases in later presentations.)

Stephen: *I felt about a one or a two.*

(Clients often give two numbers, such as "one or two," or report some range as in "between two and four." Try to get them to commit to one number. We do this because we are aiming for as much precision as possible when they discuss all elements of their lives.)

Practitioner: *OK. I know it may be hard, but I'd like you to give me just one number. Think about your reaction. Think about what you felt in your body, your stomach and muscles. Think about your thoughts and images as I delivered the barb. Now, was it more of a one or a two?*
Stephen: *I guess it was a one. I didn't feel too much.*
Practitioner: *OK, this time I'm going to say it with more force and use a sarcastic tone of voice.*

(Again, the practitioner is letting the client know what to expect.)

Stephen: *OK.*
Practitioner: *Here it comes. "You made these choices, genius, and now we*
                 both have to live with your student loans." How was that?

(The exact words that were initially delivered are used again.)

Stephen: *I felt more anger that time.*
Practitioner: *How would you rate it?*
Stephen: *I'd give it a four.*

(At this point the practitioner decides to practice the same barb statement, in the same tone of voice, until Stephen's anger reduces to two or less.)

Practitioner: *OK, Stephen, I want to say it again, the same way. Ready?*
                 "You made these choices, genius, and now we both have to live
                 with your student loans." How was that?
Stephen: *About a three.*
Practitioner: *OK, let's do it again.*

(They continue for eight more trials, until Stephen reports a rating of two on two successive presentations. Some clients report anger reductions very quickly (two or three repetitions) while others require many additional presentations. It is important to continue the session until anger is reduced. Once Stephen gives a low rating, the practitioner suggests that they add in the body posture; e.g., Jill's hands on hips.)

Practitioner: *Stephen, I'm now going to say it again. But, this time I'm*
                 going to stand up and put my hands on my hips. Do you think
                 you can still not react and stay in control?
Stephen: *Yes.*
Practitioner: *"You made these choices, genius, and now we both have to live*
                 with your student loans." How was that?
Stephen: *That was more difficult, maybe a seven. You're really*
                 starting to sound like Jill.
Practitioner: *Can we do it again?*
Stephen: *Sure.*

The practitioner repeatedly delivers the barb in a sarcastic tone, while standing with his hands on his hips, until Stephen reports a rating of two or less.

At this point a new barb statement could be created and worked on in a similar manner. *The initial goal of verbal exposure is to simply reduce Stephen's reactivity to the statements.* It may be useful to have several rehearsal sessions dealing with the verbal barbs. In our research studies (e.g., Tafrate & Kassinove, 1998) we used verbal barb exposure over the course of 12-session protocols and have achieved good results. Some clients require less repetition, depending on the number of verbal triggers and the strength of their responses.

Of course, getting the client not to react in the usual angry manner is only the initial goal of the barb exposure. We are not recommending that clients always act passively in the face of critical negative statements or advocate that they take abuse continually. Once they are in greater control of their own reactions, other techniques are added such as learning assertive responses (chapter 10) or problem solving to develop alternative courses of action (chapter 11). Self-statements that promote control and lead to productive behaviors may also be programmed into the verbal exposure rehearsal (chapters 14 and 15). For example, Stephen might practice saying to himself, *It's OK to listen to Jill's criticisms. Being honest is a healthy part of any relationship. I don't have to react with anger.* Ultimately, we want to break the conditioned dysfunctional responses and have clients develop better alternatives.

We have used verbal exposure in several treatment outcome studies with a variety of clinical problems, such as general anger and marital discord. Our experiences lead to several specific conclusions. Barbing (exposure) is a powerful and effective way to reduce angry reactions to aversive verbal stimuli. However, before using exposure make sure the client is sufficiently motivated to reduce his or her anger and use verbal exposure after the therapeutic alliance has been well established. It is likely to work best when trust and respect exists between the practitioner and client. These issues have been discussed in chapters 5, 6, and 7, which focused on the preparation phase of treatment. Also, we stress the importance of making sure that clients understand the reasons for engaging in verbal exposure and are informed at every step of what is going to happen. Finally, as illustrated in the sample dialog, clients are frequently asked how they are dealing with the exposure and they are given the option

Figure 12-3.

Contraindications for Using Exposure with Angry Clients

(Be Cautious with New Methods)

- Client does not see his or her anger reactions as problematic
- Anger is the result of a contributing medical condition
- Client is engaged in active substance use
- In addition to anger problems, client also suffers from a significant mood disturbance
- Client has a schizophrenic spectrum disorder
- Client has a significant history of assaultive behavior
- Client exhibits significant psychopathy or antisocial behavior

to stop it at any time. We have followed these simple guidelines and have not had any negative experiences with this technique. We find it to be well tolerated by community clinic clients with anger problems.

There are some situations where exposure is not recommended. These are listed in Table 12-1. It is also worth noting that in our experiences the practitioner or researcher has always delivered the verbal barbs. We have not had significant others or family members deliver the barb statements. While it may be potentially useful to have people from the client's life involved in the treatment process, it may also increase risk. For example, others might deliver the barbs in a mean-spirited manner or bring the technique up at times that might be embarrassing for the client.

When using the barb technique in a group setting, the first session or two can be devoted to self-monitoring and identifying the types of statements and body language that precede anger, as well as each client's typical response. Following sessions can be focused on barb development. Finally, as group leaders deliver barbs, other group members can give feedback by noting the client's body language, muscle tone, and facial expressions. Once a client can tolerate the statements and maintain control, the other group members might help to conduct problem solving to develop productive responses. However, we do urge some caution with this technique when applied in a group setting. Clients often report that they can tolerate barbs because of the privacy provided by individual treatment and their faith in the practitioner. In addition, we believe it is important to deliver barbs in a graded manner, until they elicit little or no anger. In a group format, there is less control over these variables.

❖ Pairing Imaginal Exposure With Relaxation and Cognitive Interventions

Some anger triggers do not lend themselves to verbal exposure. Becoming angry while driving in traffic is one common example. Another is becoming angry in response to an inanimate object, such as a VCR that is not easily programmable or a computer that gives constant "error" messages. Other anger experiences can be abstract, such as becoming angry in response to thoughts of institutions, or practices that may be perceived as corrupt or unfair (e.g., the American tax penalty on married couples, or forced female circumcision as practiced in some African countries). In such instances, verbal exposure cannot be used in the practitioner's office. However, for these situations exposure can be implemented in imagery or visualization. Exposure in imagery can also be used along with verbal barbs, as imagery allows for a more complex presentation of difficult interactions.

The first step in using imaginal exposure is, again, to conduct a careful assessment of the client's anger episodes. Once a relevant situation is identified, an imagery scene is created around the trigger. The *Imagery Scene Development Form* (at the end of this chapter) can assist the practitioner and client in developing scenes in a collaborative manner.

Stephen, for example, was asked to describe an argument with Jill and write it out on paper. He was asked to include specific details in order to make the scene more realistic (e.g., the room they were in, the temperature, what Jill was wearing, how Jill's facial expressions changed, etc.). The goal is to create a scene where the client can imagine himself or herself as participating in the events and not just observing them. A sample anger scene for Stephen is provided below.

> *I'm coming home after a long day at work, on a bright sunny day. I can see the yellow daffodils on the garden at the side of the house as I walk to the front door. The door is blue and I notice a crack on the railing. I'm feeling relieved to be home after a hectic day.*
>
> *As soon as I open the door I see Jill sitting at the table doing the bills. She is wearing her brown t-shirt, jeans, and a pair of sandals. She has an aggravated look on her face and doesn't smile as I walk in. I'm thinking to myself, "Uh-oh, she looks pissed off and I bet we are going to have another fight." I feel the muscles in my back get tight and my stomach starts to contract. When she sees me she says, "We have money problems again." I'm thinking "What a bitch. She doesn't even say hello. She just starts in with me the second I get home."*
>
> *I try to remain calm as she continues to explain that the situation is serious and that we have to do something to decrease the loan payments. She, of course, uses a sarcastic and accusatory tone and points her finger at me. I immediately take it to mean that she is blaming me for our problems. I start to feel my face getting hot and my hands tremble. Before I can stop myself I say, "Look, this is the situation we are in and just deal with it. Maybe instead of blaming me all the time you could pick up more hours at work."*
>
> *Jill gets up and puts her hands on her hips and says, "Why are you acting so immature? You created this situation, Mr. Genius, and you are acting like a child."*
>
> *I stomp out of the room and go up the carpeted stairs to the bedroom. The walls are white and the bed has a light green blanket on top of it. I sit on the bed and think of how unfairly Jill is treating me. I stay there for about 30-minutes. Part of me wants to go downstairs and have it out with Jill and tell her how I feel. However, I know that I will over-react and start to yell. So, part of me wants to avoid her. Since I am getting hungry I finally go down stairs to the kitchen to make something to eat. I ask Jill if she wants anything and she says*

"No" in a biting tone. She doesn't even make eye contact with me. I'm thinking "I'm offering to make you dinner and you treat me like crap." I walk to the kitchen door and slam it behind me and walk out of the house.

When writing scenes it is useful for clients to develop an initial draft. The practitioner can then ask for more elaboration, if needed, and help focus the client. It is not unusual for clients to feel some degree of anger as they are writing the scenes. This is actually desirable and indicates that the scene is on target.

Sometimes, simply having the client systematically rehearse an anger scene in imagination automatically leads to anger reduction (Grodnitzky & Tafrate, 2000). However, better results are likely if the scene is paired with relaxation. To combine anger imagery with relaxation, in a "desensitization" approach, begin by having the client relax (see section on Progressive Muscle Relaxation; chapter 9). Once relaxed, instructions are given to review, in imagination, the anger scene — step by step. You may verbally guide the client through the anger-provoking situation. Give an instruction to keep the eyes closed and to imagine the situation is *actually happening*. Anger and tension are allowed to build as the scene unfolds. The client is not to get up or respond verbally. Once the scene is finished, the client is told to once again practice relaxation by sequentially tensing and releasing the various muscle groups, and to breathe deeply and rhythmically. After the physical activation is reduced, repeat the anger scene again (Evans, Hearn, & Saklofske, 1973; O'Donnell & Worell, 1973; Rimm, DeGroot, Boord, Heiman, & Dillow, 1971; Wolpe, 1958, 1990). A practice session might begin with relaxation followed by the anger scene and a return to relaxation. Then, the anger scene would be presented once or twice more, followed by relaxation. Always start and end each session with relaxation.

Clients are then instructed to practice relaxation in response to their anger scene before the next session. After a number of practice sessions with the first anger scene it will become increasingly difficult to feel anger. When this happens, start with a second anger scene. The *Imagery Scene Development Form* at the end of the chapter guides clients in developing both moderate and strong anger scenes. Follow the same procedures as with the first scene. Of course, it is appropriate to create additional scenes for new situations that arise. However, practice makes better! So, don't get lured into discussion of new problematic events. Provide a relaxation response and scene review over the course of several sessions if success is to be achieved.

Alternatively, clients can be exposed to their anger scenes while also practicing cognitive coping statements. In the case of Stephen, self-statements were developed that led to less anger expression and more positive behaviors with Jill. The goal is to agree on statements that will interrupt the usual angry thoughts. It is useful to write the statements on cards so that the client can begin to rehearse them easily.

The first step is to develop and agree upon a self-statement and have the client commit it to memory. Next, clients are then instructed to rehearse in imagery or listen to an audiotape recording of their anger scene. As they imagine themselves in the anger situation, clients are to practice using the self-statement to reduce their anger. For example, Stephen used the following self-statements: "It's OK to listen to Jill's criticisms. Being able to be honest is a healthy part of any relationship. I do not have to react with anger." As he listened to a recording of his anger scene, he rehearsed the self-statement. As always, repetition is important and Stephen rehearsed his scene many times using the self-statement until he felt little anger (two or less on a ten-point scale).

As a footnote to this discussion, let us point out that we might suggest to Stephen that he and Jill consider couples counseling to help them deal more effectively with their communication issues. Our purpose here, of course, has been solely to illustrate the exposure treatment for anger problems.

❖ *In-Vivo Exposure*

Once some degree of success has been achieved in an office setting, it is useful to discuss structured homework assignments, where clients intentionally put themselves in difficult or provocative situations and actively work to prevent their usual responses. For example, we might have had Stephen return to the Department of Motor Vehicles intentionally with the wrong paper work in order to hear the worker dismiss him. He, of course, would be instructed to use the self-statements already practiced in the office and to not respond with angry verbalizations. He would also be instructed to thank the worker for the clarification. He might even go to several branches of the Department of Motor Vehicles, each time intentionally producing the wrong documents in order to practice maintaining control. As with all exposure interventions with angry clients it is important to ask about their ability to successfully complete the assignment. If there are significant doubts about a client's ability to deal with a difficult situation then more practice in the office may be required.

(N.B. Discretion should be exercised in assigning "artificial" homework that may burden other people or agencies – such as the

DMV example above. Practitioners are urged to make *in vivo* assignments as realistic as possible in service of the client's needs, and to balance those needs against the rights and limitations of other people and public service agencies. In the 1970s, for example, some less-than-respectful assertiveness trainers urged clients to go into service stations and ask to have the windows washed without buying anything. Such activities not only burdened the attendants, but gave the trainees an erroneous sense of their "rights.")

Exposure and response prevention can be applied in a number of ways to successfully help clients reduce their automatic conditioned anger reactions to specific stimuli. Exposure also enhances growth by having clients face their triggers with less arousal, thereby making them better able to develop new skills. Naturally, exposure may not be appropriate for all clients. Nevertheless, it is a powerful and effective mode of treatment for anger, especially when paired with relaxation and cognitive coping strategies.

Imagery Scene Development Form

Scene #1: Pick a situation in which you typically experience anger. For the first scene, it is best if the situation is associated with a *moderate* level of anger. A situation that does not produce anger would be rated as "0" and a situation that is associated with extreme anger would be rated "100." Choose a situation where your anger is typically at 50.

My anger situation for scene #1 will be (describe briefly):

_____

_____

Anger Intensity

0.........10.........20.........30.........40.........50.........60.........70.........80.........90.........100
none   mild   moderate   strong   extreme

Now that you have identified a situation, the next step is to develop a *detailed* scene on a separate sheet of paper. Pretend that you are writing a mini-movie script. Include the details that would normally be part of this situation. The following is a list of items to include:

Other people who were present	The clothes people were wearing
The place (describe it in detail)	Sights, smells, sounds that were part of the situation
What others said (also, tone of voice)	Facial expressions of others
Physical sensations that you felt	Thoughts that you had
Things you said	Things you did

Describe how things unfolded from start to finish. Make sure that the scene is written in such a way that you can really imagine yourself as a participant and not just an observer.

Scene #2: Now, choose another ongoing situation where you typically experience anger but this time use a situation that is usually associated with a *strong or extreme* level of anger. Repeat the same procedures to develop the second scene.

My anger situation for scene #2 will be (describe briefly):

_____

_____

Anger Intensity

0.........10.........20.........30.........40.........50.........60.........70.........80.........90.........100
none   mild   moderate   strong   extreme

Now that you have identified a situation, the next step is to develop a *detailed* scene on a separate page.

[Howard Kassinove, Ph.D. and Raymond Chip Tafrate, Ph.D. *Anger Management: The Complete Treatment Guidebook for Practitioners* © 2002]

ACCEPTING, ADAPTING, AND ADJUSTING

Fostering Cognitive Change I: Seeing the World Realistically

The great enemy of the truth is very often not the lie deliberate, contrived and dishonest but the myth persistent, persuasive and unrealistic.

— John Fitzgerald Kennedy

V arious forms of cognitive restructuring have grown out of the pioneering work of Beck (1964) and Ellis (1962), and have become increasingly popular among practitioners from a variety of backgrounds. As a group, cognitive restructuring proponents share a basic theory of psychopathology and disturbance, provide practitioners with a clear and consistent set of tools to use with clients, and value research attempts to support the effectiveness of their interventions.

Since the 1960s, many scientific articles have been published supporting the use of cognitive interventions for a variety of client problems, such as depression, anxiety disorders, and eating disorders (Agras, et al., 1992; Abramowitz, 1997; Butler, Fennell, Robson, & Geldeer, 1991; Clark, 1996; DeRubeis, Gelfand, Tang, & Simons, 1999). Unfortunately, the cognitive therapy literature is sparse when it comes to working with clients with anger problems. Nevertheless, we are optimistic, since the few studies that have been conducted suggest that cognitive interventions can indeed be applied to angry clients and appear to lead to significant anger reduction (Deffenbacher, Dahlen, Lynch, Morris, & Gowensmith, 2000; Deffenbacher, Story, Brandon, Hogg, & Hazaleus, 1988; Tafrate & Kassinove, 1998).

Cognitive researchers and theorists have also produced a great number of books and treatment manuals. Some of these help practitioners develop basic therapeutic skills (Beck, 1995; Walen, DiGiuseppe, & Dryden, 1992) while others focus on the application of cognitive techniques to specific client problems, such as personality disorders, substance abuse, anxiety, and depression (Beck, Freeman, & associates, 1990; Beck, Wright, Newman, & Liese, 1993; Leahy & Holland, 2000). Again, fewer materials are available which target angry clients (see Beck, 1999, and Ellis & Tafrate, 1997, for exceptions).

Since there are many variations in the application of cognitive restructuring, and some techniques have been designed for specific client groups, covering all the models of cognitive treatment is well beyond the scope of this book.

In this chapter, we present some basic issues regarding cognitive interventions and we then focus specifically on the work of Beck and his associates. In Beck's model of cognitive therapy, clients are provided with skills to assess their typical thoughts related to anger triggers in order to help them perceive situations more accurately and realistically. His approach also involves identifying basic client assumptions and core beliefs that predispose clients to anger experiences. In the next chapter, we present the work of Ellis and colleagues. In his Rational Emotive Behavior Therapy (REBT) the emphasis is on fostering a more flexible and accepting philosophy in response to life's adversities. By helping clients become less demanding and more able to tolerate difficulties they become less likely to react with anger.

❖ Basic Principles and Practices

All forms of cognitive intervention share the following premises:

• Humans constantly sense, perceive, interpret, and think about their experiences (past, present, and future). They are not mere reactors to the environment; rather, they actively *interpret* the environment. Thus, humans are also capable of thinking about their thinking.

• The nature of thinking, or the specific manner of thinking about events or experiences, has a powerful influence over feelings and behavior.

• Over time, and with repetition, thinking first becomes automatic and then it becomes inflexible. Like so many human functions, typical thinking responses become ingrained and less noticeable to us as we exhibit them. Thus, angry clients remain unaware of their own thinking when common triggering events appear.

• Changes in thinking are likely to be helpful in terms of reducing maladaptive emotional experiences and expressive behaviors. In addition, although it is recognized that emotional and behavioral change can be accomplished by other means, it is only through changes in thinking that lasting improvement in functioning will occur.

• With increased awareness, thoughtfulness, and practice, thinking patterns can be modified. Such modifications are likely to lead to changes in experienced and expressed anger, and patterns of interactions with others. However, as noted in chapter 1, rigid and ingrained thoughts are more difficult to change than are surface thoughts.

It is certainly true that various cognitive theorists and practitioners vary in their approach to angry clients. Yet, they all seem to share a belief in these basic principles. Thus, there are similarities in practice. For example, once an anger trigger has been identified, the first step in using a cognitive intervention is to conduct an assessment of what the client is thinking *when* anger is experienced. Although clients have many different anger-related thoughts, those that are *most immediately connected to the emotional experience* are the ones of interest when practicing cognitive psychotherapy. Some of these thoughts are conscious and persistent, and are part of the client's report to the practitioner. Other thoughts are fleeting and may be below the level of conscious awareness. Such simple strategies as practitioner *questioning,* client *self-monitoring,* and *role playing* are helpful in making these thoughts explicit.

Some cognitive theorists refer to the thoughts most connected to emotional experiences as "hot thoughts" (Greenberger & Padesky, 1995). For example, when describing a problematic emotional experience, a client may note that it occurred in the lunchroom at work, or at about 11:00 a.m., or that it was raining. These thoughts are likely to be "cold" in that they are important but do not usually set off emotional arousal. Other thoughts are "hot" in that they instigate the emergence of feelings because they are misinterpretations of reality, exaggerations, or lead to a maladaptive response. For example, depressed clients tend to have thoughts related to self-blame and self-denigration, beliefs about low self-efficacy, and negative predictions about the future. Anxious clients tend to overestimate the probability of negative outcomes, and view certain events as dangerous, catastrophic, and unmanageable.

Although there have been fewer studies on the thinking of angry clients, a few patterns are known based on research and clinical experience. Some of these were reviewed in chapter 2, in the discussion of appraisals of anger triggers, and some are presented in detail in the next chapter. Generally, they include misinterpretations of the trigger (i.e., a tendency to interpret neutral or ambiguous situations as negative and/or malicious), demanding that unfair or unpleasant situations not exist, believing that triggers are not tolerable, exaggerating the potential hardship associated with aversive life events, and describing oneself or others in harsh, judgmental and overly critical terms. A list of typical questions that elicit client thinking is provided at the end of this chapter.

Distinguishing Between Thoughts and Feelings in Practitioner-Client Discussions

❖ ━━

In chapter 1, we noted the importance of developing an emotional vocabulary. Indeed, a common problem when conducting a cognitive assessment is that many clients do not know how to make a distinction between *thoughts* and *feelings*. For example, a client might say,

"I feel as if I was treated unfairly, " or

"I feel like slashing his tires," or

"I feel like quitting."

In actuality, these are evaluations or desired actions, in spite of the client's use of the phrase *I feel*. Also, some clients respond to the question, *What was going through your* mind *when you were arguing with Bill?* with, *I was pissed off.* That is an emotional experience and does not adequately get to *content* of the thoughts.

We suggest that practitioners be alert to whether or not a client can distinguish between feelings and thoughts. If not, many can easily learn this discrimination if you repeatedly say,

That's what you were **feeling**. *Now, what were you* **telling yourself** *about the situation?,*

or

That's what you **thought**. *But, how did you feel?*

Cognitive therapy is based on the idea that thoughts are major causes of feelings. Thus, it is critical to be able to recognize the difference between these two classes of events. Also, it is important that clients be able to distinguish among the many levels of anger. The *Anger Thermometer*, presented in chapter 1, is often helpful.

It may take several sessions of reviewing self-monitoring forms, asking questions about anger episodes, role playing, and clarifying thoughts vs. feelings, to identify specific thoughts that directly contribute to anger episodes. Once relevant beliefs are identified and clients have some awareness of the role of their own thinking, it's time to begin the process of challenging those thoughts and replacing them with more accurate and functional alternative views. The models proposed by Beck and Ellis differ in emphasis and utilize slightly different techniques and strategies to modify client thinking. For the balance of this chapter, we move to the cognitive model developed by Aaron Beck.

❖ *Beck's Cognitive Therapy*

As originally formulated in the 1960s, the emphasis in Beck's version of cognitive therapy was to help clients identify *distortions in thinking about the reality of life events*, and to replace those distortions with more *accurate and realistic perceptions and appraisals*. While this is still a major focus, the Beck model has evolved to include three levels of cognitions: automatic thoughts, assumptions, and core beliefs.

Automatic Thoughts. Human beings are constantly thinking and making evaluations about the world around them. Automatic thoughts are part of this ongoing inner dialogue that naturally occurs with everyone. They are *spontaneous and fleeting,* and are thought to exist *just below the level of conscious awareness.* They may also take the form of images or memories. With minimal effort, most people are able to tune into this inner dialogue and identify specific thoughts as they occur moment to moment.

For example, you had an automatic reaction in the form of thoughts when you first encountered this book. You may have had a *positive* thought (we hope) such as *"I've been looking for ways to better work with angry clients. This book is exactly what I need!"* In this case, the thought is likely to be associated with positive feelings such as enthusiasm, as well as actions such as reading the book from cover to cover (even the parts that might seem unappealing at first glance). A *neutral* thought such as *"This looks interesting. I guess I'll give it a try"* is likely to be connected with a more moderate emotional reaction and slightly less motivation. Perhaps, however, you had a *negative* automatic thought such as, *"I've come to the conclusion that my personality is not suited to being a caring and empathic therapist and this book certainly isn't going to help."* Of course, this reaction, unless countered with different thoughts, makes it unlikely that you would have read the book or have done anything else to pursue developing additional therapeutic skills. Also, this negative thought would likely be associated with feeling sad. Once brought to light, it is easy to see how fleeting verbal messages influence one's mood and behavior.

In terms of working with angry clients, it is important to identify those automatic thoughts that are negative, distorted, and associated with anger episodes. Initially, the focus is on helping clients notice the thinking that takes place when they have strong anger reactions. Again, it is important to assess the automatic thoughts exactly as they are experienced when anger occurs.

Let's consider the case of Vincent, a 17-year-old adolescent who was referred because of a history of explosive anger episodes at school. Keep in mind that the practitioner and Vincent, in earlier sessions, have already established a good working alliance, and Vincent has agreed that it is in his best interest to have better control over his anger outbursts.

Practitioner: *Vincent, were there any times during the past week when you felt strong angry feelings at school?*

Vincent: *Yeah. They finally let me back into my history class with Mr. Fox. I missed three days because of the suspension. When I got to class I found out that there was a paper due on Friday. I asked for an extension and he blew me off.*

Practitioner: *What did he say?*

Vincent: *He said that he can't give me any more breaks and that I have to hand in the paper at the same time as everyone else. I told him it wasn't fair because I wasn't allowed to be in class and he said it didn't matter.*

Practitioner: *What was going through your mind when he said that?*

Vincent: *That he is out to get me. No one at this school gives a shit about me. I'm going to fail the class.*

At this point, three specific thoughts have been identified. Each would be subjected to a *logical analysis* to determine whether or not Vincent's interpretations about the situation are supported by available evidence. Through practitioner questioning, additional evidence for the veracity of each thought is considered, as is any alternative evidence that might contradict each thought. The goal is to help clients think clearly and objectively about the anger-related situation. Additional interactions from Vincent's case illustrates this process. Only the first thought is addressed fully in the dialogue below.

Practitioner: *Vincent, you have identified three specific thoughts that you had as you felt your anger start to build. The first was, "Mr. Fox was out to get me." The second was, "No one in the school gives a shit about me." The third was, "I'm going to fail the class." Let's look at those thoughts one at a time.*

Vincent: *OK.*

Practitioner: *In terms of your relationship with Mr. Fox, has he done anything else that would lead you to believe that he is out to get you?*

Notice how the practitioner first seeks client information that might be potentially supportive of the original automatic thought. Angry clients have a tendency to view challenges to their thinking as invalidating their point of view and may see the practitioner as taking the other person's side. Exploring support for the client's thinking helps to communicate that the practitioner is taking the client's view seriously.

Vincent: *Yeah. He gave me a failing grade on my midterm project when I thought I deserved better.*

Practitioner: *OK. Anything else?*

Vincent: *No. Not that I can think of.*

Practitioner: *In considering the other side of things, has Mr. Fox ever done anything that seemed helpful or supportive?*

Vincent: *Yeah. I guess so.*

Practitioner: *What has he done that seemed supportive to you?*

Vincent: *Well, he got me another book for the class when I lost mine. And, uh, he didn't make me pay for it.*

Practitioner: *Anything else?*

Vincent: *Well, he has told me a few times that he thinks I could do better.*

Practitioner: *How is that supportive?*

Vincent: *Well, I guess maybe he thinks I'm smart and can do the work.*

Practitioner: *OK. Anything else?*

Vincent: *Not that I can think of.*

Practitioner: *Have you ever received any good grades from him?*

Vincent: *Yeah, I got a couple of B's on tests.*

Practitioner: *So, when you consider all of the contacts that you've had with Mr. Fox over the course of the year does it still seem like he is out to get you?*

Vincent: *I guess not.*

In the final step, Vincent is taught to respond to his automatic thoughts with new thoughts that are more realistic and based on an analysis of available evidence.

Practitioner: *Vincent, what would be a more realistic way to describe your relationship with Mr. Fox?*

Vincent: *I guess he is a good guy in some ways. But, I still think it's unfair that I can't get an extension on this paper.*

Practitioner: *So, how do you pull those two opposing views together? On the one hand, he has really been a good guy, and on the other he has done something that you believe is unfair?*

Vincent: *I'm not sure.*

Practitioner: *Can both exist together?*

Vincent: *Yeah. Sure.*

Practitioner: *So, if you were to continue to think that Mr. Fox is out to get you, how could you talk back to that specific thought. You know, in your mind. What could you say to yourself that would be most accurate about the situation?*

Vincent: *Mr. Fox treats me pretty well. But, he doesn't always do what I want.*

Practitioner: *Does that seem less exaggerated and more accurate?*

Vincent: *Yeah.*

Practitioner: *Let's contrast the two thoughts, the old and the new. The old one is that 'Mr. Fox is out to get you,' and the new one is*

> that 'he treats you pretty well even though he doesn't always
> do what you would like.' Which leads to less anger?

Vincent: The new one.

Through this kind of Socratic questioning, Vincent also evaluated the remaining two automatic thoughts. It soon became clear to him that he was exaggerating and distorting the evidence and seeing others and the situation far more negatively than was realistic. Below is a summary chart that provides alternative evidence and more accurate responses for Vincent's three automatic thoughts.

A blank client worksheet for recording automatic thoughts, alternative evidence, and alternative realistic conclusions is presented at the end of this chapter. The worksheet can be completed in session with the practitioner or individually by the client as homework.

Automatic thought	Alternative evidence	Alternative realistic belief
Mr. Fox is out to get me.	Actually, he has helped me out a number of times. He gave me a new book when I lost mine. I have also gotten a few B's on his tests. He said I am capable of doing well.	Mr. Fox treats me pretty well even though he doesn't always do what I want.
No one at this school gives a shit about me.	There are several teachers who seem to really care. I have lots of friends at school. My guidance counselor spends a lot of time talking with me and said his door is always open for me.	There are many people who do care about me. There are also some that don't care at all.
I'm going to fail the class.	I have done well on most of the other assignments. Even if I hand this assignment in late I can still get a passing grade on it.	As long as I hand in something, it is unlikely that I will fail the class because of this one paper.

Initially, it may seem as though clients report a wide variety of automatic thoughts related to their anger experiences. However, in a short time you're likely to notice recurring patterns. In addition, once the other underlying cognitions (assumptions and core beliefs) are identified, the content of automatic thoughts becomes more understandable and easier to predict.

Assumptions. Assumptions can be conceptualized as *rules* or *attitudes* that guide daily actions and also set expectations (Greenberger & Padesky, 1995). These assumptions are often not directly expressed verbally by clients, as they may themselves be unaware of them, and therefore they are not easily accessible to the practitioner. Since assumptions give rise to the automatic thoughts, one way to identify them is to make *inferences from recurring themes* found in automatic thoughts. Assumptions, when stated, typically take the form of "if-then" statements, or "should" or "must" statements. For example, "If I let others get close then they will hurt me," or "Even if I try hard, (then) I probably won't succeed anyhow," or "I must not appear weak in front of others." Assumptions can be problematic to the extent that they are exaggerated, distorted, and are maladaptive when applied rigidly across situations. Assumptions are believed to develop in response to early childhood experiences and interactions with others. Persistently negative or even traumatic experiences can lead to negative assumptions about oneself and result in negative expectations or attitudes regarding others.

Core Beliefs. Core beliefs are proposed as the "deepest" or most abstract level of cognition. Deep is a misnomer as we never really mean deep, as in "two feet deep." We really mean *abstract*, and we prefer this term. Core beliefs contain the most centrally held ideas related to self, other people, and the world. Recall that in chapter 1 we noted that some beliefs are centrally held with great conviction. These are core beliefs. Negative core beliefs underlie maladaptive assumptions and distorted automatic thoughts. Thus, core beliefs may determine the way an individual automatically interprets reality, especially in ambiguous or stressful situations.

In the diagram below, we show one of Vincent's basic assumptions regarding others which can be inferred from several of his automatic thoughts. In addition, we show Vincent's core belief regarding other people, along with the connection between the three levels of cognition.

The advantage for practitioners in conceptualizing maladaptive assumptions and core beliefs lies in the larger roadmap that it provides to help direct interventions in the most effective manner. For example, if Vincent deep down believes that *others are hostile*, and that he *should not trust people*, and if in interactions with others he *distorts* situations in the direction of *believing that people are treating him poorly*, he will invariably experience more anger and be likely to behave inappropriately in interactions with others. His anger and defensive behavior will certainly influence the way others react to him. His behavior will frequently be met with rejection, indifference, or punishment. Thus, his negative core

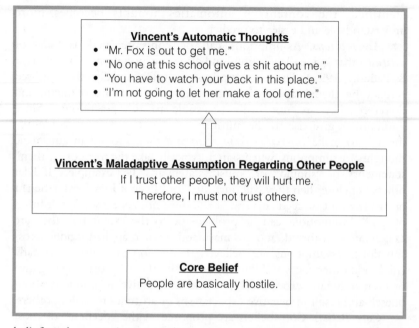

Vincent's Automatic Thoughts
- "Mr. Fox is out to get me."
- "No one at this school gives a shit about me."
- "You have to watch your back in this place."
- "I'm not going to let her make a fool of me."

Vincent's Maladaptive Assumption Regarding Other People
If I trust other people, they will hurt me.
Therefore, I must not trust others.

Core Belief
People are basically hostile.

beliefs and assumptions regarding others are continually being supported in a *self-perpetuating cycle*. It is through the understanding of this cycle that the practitioner can help Vincent modify his current patterns. So, in addition to challenging his overly negative automatic thoughts regarding others, we might work more behaviorally, moving him to act less angrily while increasing his trust in his existing relationships. The goal would be to provide him with experiences that challenge the basic ideas that drive his emotional reactions and behaviors.

Unfortunately, as noted above, there has been relatively little theorizing in the area of core beliefs for angry clients. However, Beck (1999) has recently proposed that people who react impulsively, with anger and aggression, have a tendency to view themselves as vulnerable and to see others as hostile. For a more detailed description of how to conceptualize various levels of client cognition, we refer the reader to Beck (1995).

Readers are invited to compare and contrast Beck's cognitive approach with that of Albert Ellis, as described in some detail in the following chapter.

Modifying Anger-Related Automatic Thoughts

As you know from our discussions, it is important that your thoughts about anger triggers be as realistic as possible. On this form, please write in the automatic thoughts you had about a recent anger experience, along with the evidence to support those thoughts and what alternative, more realistic thoughts might exist. First describe the trigger. Then, complete the three columns. Anger trigger or event: _____

Automatic thoughts	Alternative evidence	Alternative realistic belief
Describe the thinking in your mind, which occurred when your anger appeared.	Describe the actions of others or other evidence to support an alternate, more realistic belief.	Write in the more realistic belief, that properly describes the anger trigger.
1.	1.	1.
2.	2.	2.
3.	3.	3.

[Howard Kassinove, Ph.D. and Raymond Chip Tafrate, Ph.D. Anger Management: The Complete Treatment Guidebook for Practitioners © 2002]

Questions That Elicit Anger Causing Thoughts

- What was going through your mind *just before* you started to feel angry?

- What were you telling yourself *when* you were feeling angry?

- How were you looking at the situation *when* you were feeling angry?

- How did you interpret (see, or view) the situation *when* you were feeling angry?

- As you think about what happend, what does this mean about the other person (the perceived anger instigator)?

- What does the whole episode mean to you?

- What does the whole episode mean about you? Your life? Your future?

- What is going through your mind right now? (When clients appear angry in session.)

- Now that it's over, as you recall the situation what do you think about that person?

[Howard Kassinove, Ph.D. and Raymond Chip Tafrate, Ph.D. *Anger Management: The Complete Treatment Guidebook for Practitioners* © 2002]

Fostering Cognitive Change II: Building a More Flexible Philosophy

No one can make you feel inferior without your consent.
— Eleanor Roosevelt

No matter how long you work to help clients change their life skills to deal better with their anger triggers, or to perceive their anger triggers more realistically, you can bet that life will continue to present them with new and unanticipated problems. And, many of these problems will be *objectively* bad and will be perceived *realistically* by your clients. For example, long-held jobs will be lost, illnesses will develop, happy marriages will disintegrate, children and friends will act foolishly, good intentions will be misunderstood, gossip will emerge, teachers and supervisors will not be fair, students will misunderstand their teachers, etc. For this reason, it is important to help clients develop or strengthen philosophies to re-conceptualize aversive situations for what they are — *unpleasant, problematic inconveniences.* This is the main goal of Rational Emotive Behavior Therapy, a form of intervention very useful for the reduction of anger. As noted in chapter 9 (Managing Physical Arousal), the overwhelming majority of modern triggers are social in nature and do not threaten our lives. That's why we refer to them as *inconveniences.* As opposed to the time when the fight or flight reaction developed to protect human lives, social triggers usually cause little more than the loss of time, prestige, and money.

In contrast to Beck's approach presented in the previous chapter, which helps clients to perceive triggers more accurately, the REBT approach helps clients *adjust* to triggers — *whether or not they have been accurately perceived.* Since clients often come into treatment with philosophies that are highly negative and rigid, they are prone to *catastrophize* when things go wrong, and typically think they do not have the ability to *tolerate* aversive events. Thus, it is important to help

209

them place their triggers in perspective. In that sense, REBT is the most elegant of approaches, since the goal is to develop a lowered level of angry reactivity through a philosophical shift about the world.

Rational Emotive Behavior Therapy was formulated in the 1950's by Albert Ellis, a practicing psychologist who was dissatisfied with the psychoanalytic and non-directive approaches of the time. REBT has become exceptionally popular as a form of intervention for many problems, and thousands of articles and books are available for the reader who wants a more in-depth presentation than we can give in this chapter (e.g., Ellis, 1962, 1973, 1994; Ellis & Dryden, 1987; Ellis & Harper, 1975; Ellis & MacLaren, 1998; Walen, DiGiuseppe & Dryden, 1992). However, we believe that the beauty of this approach lies in its simplicity; it can be learned in a very short period of time. As we present below, if clients can learn and accept *four rational thoughts* about aversive triggers, much of their anger will be diminished. In that sense the approach is very *simple*. At the same time, it is not *easy*. Thoughtfulness, discussion, and practice are required to learn to respond rationally to the aversive parts of life.

Although this approach may appear similar to Beck's cognitive therapy, there are important differences. In the REBT model initial perceptions about the trigger and the automatic thoughts are neither debated nor challenged. Client *perceptions and thoughts about the trigger are assumed to be true*. Rather than debate their veracity, the practitioner explores the evaluations and meanings the client holds about the trigger in order to reduce anger. Thus, REBT focuses on the second step of the anger episode model (outlined in chapter 2) — trigger appraisal.

In the anger episode model, triggers are appraised in ways that lead to angry experiences and expressions. In the REBT model, triggers are called *Activating Events*. Appraisals are called *Beliefs*, which can be rational or irrational. That is, they can be appropriate descriptors of the trigger or they can be beliefs which magnify the trigger out of proportion to reality. Finally, angry experiences and expressions are called *Consequences* in the REBT model. The following samples of practitioner-client dialogue illustrate some of the basic REBT principles.

❖ Describing the Activating Event (the Trigger)

Joan was a 46-year-old psychotherapist at a large community mental health center. She often responded with anger when she perceived that other members of the staff were asked to see fewer and easier cases. Joan also thought that another colleague, Jack, was given preference over her for office space and an updated computer, even though she had worked longer at the clinic. Joan would seethe, complain to her friends and family members, and would ruminate for days on end about her problems at work.

As part of her presentation of the "facts," Joan said, "It's unfair! I'm working harder than Jack and I've been at the clinic much longer than he. Yet, Phyllis — she's the office manager — gave the best office to Jack and it has a new computer in it. I'm furious! He just began here two months ago. Why did Phyllis do that? She doesn't even know about some of the hard feelings she causes. I don't know what the hell is going on."

The REBT practitioner response was, "It sounds like you are really upset about this situation at work. Now, *let's begin by assuming that you are correct.* You *are* working harder than the others, it *is* unfair, and the office manager is oblivious to your feelings." Note that the practitioner did not challenge Joan's perceptions of the situation. Instead, her presentation of the facts was simply accepted as she stated it.

This up-front acceptance comes as a pleasant surprise to clients, who often feel challenged when they present the "facts" to others. In that sense, the REBT practitioner sidesteps the initial confrontation that exists with many psychotherapy strategies. Consider these common life scenarios.

Adolescent: *I'm so frustrated. My French teacher talks so fast that no one can understand what he says.*

Parent: *Maybe you are not listening carefully enough!*

— — —

Salesperson: *Those customers are really pushy. They make me so angry.*

Supervisor: *They're not that bad and, anyway, your job is to provide good service to everyone.*

— — —

Mother: *I'm so angry at my husband. Over and over again, I punish my son by sending him to his room. Then, after about two minutes, my husband goes and tells him the punishment is over. He's undermining my authority as a mother!*

Practitioner: *Well, I don't think so. Try to see it from your son's perspective. A few minutes can be a long time to a child.*

— — —

Teacher 1:   *I feel so angry. When I was sick yesterday, the substitute teacher told the class that they didn't have to study for the spelling test. She said the test would be postponed. She had some nerve! Now, my whole lesson plan for the week is ruined.*

Teacher 2:   *Maybe you are just blowing it out of proportion. Don't be so angry.*

—   —   —

Woman: *I'm furious because my boyfriend promises and promises, but never buys me any gifts. And, he calls less often. I think he's just waiting to dump me.*

Friend: *He's probably just busy with work. Don't think that way. All men are insensitive jerks.*

—   —   —

Professor 1:   *Last night, when I gave my lecture on the history of Sri Lanka, at least four people walked out of class. They came back later, but I think they were bored with me. I was really offended. Why did they take the class? They knew what they were getting into!*

Professor 2:   *They probably just went to the bathroom, or to make a telephone call. I'm sure you gave an interesting lecture. Don't get so offended. You have to develop a thick skin.*

—   —   —

These interactions represent rather typical responses. In each case, the respondent questions the statement of the reporter. Little or no credibility is given to the reporter, or to the annoyed and angry feelings. And, there is little chance that the response is helpful in any meaningful way. The REBT practitioner, in contrast, would accept the reports at face value. It would be assumed that the French teacher does speak very fast, that the customers are pushy, that the husband does undermine the mother's authority, that the teacher's lesson plan is ruined, that the woman is about to be "dumped," and that the lecture was boring to many people. The REBT intervention is aimed not at finding the truth, but at developing reasonable *interpretations* (appraisals) of the triggers. This is not to say that the REBT practitioner totally ignores accurate appraisals of reality. Rather, it is assumed that reasonable interpretations (appraisals) about the adversities of life will lead to reduced anger and to an increased possibility of solving problems. This is accomplished by listening to many stories told by the client, accepting them as fact, and helping the client replace negative and rigid interpretations with those that are more flexible and moderate.

❖ *Teaching Clients About The Causes of their Anger*

In almost all cases, clients wrongly believe that their anger is caused by the trigger. That is, they believe that external stimuli (activating events or triggers) cause their anger. The practitioner works to teach a different conception. Returning to the case of Joan, the clinic psychotherapist, the goal is to now inquire about her view of the cause of the anger.

Practitioner:	*Joan, I understand that Jack is being treated better than you, and that you are getting quite angry. But tell me, what is it that makes you angry?*
Joan:	*She makes me angry. Phyllis does it to me. It's gotten to the point that when I just see her my blood starts to boil.*

The practitioner now shows Joan that in actuality she makes herself angry. The goal is to give her an awareness that she is in control of her reactions. REBT is empowering since it takes away control from others and returns it, rightfully, to the client.

Practitioner:	*Joan, it seems to me that you think Phyllis is in control of your feelings, your anger. But, I would like to show you that there is another way to look at the situation. I think that you are in control of your anger, not Phyllis. I think your feelings are caused by **your** interpretation of her actions. Let's assume, just for a moment, that Jack was not only a younger worker, but that he was also your son. Phyllis likes him and gave him some easy cases to work on, and she gave him the best office with the new computer. How would you feel?*
Joan:	*Well, that would change things. I guess I would be happy that things were going well for my son. But, I still would want good things for me.*
Practitioner:	*That sounds reasonable. And, you wouldn't be so angry because . . ?*
Joan:	*Because it was my son, not some stranger who was getting the best office.*
Practitioner:	*So, if it was your son you would be less angry than if it was a stranger — even though in both cases you would not have the better office or computer. That suggests your anger was not caused by not getting the office or by your working harder than others. Other things caused the anger. OK, now let's take another example. Suppose the younger worker was physically challenged? Perhaps he was*

>   *in a wheelchair and the best office was more accessible*
>   *than others. Would you still feel so angry?*
>
> Joan: *Of course not.*
> Practitioner: *You see, Joan, you become angry when you interpret the*
>   *trigger in one way and not angry when you view it in*
>   *another way. If another person gets a better office than*
>   *you do, but you think it is OK because he is a member of*
>   *your family or is handicapped, then you don't get angry.*
>   *If you can't find an acceptable reason, and you think it*
>   *is unfair and shouldn't happen, then you become angry.*
>   *But, in all cases you don't get the better office! The*
>   *outcome is the same but your interpretations determine*
>   *whether or not you become angry. You control your*
>   *interpretations and you are in control of your anger. I*
>   *want to give you back control over your feelings.*

❖ *Teaching Rational Interpretations of Triggers (The Appraisal)*

Once Joan recognizes that it is not the trigger that directly makes her angry, rather that it is *her view* of the trigger that causes the anger, the practitioner moves on to present the four irrational beliefs that contribute to anger development. These are contrasted with four rational beliefs, that are to be adopted by the client.

The overall goal is *semantic precision*. That is, to *precisely describe and evaluate the trigger without minimizing or maximizing it*. An important part of this process is to teach the client these four rational ideas that are used to evaluate current and future aversive triggers, in order to minimize the development of anger. In the REBT model the *four core irrational beliefs* are labeled as *awfulizing, low frustration tolerance, demandingness*, and *global ratings*. Each one has a rational alternative that assists clients in interpreting triggers in a more flexible and moderate manner.

Awfulizing. First, angry clients almost always *exaggerate the consequences* or level of hardship associated with aversive events. They conceptualize almost all negative events as *awful, horrible* or *terrible*, rather than simply unfortunate, bad, or very bad. Such exaggerations place undue focus on the negative and reduce the opportunity to generate solutions and see into the future, to a time when the event will be less meaningful in the client's life. *Awful, terrible* and *horrible* are exceptionally strong words which, if examined carefully, really mean that everything has been lost. In our common language, we use these words to describe the massive and often final devastation due to earthquakes, airplane disasters, tornados, or the holocaust. In these cases it is often life itself that is lost.

The goal at this stage of REBT is to show clients that such evaluations are too strong for what they usually are talking about, such as a job loss, a dating failure, infidelity, money lost in the stock market, or not getting into a desired college. In fact, even when talking about very, very serious problems it is helpful to look at long-term outcomes when interpretations are made. For example, most people recover quite well psychologically even after major personal accidents where they are left severely handicapped. In fact, research data shows that happiness levels of quadriplegics, after about one year, actually return to their pre-accident levels (Diener, 1984).

Although we use words such as "terrible" immediately after such accidents, it is important to ask clients what that kind of evaluation means, and whether there are better words or phrases that can be used. In most cases, *very bad* or *very difficult* or a *major inconvenience* are better evaluations of the trigger. These terms are not meant to minimize the seriousness of triggers or the discomfort they cause. No one wants to be rejected or hurt; no one wants to lose money, a job, or prestige. Rather, the words are offered as *more realistic* descriptors. With the exception of loss of life, almost all aversive triggers are costly simply in terms of time or money or prestige. Over time, these costs can be recovered. Words such as awful or terrible suggest a magnitude well beyond partial loss and increase the intensity and duration of anger. They diminish focus on the remainder of the client's life, which usually has many very positive aspects.

Low Frustration Tolerance. Clients also typically underestimate their ability to deal with discomfort or adversity. When unfairness exists, the issue with regard to anger is, as noted in the case of Joan above, *can it be tolerated or is it really "intolerable?"* It is actually quite amazing how often our clients (and friends, family members, and colleagues) use words suggesting an inability to deal with problems. We say we *can't stand it* when waiting in a long, slow moving line, when a child spills juice on the rug after being warned to be careful, when a spouse cheats, when demoted at work, when not invited to a party we wanted to attend, and when similar setbacks occur. In fact, a better evaluation would be that we *truly don't like it,* and *wish it didn't happen.* Again, if clients can be helped to see the world more realistically, less anger is likely to emerge and there will be more opportunity to generate solutions to the problems faced. If they can be led to have a problem-solving orientation, coupled with a level of optimism about their tolerance skills, clients are more likely to be successful. Whining about an inability to tolerate unpleasant and aversive events is rarely helpful. In fact, there is no acceptable definition of *can't stand it.* Most people who are betrayed, lose their jobs, fail in school, are rejected, and so on, *do* stand it. That is, they eventually adjust and adapt. In addition, rejection and other negative triggers sometimes provide opportunity for much better things. The reader may recall the case of the behaviorist John Watson. After losing his job at Johns Hopkins University, where he struggled on an early-twentieth-century professor's salary, he went into the world of business and earned much more than he could have dreamed about in academia. Clients who learn to describe aversive triggers as difficult and frustrating will do better than if they whine and moan about how they can't stand or cope with them.

Demandingness. Clients often elevate personal *desires* to absolute *dictates* or *unbendable rules* that are imposed on the self, others, and the world. By engaging in such *demandingness* they forget that the aversive behavior of others is determined by biology, modeling, learning history, and sub-cultural norms. Demandingness ignores reality, places dictatorial rules on others, and leads to trouble. Clients will experience less anger if they learn to differentiate *preferences* from *demands.*

Demandingness is reflected in client words such as *must* or *should* or *has to.* These words suggests no alternative. Now, some things in this world "must" happen. We agree that we must eat, sleep, urinate, etc. There is absolutely no choice with regard to these behaviors. But, even if you are very bright, *must* you go to Harvard? *Must* your boss appreciate your work? *Must* your spouse be faithful, even if you have been 100% faithful? (After all, look at the data. About 55% of men and 30% of women have extramarital affairs during marriage.) Is it rational and wise to say they are all doing what they *must not* or *should not* do? We think not. While these behaviors may very well be *non-preferred,* they happen and they happen quite frequently. We would be better off to look for their causes, try to rectify them if possible, and accept them if we can't. But, to simply sit back and demand that things *must* or *must not* happen will just lead to anger — without a solution.

Global Self- or Other-Rating. Most clients have a strong tendency to *over-generalize* about people. Clients *blame* or *condemn* other people "in total" for limited and specific behavioral acts. As part of this blame, they tend to use inflammatory language such as "dope," "s.o.b.," "idiot," "moron." In actuality, all of us do many good things and some bad things. Some people do more bad things than others. But even those people do some good deeds once in a while. So, in keeping with REBT and many other philosophies and religions, we recommend to clients that they look at *specific behaviors* of people and evaluate those specific behaviors accordingly.

Unfortunately, rather than recognizing the learned or environmental causes of specific behaviors, clients often attribute the bad behavior of others to internal personality characteristics. In social psychology this is called the "fundamental attribution error" (Heider, 1958). Rather than seeing the office manager as a complex person with many pressures on her that lead to a variety of different decisions, Joan sees her as *totally stupid* and *evil*. By that, she means the manager's behaviors are almost always unfair and caused by a bad personality. It is important that Joan learn to see her as a woman who does many things — some good and some bad — and not to characterize her whole personhood based on one set of acts. If she can learn to do this, she is less likely to become angry in future interactions with her.

The chart below illustrates the core irrational beliefs that were pursued with Joan, the angry psychotherapist, around the issue of fairness.

Irrational beliefs	Rational beliefs
It's *terrible (or awful* or *horrible)* that I am treated unfairly.	While I *don't like* this *bad* situation, there are far worse injustices in the world that I could suffer. This is really just unfair and *unpleasant*.
The office manager *should* respect my seniority!	I *want* the office manager to respect my seniority. I *hope* she will.
I *can't stand* being treated unfairly. It's *intolerable!*	I *can* stand being treated unfairly. In life that is sometimes going to happen and I am a resilient person who *can cope* with unpleasant problems.
The office manager is a *real a**h****. What a *fool (or jerk)* she is!	Even though the office manager made this decision, she has treated me well at other times. She does some good and some not so good things. *I cannot characterize her whole personhood from a small group of her actions.*

Compared to the Beck approach, REBT presents more philosophical positions to be addressed with the client. In addition, the practitioner is more accepting of the client's perceptions, which increases the therapeutic bond. At the same time, the goal is to encourage client acceptance of the reality that the world is unfair and that it is quite possible to tolerate most unfair events for long periods of time. These events, clients are taught, may be truly and strongly unlikable — but they are tolerable. Thus, REBT introduces a less demanding and more tolerant philosophical view to help clients experience less distressing emotional arousal.

In REBT, irrational beliefs are disputed with the goal of teaching alternative semantically precise and rational ways of evaluating problematic triggers. A number of methods can be used to achieve this end. The primary method of dealing with philosophical issues is through logic. Thus, Joan's beliefs were challenged by asking a number of thoughtful questions and presenting her with better alternatives.

Practitioner: *Joan, assuming that the office manager was unfair, why is it* awful *rather than* unpleasant?

Joan: *Well, it's just terrible that she did what she did.*

Practitioner: Unpleasant *means distasteful or disagreeable, which it certainly was.* Awful *and* terrible *imply far more severe consequences. Those words imply dread, terror, horror, or a very high intensity of fear. Which word precisely describes her actions, unpleasant or awful?*

Joan: *I guess what she did was really surprising, and very unpleasant!*

Practitioner: *I agree. Let's call her actions very unpleasant.* (Pause.) *You also said you can't take it anymore. What did you mean by that?*

Joan: *I meant it's so unfair.*

Practitioner: *I agree. But, you obviously can take it. By that I mean you can just continue to work on your cases, including the difficult ones, in your current office. You don't have to like it, but I have faith in you. You can tolerate it, right?*

Joan: *I guess I can. But I don't like what she did.*

Practitioner: *Again, I agree. You don't like it, but can tolerate it.* (Pause.) *Now, why should she have acted any differently than she did?*

Joan: *Because I worked at the clinic much longer, and I take on difficult cases.*

Practitioner: *Right. That's why you expected her to give the better office to you. But, why should she do what you wanted or expected?*

Joan: *I don't understand.*

Practitioner: *You are basically believing that because a set of events is* logical, *and* expected, *that they* must *or* should *or* ought *to happen. It's like believing that because a train is scheduled to arrive at 8:15 a.m. that it* must/should/has *to come at that time. In fact, it's just an expectation or prediction. And, while expectations and logic often prevail, sometimes they don't. In your case, you would be better to stick to, "I fully expected to get the better office, but it doesn't have to happen." That would be similar to "I expect the train to arrive at 8:15 a.m. but it doesn't have to."*

Joan: *I see. I really never thought of it that way.*

Practitioner: *Right. I'm not suggesting that what happened was right or correct or logical or that you like it. Just that you accept the reality that lots of expected things don't happen in life and you have lots of capacity to tolerate them. You could talk to her, ask to be considered for the office or to be considered when another good office comes along. Or, you could forget about it. You have choices. But whether or not you get what you want, I would like you to describe the situation precisely and realistically.*

Joan: *OK.*

Practitioner: *What about the manager? You said she was a real jerk. Did you mean that?*

Joan: *I thought so.*

Practitioner: *Well, the final point I would like to make is that she does lots of things during the day, many of which affect you. Some are real bad, some are just OK, and some are good. Remember, you told me two weeks ago that she gave extra time off to a secretary who had a medical appointment?*

Joan: *Yeah.*

Practitioner: *So, it would be more accurate to limit our statements to her* behavior – *not her* total personhood. *Let's say her behavior was bad. OK.*

Joan: *Well, I do agree with you there.*

Of course, the above dialogue is condensed. It requires a number of sessions to adequately discuss and replace each irrational belief with a more flexible alternative. The ultimate goal is to get Joan to stop insisting that the unfairness must not exist and to accept the reality that unfair situations are part of everyone's life. At the same time, it is important to communicate that it is reasonable to dislike what she perceives as unfair treatment. Also, while accepting that unfairness exists, Joan could still choose ways to try to change the situation or even decide to seek a new job. The outcome is to have her give up her demands and, ultimately, her anger.

There are various ways to dispute imprecise, irrational, exaggerated thinking. Most of the examples given above reflect *logical* challenges. Another possibility is to question the *functionality* of holding on to a specific position. For example, when targeting the beliefs about awfulizing and low frustration tolerance, Joan was asked the following questions:

How does believing the situation at work is terrible lead you to feel?

Does believing the situation at work is terrible lead you to a solution?

Does believing that you can't stand the situation at work help you do a better job with your clients?

How does believing that you can't stand the situation help you to change it?

How does believing that you cannot tolerate the situation help give you confidence to face other challenges?

How would you feel if you chose to believe that you were strong enough to deal with the situation?

The goal of this line of questioning is to help Joan realize that believing the situation is *terrible* and that she *can't stand it* is not helping her to achieve any of her goals. By recognizing that she can tolerate the unfairness at work Joan would actually be less emotionally upset and angry, and would have more confidence to take constructive action.

Completing the *REBT Anger Analysis Form*, presented at the end of this chapter, is one way to "chip away" at irrational ideas. Clients are asked to fill out one or two forms prior to each session. This urges them to think about the model before arriving in the practitioner's office, where the episodes can be discussed at length.

Rational role reversal is also useful (Kassinove & DiGiuseppe, 1975). In this technique, the practitioner describes an event that led to (or supposedly led to) anger. Or, the practitioner plays the client by being angry and verbalizing the client's typical beliefs. The client is then asked to help the practitioner de-awfulize, increase tolerance for the event, understand that there is no reason why the event should not have happened, and to see the instigator of anger as a multifaceted person. Clients learn more when placed in this active teaching role.

Typically, the practitioner begins by saying,

I've had a really bad week myself. I'm really angry with my colleague. He promised to buy some airline tickets so that we could go to a conference together. Now I find out that he never bought them and I will have to pay an extra $200. I just can't take him any more. Not buying the tickets was really terrible and he should have done it. I guess he's a jerk.

OK, now I want you to be my therapist. Help me get over my anger.

Most clients enter into the task willingly, but do a poor job. Yet, after three or four such role plays they become much more understanding of the differences between reasonable and rational thinking, and magnified or distorted thinking.

Disputing irrational beliefs and, most importantly, helping clients to accept precise and more moderate interpretations of anger triggers requires skill and can be challenging for practitioners who are unfamiliar with cognitive interventions. It is often useful for the practitioner to *model* how he or she has overcome adversity by adopting a rational philosophy. Many of us, for example, have been treated unfairly or have had misbehaving children, or were the recipient of some unwanted event at work. It is useful to describe to clients how, at first, the event was seen as terrible and the belief was held that it *shouldn't* have happened. Most of us, however, eventually accept such unpleasant triggers as part of life. We learn to *decatastrophize* the event and to *accept, adapt* and *adjust*. Describing such events along with the adaptation that

Figure 14-1.

Changing irrational beliefs — one chip at a time.

occurred over time is one way to model the development of rationality and precise interpretations for clients.

Some REBT materials portray clients as having an almost epiphany-like experience, resulting in a sudden change in their philosophical views. Our clinical experiences suggest that although this sometimes happens, most clients modify their philosophical views slowly, over a number of weeks or months. As with most forms of intervention, brighter and less disturbed clients may understand the system easier and quicker than less intelligent and/or more disturbed clients. We find it useful to think of irrational beliefs as large boulders to be removed. As a practitioner you do not have heavy equipment to work with, but you do have a small pick ax. Thus, the only way to remove the boulders is to "chip away" at them over time.

❖ Some Final Thoughts

The information presented on cognitive therapy in chapters 13 and 14 introduces basic principles, concepts, and methods as they are used with angry clients. They are simple to explain, but not easy to do correctly in practice. Indeed, we have worked with many agencies that claim their counselors do cognitive therapy. Unfortunately, when actually observed, it became obvious that the practitioners were not adhering to a cognitive model. REBT skills can be developed by reading, attending professional workshops, and obtaining supervision. These are worthwhile endeavors.

We recommend, when working with angry clients, that cognitive interventions be implemented following other benign techniques such as relaxation training, meditation, or skill building. It is unwise to begin with cognitive interventions since some angry clients initially react negatively to them. The process of questioning and challenging client beliefs may be perceived as invalidating their views. Remember, clients truly believe that they have suffered some transgression, no matter how distorted their thinking might be. Challenging their thinking at the beginning of an intervention program can damage the therapeutic alliance. We believe that a therapeutic alliance is an important prerequisite for the effective use of cognitive — and other therapeutic — interventions.

We also recognize that astute practitioners are typically aware of the negative thinking their clients possess and see those thoughts as targets for change. Unfortunately, some practitioners assume that to help their clients they simply have to reinforce more positive thinking. We recommend that empty affirmations (e.g., "Joan, you are really a good person") be kept to a minimum. We are not opposed to simple affirmative suggestions as a psychotherapeutic tool and they certainly have a role, for example, in hypnosis. However, powerful cognitive interventions are not simply about positive thinking. *The problem with positive thinking and simple affirmations is that they are devoid of critical analysis and self-examination.* Clients are simply told to rehearse a fluffy positive statement without examining the accuracy of the belief. Many such statements are inaccurate (e.g., "My actions have *always* been well intended and altruistic!") or represent overgeneralizations (e.g., "I *am* a good person!") and the client does not learn new cognitive skills.

Affirmations were popularized by the charismatic French psychotherapist Émile Coué (1923) who promoted cure based on optimistic autosuggestion. He had his patients repeat an affirming phrase, "Day by day, in every way, I am getting better and better," over and over and his teaching achieved a vogue in England and the United States in the 1920s. Such statements are not bad; they simply gloss over the philosophical change, the goal of REBT.

Another drawback to affirmations and positive thinking is the reality that there *are* events and experiences in life that are not positive. Clients do *not* get better every day, in every way. Life *is* difficult and learning to see difficulties accurately is crucial to facing challenges. Asking clients to rehearse some positive statement may actually contribute to avoiding a difficult problem and not taking action.

Of course, clients *are* often overly negative in their thoughts and perceptions. Thus, the goal of cognitive interventions is to help them change their exaggerated and incorrect negative thoughts about aversive situations to more realistic, accurate, and less exaggerated ones. This is quite different from simple positive affirmations.

The "Saturday Night Live" character, Stuart Smalley, best portrays our criticism of the affirmation approach. He is funny, precisely because his dependence on affirmations is not grounded in anything real. Affirmations and positive statements are not likely to provide lasting change and ultimately undermine the credibility of the practitioner.

Figure 14-2.

Stewart Smalley — the affirmer!

REBT Anger Analysis Form

A. Activating Trigger: Describe the triggering stimulus which began the anger episode. What did the person or persons do? How was it done?

B. Beliefs about the trigger. How did you **appraise** it? [Hint. You didn't tell yourself it was wonderful. And, you didn't tell yourself it was neutral or that you didn't care. You probably believed it was *awful* or *terrible*, and that you *couldn't tolerate it,* and that it shouldn't have happened. What did you believe about the person. Did you believe the person was a *jerk,* or a dope?]

C. Consequences of your beliefs and appraisals. What did you *feel?* Was the anger strong? How long did it last? What did you do?

List **alternate, precise, constructive, rational, reality-based beliefs.** [Hint. What are the realistic facts? Was the event *unpleasant*? If it continues, *could you tolerate it?* What if you were paid money, then could you tolerate it? Why *must* what you want come true? Since the other person has probably done many good and bad things, how can that person be accurately described?]

[Howard Kassinove, Ph.D. and Raymond Chip Tafrate, Ph.D. *Anger Management: The Complete Treatment Guidebook for Practitioners* © 2002]

ACCEPTING, ADAPTING, AND ADJUSTING
Forgiveness

>*Without forgiveness there is no future*
>— Bishop Desmond Tutu

T he harsh reality is that life is filled with disappointment, aversion and conflict. In most cases, these problems are objectively minor and do not involve aggression. Most typically, relationships with friends, acquaintances, family members, coworkers, and others are marred by interpersonal offenses such as neglect, rejection, or deception. Sometimes, however, major problems — caused by rape, murder, war, religious and tribal conflict, traditions of slavery and apartheid, terrorists, and other outside forces — do affect our clients. Practitioners may work with clients who have experienced aggression, sexual assault, or, perhaps, the death of a loved one at the hands of a stranger. Clients may have been victims of oppression or torture that seems almost impossible to comprehend. Indeed, torture victims may not even be willing to tell their stories for fear that no one will believe them (Gorman, 2001). Yet, their anger and bitterness still exist. In sum, clients come to our offices as a result of many different kinds of aversive triggers. For some, their anger experiences are associated with a severe trigger — e.g., an intense and pervasive drive for social justice and retaliatory revenge, bitterness, obsessive thoughts — and an inability to move forward with life.

Forgiveness interventions, as presented in this chapter, are extensions of cognitive change strategies. In addition to perceiving situations more realistically and/or accepting the realities of life, forgiveness interventions focus on *perspective taking* and *letting go*. This approach, while applicable to the more common anger triggers seen by practitioners on a daily basis, is particularly useful for *major* anger triggers that have occurred in the past. Traditionally, the techniques of forgiveness have been left to religious leaders who try to help large groups of people understand and come to grips with the atrocities of civilization. However, mental health professionals also have much to offer to the process of forgiveness, and individual clients can learn to personally let go of the past and live a more fulfilling life in the future. Since many clients are unaware of the benefits of forgiveness interventions, we have provided a Client Information Sheet to stimulate thinking about this strategy (at the end of the chapter).

❖ *Why Forgiveness is Important*

The two most important unforgiving responses of clients are *rehearsing past aversive events* and *harboring grudges*. These are typically associated with repetitive thoughts of blame, revenge, hostility, and remaining in the role of victim. In turn, these cognitive reactions are associated with self-defeating behaviors, high levels of physiological arousal, and life-threatening medical problems such as coronary heart disease.

Forgiveness and lack of forgiveness influence cardiovascular disease, stroke, and mental health by producing changes in what is known as *allostatic load*. This load refers to the total of normal and natural responses of the body to stressors. When threatened, or when we feel angry and hostile, our bodies react by producing stress-fighting responses in the nervous and endocrine systems. We become energized and ready to fight, and this is a good reaction in the initial stages. However, when these reactions continue over time the load becomes overwhelming and the body begins to break down. This process is well known as the *general adaptation syndrome* (Selye, 1946) and it includes three phases. In the first, there is an initial *alarm* reaction that alerts and energizes the body to the stressor. In the second, there is the continued development of active and successful *resistance* to the stressor, called *adaptation*. Then, if there is continued bodily excitation and failure to resolve the problem, there is *exhaustion*. Coping skills and adaptive resources are required for stress resistance and improved life functioning over the longer term (Holahan & Moos, 1990). Forgiveness is a coping skill to be used in cases where clients have been exposed to longer-term, often intense, stressors and where alarm and resistance have continued to the point where they are more detrimental than helpful. It is, of course, also useful for more common aversive triggers.

For ethical and moral reasons it is impossible to do controlled experiments to assess the effects of forgiveness interventions on victims of rape, torture and other forms of evil. We have learned much, therefore, from case histories, some of which are presented below. One study, however, has shown clearly that unforgiving thoughts and fantasies of blame and revenge were causative of increases in physiological stress responses while forgiving responses led to decreases in physiological stress responses (Witvliet, Ludwig & Laan, 2001). Subjects were first taught how to be unforgiving (i.e., to rehearse hurtful events and harbor grudges) and forgiving (i.e., to develop feelings of empathy for offenders and forgive while not denying, ignoring, tolerating or forgetting the offense). Then, they were asked to recall the offenders and their offenses, and to alternate between thinking of forgiving and not forgiving the perpetrator. As often seen in practitioners' offices, the triggering events were typically betrayals of trust, rejections, and insults committed by friends, romantic partners, and family members. The results were very impressive and showed the importance of forgiving. When thinking of unforgiving responses, the victims reported feeling more angry, aroused, sad, and less in control. However, when thinking of forgiving responses the victims reported feeling more empathy toward the offender. In addition to these self-reports, physiological data showed that while rehearsing the offense and thinking about holding a grudge, there was more tension in facial muscles, higher arousal as measured by skin conductance, increased heart rate, and increased diastolic and systolic blood pressure. Thus, "Chronic unforgiving, begrudging responses may contribute to adverse health outcomes by perpetuating anger and heightening SNS (sympathetic nervous system) arousal and cardiovascular reactivity. . . . Although fleeting feelings of unforgiveness may not erode health, more frequent, intense and sustained unforgiving emotional imagery and behaviors may create physiological vulnerabilities or exacerbate existing problems in a way that erodes health" (Witvliet, Ludwig & Laan, 2001, p. 122). It seems important that, at the right time, practitioners suggest the possibility of forgiving as a response to continued agitation, anger and victimization.

❖ Definition

There is no universally agreed-upon definition of forgiveness. Rather, it is based on philosophical thinking and other traditions (e.g., Hebrew, Christian, Islamic, Confucian, Buddhist), as well as principles gleaned from professional readings, and stories of forgiveness written by volunteers. As noted above, the practice of forgiveness was previously left to religious leaders who generally preached tolerance, love and acceptance. Indeed, all major religions prescribe forgiveness as part of their teachings, although they may place limits on the manner in which forgiveness is to be approached. Consider, for example, the Christian position as reflected in these biblical quotations.

> Father, forgive them; for they don't know what they do. Luke 23:34
> If you forgive sins of any, they are forgiven; if you retain the sins of any, they are retained. John 20:23

Therefore I tell you, every sin and blasphemy will be forgiven men, but the blasphemy against their Spirit will not be forgiven. Matthew 12:31

I tell you, there will be more joy in heaven over one sinner who repents than over ninety-nine righteous persons who need no repentance. Luke 15:7

Thus it is written, that the Christ should suffer and on the third day rise from the dead, and that repentance and forgiveness of sins should be preached in His name to all nations, beginning from Jerusalem. Luke 24:46-47

For if you forgive men their trespasses, your heavenly Father also will forgive you; but if you do not forgive men their trespasses neither will your father forgive your trespasses. Matthew 6:14-15

Presbyterian minister Charles Henderson, who served as chaplain at Princeton University, notes that forgiveness is central to Christianity, but that it is sometimes a difficult undertaking (Henderson, 1986):

In some cases it seems impossible to forgive once, let alone 70 times 7 as Jesus required. . . .Yet forgiveness was at the very center of Christ's teaching. It was his principal concern at the very hour of his death. As he hung there bleeding on the cross, with pain as great or greater than any of us will ever experience, he said so directly of those who delighted in his own death: "Father, forgive them, they know not what they are doing."

Others have also commented on the centrality to Christianity of forgiving. On his internet site, Pastoral counselor Don Dunlap writes that, "Refusing to forgive is one of the most serious sins a Christian can commit." He believes that, "a lack of forgiveness results in some of the most severe emotional and spiritual problems a person can experience" (www.christianity.com). Thus, Christianity places high value on both repentance and forgiveness and promotes the idea that a person who has not learned to forgive may well suffer continuing and severe problems.

Judaism also stresses the importance of forgiveness as well as restitution, especially on Yom Kippur, the day of atonement. In the *Tefilah Zaka,* it is written:

I extend complete forgiveness to everyone who has sinned against me, whether physically or monetarily, or spoke *lashon hara* (negative speech) about me or even false reports. And (I also forgive them) for any damages, whether on my body or my property, and for all sins between a man and his fellow except for money which I can claim in a court of law and except for someone who sins against me saying, "I will sin against him and he will forgive me". Except for these I grant complete forgiveness and no person should be punished on my account. And just as I forgive everyone so should you grant me favor in the eyes of all men that they should completely forgive me.

In addition, in Teshuvah 2:9-10, it is written:

Sins between one man and his fellow, such as striking, cursing, or stealing are never forgiven until one pays up his debt and appeases his fellow. Even if he returns the money he owes he must still ask for forgiveness. Even if he only spoke badly about him, he must appease and beseech until he is forgiven....It is forbidden to be cruel and difficult to appease, rather, a person must be quick to forgive and difficult to anger and when the sinner asks for forgiveness he should forgive him willingly and wholeheartedly...

Forgiveness is central to Islamic beliefs as well (see N. Ali, Al-Noor, Vol. 1, No. 6, Jamadi Al-Thani, 1412 A.H. - Dec. 1991 A.D., pp 10-11). The Koran praises forgiveness, which is defined as overlooking the offenses of a person who has done you wrong by insults, physical aggression, or harm to your property. Two types of forgiveness are delineated. First, there is forgiveness when vengeance is unavailable. However, this is actually seen in Islam as patience and tolerance in the face of helplessness, not true forgiveness. In contrast, the most desired behavior is forgiveness when the power to take revenge does exist. Of course, granting a pardon to an oppressor and abstaining from seeking vengeance are not considered to be simple tasks. To accomplish them, the Koran notes that a greater spiritual power (Allah) is required.

We are certainly respectful of such religious teachings, and they are consonant with current scientific materials. However, while reading the Bible, Koran, or the Talmud may indeed be helpful, *more than reading or listening to religious sermons is often necessary to produce forgiveness.* Knowledge about the cognitive, behavioral, and physiological benefits of forgiveness may increase client acceptance of this option. Once accepted, behavioral actions and practice, with the collaborative guidance of a mental health professional, increases the specificity of forgiveness as a treatment and increases its likelihood of success. We hope that the materials on forgiveness presented in this chapter will provide clarification of the concept and the methods that can be used by practitioners to help clients forgive.

Returning to the issue of definition, we note that *forgiveness is a cognitive concept* that emerged from the abstract works of philosophers, religious leaders, and other theoreticians. Forgiveness involves a *cognitive shift*; that is, turning the focus to the good side (goals and actions) of the offender in the face of wrongdoing. This attitude leads to *lowered physiological reactivity* and *more adaptive patterns of behavior.* Forgiveness involves *minimizing the frequency, intensity, and duration of thoughts of resentment and the pursuit of revenge.* Surprisingly, it may even involve unexpected generosity to the offender and offering personal interactions such as attention and time that contribute to the betterment of the offender. Paradoxically, it is the minimization of anger, resentment, bitterness, and the desire for revenge, and the giving of understanding to the offender, that lead to the improvement in the victim.

❖ *Forgiveness is a Process That Occurs Over Time*

Forgiveness involves *diminished focus on*, or *letting go* of negative attitudes and feelings such as hostility and anger, and adopting a perspective of mercy, compassion, and good will toward the offender. The goal for practitioners who work with offended, hurt, bitter, furious, vengeful and angry clients is to assist nature's healing process. The passage of time, of course, is helpful in many situations. Forgiveness interventions shift the time frame, to allow clients to return to a more normalized life as soon as possible, without forgetting the offense.

In the early stages, most angry and bitter clients who are victims of major offenses benefit from ventilation, support, and the re-establishment of safety. Indeed, in the treatment of victims of domestic and sexual violence, as well as veterans of combat, the first stage is the establishment of safety (Herman, 1992). Traumas such as rape, other forms of abuse and torture take away power and control, and often lead to a muted life where all feelings are extinguished (see, for example, Levi's 1959 description, *Survival in Auschwitz*). Therefore, the first step in recovery is to *establish a safe environment* where personal control over daily life activities is reestablished within a supportive relationship. Then, when the survivor feels safe, the events can be reported and feelings of anger and rage may reemerge along with desires for revenge. The next phases are reconstruction and reconnection.

In reconstruction, the client develops a narrative of the triggering events. As the narrative is told and retold, many times to many people, the story is naturally modified. Since most people have not suffered from atrocities, the angry victim learns how to present the facts to audiences of friends, family, and professionals in a way that will be understood. Many victims of severe violence, abuse and torture find that listeners cannot comprehend what happened, since it is so far removed from their reality. Thus, in their repeated reconstructions the victims leave out many parts. To help in the full expressiveness of their story, practitioners will find use in the poetry, artistic and musical expressions, writing of books and journals, and religious traditions of the client. Over time, the reconstructed story becomes filled with more details. Of importance, these details are not only those about the subjugation, humiliation, and/or shame which may have been experienced. Rather, they also include aspects of dignity and determination, as well as anger and blame and a desire for revenge. Then, at some point, the practitioner will observe a new openness in the client to discussing the experience from a different perspective. At that point, when the practitioner deems it to be the right time, the client may benefit from discussions about the process of forgiveness.

❖ *Discriminating Forgiveness From Other Concepts*

When forgiveness is initially mentioned it may seem foreign and unacceptable. To help, it is useful to distinguish forgiveness from related but different concepts. The procedure can be seen as a form of *cognitive discrimination training*. Through discussion, clients are taught to differentiate forgiveness from other possible responses to an offense. Consider differentiation of these words and concepts for clients.

Accepting. This word implies indifference and a lack of motivation to change the aversive parts of the world around us. In contrast, forgiveness leaves open the option of working toward change. For example, accepting the behavior of specific students who cheat on examinations, and forgiving them, does not imply accepting cheating as inevitable. Accepting educators still want to change conditions to minimize the probability that students will cheat in the future. Likewise, forgiving a child who sets fires or who assaults other children in the neighborhood does not imply indifference to those behaviors. It would remain important to work to change the behavior of those children to the best of one's ability.

Excusing. This word implies minimization. Clients may say, "It's not so important that she wasted all of our money at the slot machines. After all, she's a good person and it won't happen again," or "So, he drinks and yells at me. There are worse things in the world. At least he keeps a job and provides for us. And, he has never hit me. So, it's not that bad." Forgiving is quite different from simply excusing. Forgiving implies admitting that the behaviors (from failing to keep promises and poor school achievement to drinking to excess and using drugs to rape, violence, and torture) are negative. Forgiving does not imply minimizing the problems, nor does it imply ignoring the need to seek solutions.

Neutrality. This word implies that no sides are to be taken in conflicts. Certainly, we do not expect victims to be neutral with regard to the actions of terrorists, tyrants and other evil-doers. Their actions led to suffering, and neutrality may lead to more problems in the future. Victims are on the other side from perpetrators, whether we are talking about discrimination in the workplace or the repeated attacks of serial killers and strong actions may be required to repair such situations. Sides are taken; yet, it is the victim who chooses to forgive the perpetrator.

Forgetting. Douglas, a very good friend of ours, was killed in a needless car accident more than 35 years ago. He has never been forgotten, as forgiveness does not mean forgetting, and the memories of good times with him linger to this day. Forgiveness, however, has allowed for a change of focus. Instead of obsessively recalling the very inappropriate behavior of the speeding, reckless driver who caused the crash, the memories are now focused on the good times enjoyed with Douglas. Memories of the crash and fantasies of blame are less frequent now than when the accident occurred. And, hopefully, the reckless driver has changed his habits. Douglas, however, has never been forgotten.

Justifying. Consider Fran, who is frequently beaten by her husband after he drinks excessively. In a clear case of justification, she says, "It's the liquor that makes him do it. He really loves me and it's really not him who hits me. It's like it's some other person." Although forgiveness does imply analysis of the causes of behavior, it is not a justification for the aversive acts of others.

Calming Down. Consider Fred, who moved out of his apartment in downtown Chicago and found that his landlord would not return his security deposit of $1900. The landlord claimed that Fred had broken the dishwasher and had left the apartment in such a dirty state that it would take much more than $1900 to repair the damages. Fred was furious and had a number of shouting matches with the landlord. However, after a few weeks in his new apartment Fred spoke about the problem in a much calmer tone. In fact, two weeks later he initiated proceedings to sue the landlord for the $1900. When he relayed the story to a lawyer, he did so in a rather calm and subdued manner. This does not mean the event meant less to Fred. Rather, he had put it in perspective and was now going to let the legal process proceed (now in small claims court). Becoming calm is very useful but it is not synonymous with forgiving. Part of forgiving, in this case, is an awareness of the fact that conflicts exist in life and that we have a legal process to resolve disputes. Fred does not have to agree with, or accept, or be neutral about, or justify, the landlord's behavior. Rather, forgiveness implies letting go by reducing arousal, changing thinking, and allowing others to help solve the dispute in a fair manner.

Forced Forgiving, Truces, and Pseudo Forgiveness. Consider Marc and Joe (both age 12) who were fighting during school recess. Marc said that Joe's mother was retarded and that Joe was not her natural son. This verbal assault was in retaliation for an earlier event when Joe threw Marc's books on to the floor during lunch period. A teacher came along and broke up the fight. He told the boys, in a rather forceful way, to apologize to each other and to "forgive and forget." So, they each said "I'm sorry" and supposedly forgave each other. Did they? True forgiving implies a process of cognitive analysis and restructuring by the offended parties. In the case of Marc and Joe, the words do not reflect such a process. Rather, the teacher simply forced a temporary truce.

Seeking Justice, Compensation, and Feeling Good. Retributive justice implies that a victim will feel good only when some sort of revenge is taken. In contrast, forgiveness is not a *quid pro quo* arrangement. It doesn't demand compensation first. Indeed, as Ghandi said, "If we practice an eye for an eye and a tooth for a tooth, soon the whole world will be blind and toothless" (Attenborough, 1990).

Forgiveness may or may not lead to good feelings. And, since forgiveness is a process that occurs over time, positive feelings may wax and wane. Unfortunately, justice and financial or other forms of compensation, and the possible good feelings they produce, will not bring back a loved one killed by a drunk driver or a friend who died in the collapse of the World Trade Center towers. And, while some transient good feelings may indeed be produced by seeing an ex-lover suffer, they certainly will not restore the client's relationship. So, forgiving means something more and different from feeling good and being compensated. Dealing with torture victims from other countries, Gorman (2001) wrote, "As refugee survivors give voice to their multiple traumas of loss, they must deal as well with the realization that there can be no adequate response or compensation to the wrongs done to them" (p. 448). At the same time, letting go of anger, bitterness, and fantasies of revenge does not mean giving up the desire for justice. The perpetrator is still to be held accountable for the crime.

Condemning. Forgiveness does not come out of a sense of condemnation, which assumes blame and denunciation. The condemning person has the attitude of, "She is a totally uncaring person who deserves to know how much she hurt me. She has no heart!" This type of so-called forgiving has a sense of moral superiority that is absent in true forgiving.

❖ The Challenge of Forgiveness

At this point the reader may agree that *many* anger-triggering persons who commit anger-engendering offenses can be forgiven. For example, recollections may emerge about a child or parent, or next-door neighbor, or good friend, who was forgiven for acting improperly. Perhaps the person wrongly revealed a secret, or engaged in inappropriate gossip, or was unfaithful.

But, is it possible to forgive *all* offenders no matter what they have done? Or, are some people who trigger anger and bitterness and hatred so bad that they are unforgivable? What about more serious perpetrators of evil? We ask the reader to think about the people described below, all of whom have elicited anger, bitterness, and a desire for vengeance. Some caused enormous suffering and the deaths of millions of people, while others committed brutal acts against individuals. Can empathic understanding of the forces that led them to behave as they did be developed in those who suffered under them? Consider these ten dictators, serial killers, terrorists and pedophiles.

Adolf Hitler, the German dictator whose final solution was to kill millions of Jews, Gypsies, homosexuals, and the infirm.

Saddam Hussein, the Iraqi President who murdered government officials suspected of disloyalty, used chemical weapons to crush a Kurdish rebellion, and attacked Iran and Kuwait.

Josef Stalin, dictator of the former USSR, under whose leadership many thousands of people simply "disappeared" while others were sent to labor camps in the Siberian Gulag, without a trial and with no knowledge of the nature of their "crime."

Jeffrey Dahmer, who strangled men he had invited to his apartment to watch sexually-explicit videos or pose for photos. He frequently had sex with the corpses, masturbated on them and dismembered his victims, photographing each stage of the process for his future viewing pleasure.

Dr. Harold Shipman, the world's most prolific serial killer. A "loner," brought up by an overprotective mother, Shipman became a drug-addicted forger who murdered more than 300 of his patients.

Nannie Doss was known as "Grandma Venom." She killed five of her husbands, and her children, grandchildren, sisters, and mother. Doss used arsenic-laden rat poison, which she fed to her victims in home-made stewed prunes.

Ted Kaczynski, known as "The Unabomber," pleaded guilty to 13 counts for attacks in three states that killed three people and injured others. Sentenced to life in prison, he was spared the death sentence. In childhood, he was emotionally abused and was the target of teasing by other children. Kaczynski was very bright and skipped grades 6 and 11. At the age of 16 he began his education at Harvard. At 25, he had completed his masters and Ph.D. After graduation in 1967, he became an Assistant Professor of Mathematics at the University of California at Berkeley. However, he quit in 1969, saying that he failed to see the relevance in what he taught.

Timothy McVeigh, who was responsible for the Oklahoma City bombing. McVeigh liked the army where there was discipline, a sense of order, and training in survivalist techniques. In 1991, McVeigh served in Desert Storm, excelled as a soldier, and earned the Bronze Star.

Osama bin Laden, who was behind the demise of New York's World Trade Center towers. A wealthy man, granted safe haven by Afghanistan's Taliban movement, bin Laden called for a holy war against the United States and the Jews. Born in Saudi Arabia to a

Yemeni family, he left to fight against the Soviet invasion of Afghanistan. The US State Department called him one of the most significant sponsors of Islamic extremist activities in the world. Bin Laden was involved in the 1993 and 2001 World Trade Center bombings and destruction, the 1996 killing of 19 US soldiers in Saudi Arabia, and the 1998 bombings in Kenya and Tanzania.

Father James Porter, a Massachusetts priest who sexually abused more than 200 children from 1953 to 1992. Although his superiors in the seminary recognized that Porter was a molester as early as 1960, multiple complaints, a criminal arrest, and several confessions from Porter did not lead to prompt or meaningful action. Instead Porter repeatedly received "spiritual counseling" and was transferred to various new locations. In 1993, he was convicted and received a sentence of 18 to 20 years in jail.

Is it truly possible to forgive such violent oppressors of people and individuals who committed acts of brutal violence? Certainly it would be more difficult to forgive if one had personally suffered because of their actions. But now, as time has passed, is it better for the victims of such people to remain angry, bitter, and vengeful? What is the likely effect of continued rumination on the emotional and behavioral functioning of former victims as the years pass by? As a mental health practitioner, what would be recommended for clients who suffered as a result of such actions?

Actions to eliminate future acts of aggression and reigns of terror are surely warranted. The words "never again" are certainly to be heeded by all of us. But, are these people eventually forgivable by their victims? If these perpetrators were all alive today, could we meet with them and be kind to them, without strong anger and physiological arousal, while still accepting their guilt and seeking justice and a better world? What is the goal for those perpetrators who are still alive? What is the goal for their victims?

What is the alternative to forgiveness? Consider the cases of psychologists Viktor Frankl and Bruno Bettelheim, both survivors of World War II Nazi concentration camps. If they were clients in a psychotherapy or counseling practice today, how would we want them to act and feel (psychologically), so that the remainder of their lives would be peaceful and productive? What recommendations regarding bitterness, vengeance and retaliation, as opposed to remembrance, prevention, and forgiveness, would we have for such survivors? Suppose our clients were Native Americans or African Americans. How would we want them to think, act, and feel as they recall oppression and slavery by whites? What about Japanese-Americans who were placed in American detention camps during World War II? And, can peaceful Arab-Americans and Muslims forgive the suspicions and anger shown toward them after the bombing of New York's World Trade towers? Could

Jews, Muslims, blacks, homosexuals, and others who have been victims be taught to meet peacefully with those who offended them and triggered their anger? Could they be taught to be kind toward their offenders, without anger and thoughts of revenge, while still accepting the guilt of those offenders and seeking proper action to prevent transgressions in the future? Is forgiveness easier if more is known about some of the unusual and abusive childhood factors that led rapists, serial murderers, and terrorists to develop their abhorrent behaviors? Could they be forgiven even if little or nothing was known about what caused the behavior of such people?

❖ *Unforgiving and Forgiving Responses*

Much of what has been presented above emerges from philosophical and religious teaching, and leaves practitioners without specifics of the appropriate forgiving responses to be developed in angry clients. Thus, we require tighter definitions for practitioners to proceed.

Unforgiving Responses. When clients are unforgiving they engage in frequent *cognitive rehearsal* about the offender or the triggering event(s). Images and thoughts about the aversive event and the perpetrator enter awareness throughout the day and night, even though they may be unwanted. Clients imagine the anger trigger in action, recall how they felt, and blame the perpetrator for evil intent and action. They ruminate about their "outrage" and think about how they can "get even." This leads to *harboring grudges*. Grudges show that rehearsal is continuing, that the client is remaining in the role of victim, and that negative angry reactions are continuing. Grudges suggest the desire for retribution, retaliation, and the payment of a debt by the offender, which is thought to somehow lead to closure. But, grudges actually bind the client to the role of the injured person. Until the client can move out of that role, improvement will be difficult.

Forgiving Responses. In contrast, forgiveness implies the development of feelings of *empathy* for the instigator of the anger event. As in the theory of Rational Emotive Behavior Therapy (REBT), clients are encouraged to think of the offending person as a whole human being with many facets, rather than defining the person totally in terms of the offending acts or actions. In that sense, forgiving is consonant with the behavioral approach of defining personality as a series of *specific behaviors*, each of which is elicited by certain environmental stimuli and reinforced by consequences. This further suggests that any one of us who may have been brought up in poverty, in a specific dysfunctional family, in Nazi Germany, or with a particular medical problem such as a brain tumor, would have the potential to behave aversively, as did the offending person. Anger and a desire for vengeance imply blame. In contrast, the behavioral approach suggests that our behaviors (both pro-social and offensive) are caused by our history where we learned to act as we do, and our biological capacities, which are certainly not in our conscious control.

Since many clients are religious, it is useful to know that a forgiveness intervention is consonant with teachings to differentiate the *sinner* who can supposedly be cognitively forgiven, from the *sin* (i.e., the behavior) that is to be changed or eradicated. The very useful phrase, "Hate the sin, love the sinner," — a quote from Saint Augustine — can be very helpful to practitioners.

The perspective of forgiveness involves stepping back and looking at the offending person in a new way. In terms of Ellis' (1994) REBT approach, it means ceasing to define offending people as totally "worthless," "incompetent," "evil," "bastards," or the like. Instead, Ellis suggests the offender be defined as a complex person with many different behaviors in his or her repertoire, some of which are acceptable and others of which are highly offensive and repugnant. Ellis suggests that no one can be an "evil bastard." However, people can engage in evil, bastardly acts. So, he too differentiates the person from the act.

Consider the case of Frank, a 33-year-old account executive, who married his long-time sweetheart, Stephanie, eight years ago. Their marriage is going very well, with one exception. Stephanie expects that Frank will respond to *every* major event, such as birthdays and anniversaries, with a card, flowers, or some kind of gift. Frank has no such expectations and views these events as representing the simple passage of time within a loving relationship. He brings many gifts and other signs of recognition throughout the year, but often does not do so for Stephanie's birthday or Valentine's Day. She, then, becomes infuriated and ruminates about how he "should" act as she expects (demands). The strain on their relationship has been increasing. Forgiveness, for Stephanie, implies seeing Frank in the broadest perspective as a man with many, many qualities – some good and others not so good. Forgiveness involves the development of an understanding of the factors that lead Frank to act as he does. That is, to step into his shoes. Perhaps Frank's father modeled this kind of behavior or perhaps the issues are financial, or relate to time constraints. Forgiveness does not suggest that Stephanie give up her desire, or that she agree with Frank, or excuse his actions. Rather, the process is one of perspective taking and understanding, which leads to lowered angry arousal and cognitive rumination.

Forgiveness means changing cognitive, emotional and behavioral reactions. When clients forgive, they *think* in different, broader terms about the life of the offender and the forces that led the offender to behave aversively. The client then *feels* less anger as the problem is imagined and may even *act* to help the offender in some way.

The case of Frank and Stephanie represents a relatively minor problem. In contrast, it would initially seem to be impossible for victims of major criminal or terrorist or dictatorial activities to forgive. Yet, there are many reported cases that illustrate that such forgiveness has occurred.

Consider the case of Ronald Carlson, which is explored in some depth on the internet (www.restitutioninc.org/forgive/carlson). His sister was murdered in 1983 and he immediately wanted revenge. After their capture, a man and a woman were found guilty and sentenced to death. Carlson seemed to be satisfied, although he continued to be consumed with anger and hatred. He had thoughts of suicide. In an attempt to help, the prosecutor suggested that he would feel better after their conviction and execution, knowing they paid for their actions. But he continued to feel upset, angry, and agitated. Then, eight years later, he confronted the murderers, one in prison and the second by letter. He indicated that he forgave them and no longer held their acts against them. Carlson reported that this forgiveness led to great relief and prevented the incident from destroying the rest of his life. Although he later witnessed the execution of one of the murderers, Carlson does not support the death penalty, believing that it creates even more victims. He believes that his forgiveness saved his own life.

Another example is provided by the case of Aba Gayle, who forgave the man who murdered her 19-year-old daughter. The murderer, Douglas Mickey, was caught, convicted and sentenced to death. Gayle initially felt overwhelmed with anger, hate, a wish for revenge, and despair. She couldn't drive her car because she would cry and couldn't see the road. As in the previous case, the prosecutor assured Gayle that when Mr. Mickey was executed, she would feel much better. However, after eight years of a desire for revenge, she began to read about forgiveness. She watched a video that showed a Jewish holocaust survivor who was able to forgive not only the German people, but also the actual guards in the camps who had killed every member of his family. This affected her outlook and she began to think she could forgive the man who killed her daughter. She began to meditate and eventually she wrote a letter to the killer in which she expressed forgiveness and compassion. She reported this as a turning point that led to relief from despair. Although it seems very surprising to outsiders, Gayle developed a "friendship" with the murderer, and she has since befriended other inmates on death row. She visits and corresponds with many of them. She wrote, "What I learned is healing and grace can be achieved by anyone under any circumstance through the miracle of forgiveness" (www.catherineblountfdn.org/aba's.htm).

We also review the case of 16-year-old Debbie (Morris, 1998). While on a date, two strangers (Robert Willie and Joseph Vaccaro) put a revolver to her boyfriend Mark's head. They shot Mark, leaving him for dead, and repeatedly raped and tortured Debbie. After their capture, one of the men was sentenced to die. He admitted to other murders, including butchering a girl. However, as in the two cases presented above, Debbie's anger and anguish did not end when Willie was sentenced to die. Justice did not relieve her negative emotions and thoughts, which continued at high frequency and intensity. Debbie did not feel relief until she was able to comprehend their actions and forgive the men. She reportedly came to the conclusion that forgiveness not only recognizes that the offender still has to pay a debt but it also allows for forward life movement in the victim.

Finally, we note that many survivors and victims use their own tragedies as a foundation from which to try and help others. Consider the Mission Statement from *Life Sentence,* an organization created by parents who have lost children to violence:

> Our goal is to educate youth, parents and the public about the devastating effects of violence. Through our presentation on choices, we share our own real life stories in a very graphic and powerful way. We bring reality to the youth of today in a way they can understand: through a mother's heart (www.lifesentence.org).

These case testimonials suggest that people seem able to forgive many types of offenses, both mild and severe. And, since they are filled with references to religion as the source of forgiveness, they will be helpful to practitioners who work with religious clients. However, it is important that practitioners know how to implement forgiveness for both religious and non-religious clients.

❖ A Forgiveness Model for Practitioners

As noted above, forgiveness is a *process* that develops over time. Although practitioners may seek distinct programmed steps, perhaps to be reassured that clients are moving forward, like other aspects of intervention it is likely that clients will not proceed in a lockstep fashion. Movement toward forgiveness, with or without the help of a practitioner, follows only a general pathway. There is no rigid sequence and clients may experience only some of the steps (Enright, 2001). Forgiving relatively minor events, such as the misbehavior of a friend or family member, is likely to proceed differently from forgiving more serious behaviors such as rape or false imprisonment. And, clients who always lived in a relatively stable and predictable world are likely to proceed through the process differently than are victims of torture and other major aversive encounters.

The following is a brief description of the four phases of forgiveness.

Uncovering Anger. Forgiveness is preceded by the development of a full *awareness* of the anger experience. Depending on the anger trigger and the associated appraisal, the client may experience hate, hostility, and bitterness, along with ruminative thoughts of revenge and self-defeating patterns such as emotional numbing, obsessive planning for unlikely future events, and sleeplessness. Patterns of expression vary from obsession with negative feelings and a cognitive desire for revenge to simple denial. Using basic skills of discussion, reflection, support and active listening, the practitioner can help the client confront the feelings, thoughts and behaviors associated with the trigger. As the anger experience is brought into the open, reconstruction of the experience and lowered reactivity can begin.

The process thus begins with the shared practitioner and client *recognition that an injustice has occurred*, that the client has experienced psychological suffering and possibly physical pain, and that the effects and outcome have been negative. For some clients, the trigger will objectively be minor. For others, it will be severe. Consider clients who have been betrayed by friends who revealed personal secrets to others, or clients who lost their money to unscrupulous stock dealers, or clients who have been the victims of other financial scams. Or, consider clients who may have been the target of major anger triggers such as racism or sexism or ageism, resulting in lost jobs and opportunities for advancement. Finally, some clients will have been physically attacked, raped, or have otherwise suffered greatly. In each case, the client is likely to experience anger, perhaps with great intensity, and to have a shifted view of the world. They are now untrusting, skeptical of the promises of others, and often cynical. They may question their religious faith, which previously brought comfort to them, and they may have developed interpersonal, behavioral, and medical problems as a result of the anger trigger. Full recognition of the triggering event, the anger itself, and the associated problems is the first step in the process.

Deciding to Forgive. Clients often get stuck in a mode of responding, even if that mode is self-defeating. Indeed, in one study pairs of subjects played a game (the Prisoner's Dilemma) and were told that *cooperation* would lead to the best outcome for both players while *competition* would generally be harmful to both of them (Kassinove and colleagues, 2001). In spite of the instructions, players who were high on the personality trait of anger repeatedly tried to compete rather than cooperate — a self-defeating behavior pattern. The outcome was that both players wound up losing.

Unforgiving anger and vengeful fantasies become habitual. Even though they lead to lack of problem resolution, the client continues along the self-defeating pathway. Thus, in this phase practitioners help the client to realize that continuing to focus on the triggering injury and the inflammatory appraisals may lead to greater and unnecessary suffering. With more empathy and support from the practitioner, and with repeated reconstructive telling of the anger-evoking story, the client may eventually entertain the idea of forgiveness as a strategy to improve life. Alternatively, the practitioner may gently suggest forgiveness. Retelling of the story is important, as each retelling allows the client to see new and sometimes less aversive elements of the negative event. At this stage, the practitioner is helping the client to commit to forgiveness as a strategy to resolve anger and bitterness and move forward with life. An important step is a shift in the *dimension of time*. Ask the client to "let go" of the past, without forgetting it. Ask the client about the future. What goals now exist and what is likely to happen? Ask the client, "What would be likely to happen if thoughts and intentions of revenge were stopped?"

Work Phase. Now the client begins the concrete and active work of forgiving the person who triggered the anger. This involves the development of new ways of thinking about the perpetrator that encourage compassion and understanding. The angry, still-bitter client may be helped to understand the childhood of the offender or to put the event(s) in context by understanding the pressures the offender was under at the time of the offense. What role did drugs, alcohol, an abusive childhood, a psychiatric illness, or a brain dysfunction play in the life of the offender? Did the offender's religious beliefs or delusions, or the learning of behaviors in a specific social or cultural context contribute to the behavior? In the offender's family or culture or religion of origin, what rules were taught about how to treat children, criminals, women, the elderly, or other people in general? Did biology and learning make the offender a victim?

The practitioner does not help the client develop this new way of thinking to excuse the offender of responsibility. Rather, the goal is to better *understand* the offender and understand the shaping forces that led to the offensive behavior. Without excusing, forgetting, accepting, or justifying, the goal is to develop a willingness to experience empathy and compassion toward the perpetrator.

The central goal of this work phase is the simple acceptance of the unjust physical pain and emotional discomfort that resulted from the actions of the perpetrator. By acceptance, we mean recall of events and recognition of what happened, without a desire to seek revenge. The challenge for the client is to see the perpetrator as a whole person who acted badly because of biological and environmental forces. When this shift is made, the client may now become ready to begin to offer some small degree of goodwill toward the offender. This may include simple restraint from a desire for revenge. It may also include an enhanced client self-definition that includes the characteristics of mercy and generosity.

Clients begin to ask, "What kind of person am I?" The shift also may, or may not, include some form of reconciliation. Giving something to the person who offended the client may seem impossible when intervention begins. For example, clients may talk of family members they haven't seen in years because of some transgression that led to intense anger and they may initially express hope that the family member will continue to suffer. Yet, there are cases of last-moment forgiveness, such as making a hospital visit to a terminally ill person who offended the client in the past. At that point, the client may give a gift of time spent with the offender, or may offer handholding, or may send a card or flowers or candy. As the offender is seen in a debilitated state, a different view is taken. Paradoxically, it is the client who is most served by this kind of forgiveness. It is the client who feels better once peace has been made.

Release and Deepening. The client now begins to realize that forgiving the offender is leading to cognitive change and emotional relief. With the help of the mental health professional, the client may partially reconstruct the past (i.e., think of it differently) and find meaning in the anger and suffering that was experienced. This meaning is discovered and enhanced in different ways, some of which can be suggested by the practitioner.

Some victims of severe oppression write books. In 1959 Italian concentration camp survivor Primo Levi wrote *Survival in Auschwitz*. His goal was to tell his story and satisfy his drive for "interior liberation" (p. 5). On multipurpose internet sites, others write poetry or stories, create films, meet with other survivors, or simply chat via email to achieve a deepening of their personal release from anger and vengeance (e.g., www.stardate.bc.ca/survivors). Some clients set up internet sites to devote total attention to their own unique case. A simple internet search for "survivors" will lead to many links so that sharing of all kinds of stories can occur.

For a rare few, meaning is discovered in true scholarship. Consider the life and work of Dr. Viktor Frankl, who developed Logotherapy and Existential Analysis. Frankl believed that human beings are not simple puppets of biological and environmental forces. Rather, they think and make their own decisions about life. Thus, he saw a "search for meaning" as a primary human motivation. In his Logotherapy, clients are helped to discover meaning in their own life situations. Logotherapists help clients to re-orient and recover from aversive life events by strengthening trust in the unconditional meaningfulness of life and the dignity of the person. Frankl's ideas are based partially on his own search for meaning while a prisoner in Nazi concentration camps from 1942 to 1945. Although we can only speculate about how he would react to Saddam Hussein or Osama bin Laden, Frankl's search for meaning certainly helped him survive the Nazi camps (see Frankl, 1984).

Frankl's view is different from ours. Scholars have argued for years about the degree to which we are free thinkers versus the degree to which we are puppets of biology and environment. Frankl takes the former view while we understand the importance of the latter. Nevertheless, the important point is that both can be used to deepen understanding of the aversive conditions of life and both can provide a means to a release from suffering.

To help establish meaning and release many clients profit from keeping a journal to address each phase of the forgiving process (Enright, 2001). The value here is that practitioners can suggest specific questions for the client to consider in the journal that may enhance movement towards letting go of rehearsing past injustices. For example, with regard to awareness, the practitioner can suggest that clients answer such questions as, "How long have you been angry?" or "What are some of the reasons to keep being angry and seek vengeance?" and "What are some of the reasons to let go of the anger, while still holding the offender accountable?" With regard to the encouragement of perspective taking and developing a broader view, clients can be asked to write about, "What do you think life was like for (the offender) while growing up?" or "How might (the offender) have tried to deal with his abusive father?" or "Can (the offender) in some ways also be seen as a victim?" The client may or may not want to share the answers with the practitioner, and each choice is acceptable. Simply considering the questions, with or without feedback, is helpful.

It is important to be respectful of cultural differences among clients. Some will enhance their improvement by meeting with others, while others want to work alone. Some will talk to strangers in the early phases of improvement while others will talk only to family members. Some will attribute their strength to a religious figure or set of religious beliefs, while others will look to science or secular resources for help. Some will want to discuss their journal entries but others will find them improper to share. We have suggested that a successful anger management program is likely to work best if it is based on a collaboratively developed plan. Such collaboration is certainly critical at this stage of the forgiveness process.

The process of forgiveness, cognitive shifts, anger relief, and the newly developed meaning attached to the offense and offender(s) lead to increased interest in, and understanding of, the self and others. Clients rediscover purpose in life and develop a concern for their community. Certainly, the forgiving client will discover the paradox of forgiveness. As time, compassion, empathy, mercy, and generosity are provided to the offender, it is the forgiver who improves.

Client Information Sheet

Anger, Bitterness, and Forgiveness

Many people harbor anger, believing that it is "appropriate" to continue feeling bad. They mentally rehearse the problem that led to their anger, think about how wrong the other person was, and believe that person should "pay" for the anger and bitterness that was caused.

Sometimes, grudges are held for years and years. Unfortunately, anger, bitterness, and thoughts of revenge are not healthy. They lead to preoccupation with the past, rather than allowing for enjoyment of the present, and keep the offended person in the role of "victim."

How long do you have to "suffer" with past events? To some extent, it's up to you. It would certainly be unwise just to ignore past injustices that led you to suffer. But, current anger and bitterness are not useful because they lead to ruminative thoughts and high levels of bodily stress. Eventually, this can lead to sleep disturbances, heart problems, and other forms of life disruption.

Forgiveness education can be the first step in moving forward from the prison of the past. It involves the development of a clear and thoughtful differentiation between the healthy response of "letting go" and "giving up the victim role," and other unacceptable forms of adjustment such as forgetting what happened. Forgiveness means giving up the belief that only continued condemnation and retribution will make you feel better. *Forgiveness education gives you power to control your own feelings, thoughts, and behaviors.* Forgiveness means living in the present, developing an understanding of what caused the other person to act offensively and, perhaps, understanding that person was also a victim of life circumstances. Forgiveness is a healing process that takes time.

"Forgiveness does not change the past, but it does enlarge the future."   (Paul Boese, author)

Ask your practitioner to help you understand why *forgiveness is not the same as*:

- Accepting the behavior of the offender
- Excusing what was done
- Taking a neutral position
- Forgetting the offensive behavior
- Justifying why the offender did it
- Simply calming down, or developing a truce

Consider what was said by psychiatrist Thomas Szasz:
> **The stupid neither forgive nor forget;**
> **the naïve forgive and forget;**
> **the wise forgive but do not forget.**

Are you wise? Discuss the benefits of forgiveness education with your practitioner.

[Howard Kassinove, Ph.D. and Raymond Chip Tafrate, Ph.D. *Anger Management: The Complete Treatment Guidebook for Practitioners* © 2002]

Relapse Prevention

I have just returned from Boston. It is the only thing to do if you find yourself there.

— Fred Allen

Many clients achieve substantial improvement from participating in a structured anger management program using the strategies described in this guidebook. However, since anger is a complex constellation of thoughts, physical activation patterns, and motor and verbal behaviors, change is unlikely to occur in an even progression. It is not uncommon for periods of reduced anger to be interrupted by the reemergence of personal anger experiences and expressions to others. Another common scenario is that in the midst of a period of improvement clients may have one strong anger episode that results in dramatic problems, leaving the client (and perhaps the practitioner) feeling defeated. When a client backslides, or relapses into prior ways of behaving, it is easy to conclude that treatment is not working and to become pessimistic, believing that the client is not capable of making substantial and lasting improvement. At these moments it is the practitioner's long-term view, and the ability to re-focus treatment, that makes the difference in the overall outcome of the case.

Relapse prevention began with the work of Marlatt and Parks (1982) and Marlatt and Gordon (1985) who noted that after success with the treatment of various behavioral problems — such as smoking, drinking, overeating, drug addiction, obsessive compulsive disorder, and gambling — clients very often fell back into their old behaviors. In fact, between 50% and 90% of clients who are successful in the reduction of overeating, smoking, and other problems eventually relapse.

Relapse is not the same as treatment failure, in which there is little or no progress at all. Rather, the terms "lapse" and "relapse" refer to slight or almost total increases in problem behaviors, after improvement has already been shown. In all likelihood, this occurs because we don't

245

focus formally on consolidating and maintaining treatment gains. Thus, an important final step in any anger management program is preparing clients, *in advance*, for the likely scenario that anger will reappear. While the anger reduction program described here focuses on interventions to reduce reactivity to known and current anger triggers, relapse prevention focuses on identifying, analyzing, and managing the warning signs of relapse that may involve unknown or rare triggers. Relapse prevention encompasses *proactive* measures to minimize the tendency for clients to backslide and respond with anger. Clients are taught that rather than engaging in self-blame and condemnation when lapses occur, it is more productive to understand what has happened and take responsibility for further maintenance of their improved behavior.

A number of methods can be utilized to get clients back to a productive path and to combat hopelessness about continued progress after anger has reemerged. Increasing treatment focus on a particularly problematic anger trigger, or on a rare trigger, increasing the frequency of sessions, or raising the intensity or frequency of practice regarding a set of new skills all help to reduce backsliding. Thus, the final part of a comprehensive anger management program involves the development of a proactive, relapse prevention strategy. This becomes part of a formal collaborative plan of action between the practitioner and client to maintain treatment gains and deal with difficult or risky situations. It involves the development of *anticipation* and *coping*, as part of a program of client *self-control*, once formal intervention has ended.

Relapse is slow and insidious, and begins with lapses. That is, in the midst of clear progress clients will experience and express anger in old ways. Thus, lapses may initially come as a surprise to both the practitioner and the client after things seem to have been going so well. Common elements of the relapse process that occur in the treatment of various addictions have been identified and we believe these also apply to the treatment of anger (Parks & Marlatt, 2000).

The relapse process begins when a sense of *perceived control* or *self-efficacy* is experienced. This may occur as clients learn to relax, to apply new cognitive appraisals to their common anger triggers, or develop the broader perspective central to forgiveness interventions. Even if the true gains are minimal, as is often the case in the beginning of any intervention program, *clients may inflate their progress*, believing they have clearly mastered anger management skills when in fact they have only experienced success with infrequent or minor triggers. As the number of common triggers that are successfully handled increases, with minimal or no anger, and as the time period of success grows, there is a corresponding *increase in the client's perception of self-efficacy*.

This may continue until a high-risk, strongly aversive, and perhaps novel trigger is experienced (e.g., "I can handle most things now, but learning that my daughter has failed out of college! Wow! That really pissed me off!"). This experience threatens perceived control, decreases self-efficacy, and eventually increases the probability of full relapse.

Alternatively, an effective preprogrammed coping response to deal with a novel high-risk trigger, such as unexpected conflict or disappointment, will diminish the probability of relapse. If the client copes effectively with the novel trigger, self-efficacy increases even further. As the duration of anger control increases, and as the client copes effectively with typical and novel anger triggers, the probability of relapse into previous patterns of anger expression is reduced. Thus, a positive feedback cycle develops.

Clients who have not learned effective coping responses to use when confronted with new high-risk situations are more prone to enter a negative cycle. For example, a lapse related to an episode of anger may result in decreased self-efficacy and a sense of powerlessness. The client feels defeated. In turn, this lowered sense of self-efficacy and defeat may be followed by a full-blown return to old anger patterns or the development of other maladaptive behavior such as alcohol and drug use, or aggression.

In practice, according to Parks and Marlatt (2000), the cornerstone of relapse prevention is coping skills training. In terms of anger management, these skills are aimed at teaching clients to:

(a) understand that lapses are part of the process of improvement and, thus, to predict in advance that they will occur. We present a *Client Information Sheet* (at the end of this chapter), to be left in the waiting room or given to clients, to increase awareness of the possibility of relapse;

(b) identify and agree upon a list of high-risk triggers (people or situations), which may either be a frequent part of the client's environment or may represent infrequent but possible situations;

(c) cope with high-risk triggers and resist the desire to return to prior angry ways by developing anger prevention skills;

(d) implement some form of "damage control" when (inevitable) lapses to anger do occur, so that the client will not see the lapse as a sure sign of failure;

(e) persist with the treatment plan after a lapse; and

(f) learn how to create a more balanced lifestyle in which novel triggers and maladaptive appraisals are less likely to appear or be bothersome. This includes assisting clients in sleeping well, eating well, and managing time effectively; ensuring that some free time is also built into the life plan for recreational pursuits. Clients will be more able to deal with novel problems if they are well rested and not overwhelmed with other difficulties.

We believe that, with regard to anger management, it is particularly important to prepare clients for lapses in progress, to develop strategies to manage setbacks, and to continuously identify risky triggers and unhelpful cognitive appraisals in order to maintain treatment gains. Specific ways to incorporate a relapse prevention philosophy into anger treatment are discussed below.

❖ *Preparing Clients for Lapses: Putting Setbacks in Perspective*

Clients typically believe that participation in individual or group counseling means that they will show consistent and steady improvement over time. Each week of treatment is expected to bring more progress, in terms of fewer anger experiences and less maladaptive expressive patterns. Of course, even when treatment is highly successful this is rarely the actual course of progress. New triggers may present themselves in the middle of treatment, additional psychopathology (such as binge drinking or gambling) may be identified as problematic, and new skills may take longer to learn and become part of the client's automatic repertoire of behavior. The new skills may be present in the office session, but may not emerge in the natural environment. Improvement is usually variable and setbacks are to be expected. It is important to provide realistic expectations about the course of change.

The time to introduce the topic of relapse is when a client first expresses disappointment about having experienced an episode of anger. A useful way to approach the situation is to ask, *"What is improvement supposed to look like?"* Have the client graphically depict his or her view of reasonable progress. Set up a simple graph with anger (frequency, intensity, or duration) on the vertical axis and time (in sessions or weeks) on the horizontal axis.

Most clients will draw something that looks similar to the striped or the dotted lines (see graph on following page). If this occurs ask, *"This seems to indicate that in almost every week you will show more improvement than the week before. How does this line take into account the major ups and downs that may occur from week to week?"*

The goal, of course, is to show that a smooth linear progression is not realistic and to reduce worrying (i.e., cognitive rumination) when a lapse occurs. Ask clients to redraw the line so it reflects a more accurate view of progress, given that stressors vary from week to week. With

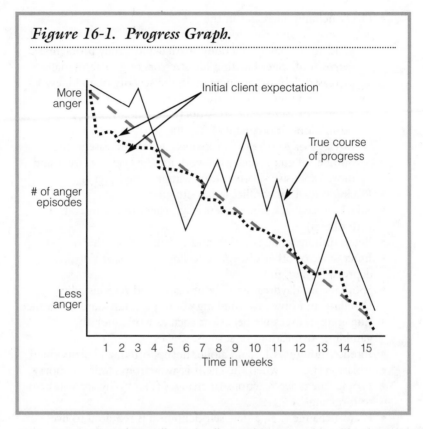

Figure 16-1. Progress Graph.

More anger

Initial client expectation

True course of progress

# of anger episodes

Less anger

1 2 3 4 5 6 7 8 9 10 11 12 13 14 15

Time in weeks

some questioning, they will eventually produce something like the solid line as a better representation of expected progress.

Several issues can be highlighted with this graph. The first is that ups and downs occur throughout the treatment process and are completely normal and expected. Thus, overreacting to a lapse may unnecessarily undermine future progress. Second, meaningful improvement is obtained over the long term and can only be judged over a longer time frame than initially expected. And third, although anger will never be completely eliminated, the frequency, intensity, and duration of anger can be substantially reduced. In other words, the real goal is to make anger much less of a problem in the person's life.

In addition to education about the likely *sequence* of progress, it is useful to educate clients about the potential *causes* of relapse. Although they will naturally differ for each client, the following are some reasons why client anger re-emerges after treatment begins to become effective.

- Overwhelming increases in the
  - *number* of anger-eliciting life stressors (e.g., new debt, a car accident, or newly emerging marital and family problems)
  - *intensity* of anger-eliciting life stressors (e.g., substantially increased debt or an increase in the severity of an illness.)
- Overwhelming increases in the
  - *number* of *positive* life stressors (e.g., a new house, a promotion, or pregnancy)
  - *intensity* of *positive* life stressors (e.g., an increase in the number of employees who work for the client, a larger and more expensive sports car, or winning the lottery)
- Placing oneself in conflict-laden situations
- A lack of feedback from others (e.g., client does not consult with others)
- Being dishonest, unassertive, and untrusting of others
- Emergence of other disruptive feelings, such as anxiety, depression, and guilt
- Spontaneous daydreaming about blame and responsibility
- Dwelling and obsessive thinking about past hurts and vengeance
- Engaging in excessive behaviors such as work-aholism, gambling, overeating, or sexual excesses
- Intense thoughts of being alone, unsupported, and abandoned
- Isolation (i.e., as when the client is away from family support)
- People's negative reactions to changes (i.e., "Why are you being so forgiving?")
- Fear of change (i.e., a new self-definition is required to live without the anger disorder to which the client is so accustomed)
- Interruption of treatment sessions (e.g., holidays or illness lead to a longer than usual period between treatment sessions)
- Stopping or beginning new medication
- Drinking and drug use
- Skipping treatment appointments
- Feeling overconfident — thinking that formal professional support is no longer needed
- Setting unrealistic goals for others or being too hard on oneself
- Changes in eating and sleeping patterns, personal hygiene, or energy levels
- Lack of social support from friends, family, colleagues, students, supervisors, etc.
- Emergence of, or changes in, psychiatric symptoms
- Avoidance and lack of resolution in facing personal problems and other problems of daily living, until they have built up
- Ignoring relapse warning signs and triggers

❖ *Strategies for Managing Setbacks*

Although treatment in outpatient settings is traditionally provided to clients in an interval of one meeting per week, other options may be considered. Flexibility may be especially possible in school, in-patient, correctional, or independent practice settings where frequency of meetings can be tailored to client functioning. In addition, telephone and internet contact may be used as adjuncts to face-to-face contact. Thus, one way to handle setbacks is to increase the frequency of therapist-client contact.

For example, consider the case of Ryan, a 38-year-old executive and father of three with a history of anger outbursts on the job. In the past, his anger has contributed to losing several important customers for his company. This, in turn, has led his supervisors to question whether or not it is wise to consider him for more responsibility and promotion. Such a promotion would be accompanied by a substantial salary increase, which would be much appreciated in a family of five. Unfortunately, the decision has been to withhold advancement based on his difficulty with customers. And, Ryan's lack of upward mobility in the company during the past two years has become an additional source of anger, rumination and resentment. As is common in clients with anger disorders, he believes that he is not completely to blame for the difficulties that have occurred and insists that he was assigned to work with a group of particularly "difficult customers." His supervisors have not been supportive of his analysis, leading Ryan to see them as "out to get me." There are a number of negative evaluations of his job performance in his personnel file.

Ryan came to treatment because his wife urged him to get help. He did well in the early sessions, meeting with the therapist about once a week. He was able to examine how his angry thoughts and behavioral reactions (e.g., sulking and desires to punish others) had interfered with his career success. He was also able to work collaboratively with the therapist and he appeared committed to learning new ways of responding to disappointment, disapproval, and negative feedback. In the fifth session Ryan came in upset and embarrassed. He had gotten into a "shouting match" with one of his supervisors regarding how to handle a difficult and highly demanding customer. Once again, Ryan viewed the supervisor as taking the customer's side in the dispute and believed that he was treated unfairly.

Although Ryan had shown a meaningful decrease in the number of anger episodes he was experiencing at work since treatment began, this one incident was important because he was now at risk for losing his job. Ryan was confused about how to deal with the "unfair" supervisor and was unsure if he could continue to manage his anger in light of what happened. Clearly, Ryan's progress in treatment was in jeopardy, along with his job.

Ryan and the therapist agreed to meet three times during the next week to help him better handle the current situation and to get treatment back on track. In addition, Ryan was encouraged to contact the therapist by phone or email if immediate, additional problems emerged. (Another helpful alternative, although not used in this case, would be the use of a computer "instant messenger" or visual "net meeting" service.)

Increasing the frequency of sessions and other forms of contact when clients have setbacks has a number of advantages. Some are readily obvious while others are more subtle. Among the more obvious, increasing contact provides for better monitoring of reactions to daily triggers. Thus, the therapist is in a better position to assess risk in terms of danger to self or others — or, in Ryan's case, a potential loss — and to intervene and prevent serious negative consequences from occurring.

Second, more frequent contact allows the practitioner and the client to put in greater effort to reduce anger in response to a specific ongoing trigger. Skills such as relaxation, alternative ways of appraising and thinking, planned avoidance, and even forgiveness can be rehearsed with greater frequency and intensity. In Ryan's case, managing his physical activation in relation to the event through relaxation was important, as were practical suggestions for avoiding further conflict. Problem solving was conducted to help Ryan develop a plan of action aimed at repairing the damage to the relationship with this supervisor. New skills were added, such as replacing inflammatory thoughts (e.g., "This s.o.b. never gives me the benefit of the doubt and always takes the client's side") with more realistic alternatives ("My supervisor's job is to make money for the company. So, he has to maintain customer relationships. I can see it from his side, and don't have to take this personally").

Subtler benefits of increased session contact are embedded in the message that this course of action sends to the client. Increasing session frequency signals that the situation is serious and problems that develop in the client's life are important. Further, it shows that the practitioner is concerned and supportive. Scheduling more frequent sessions also demonstrates that the practitioner is willing to work harder with the client, and is not giving up. In fact, this simple action models the basic idea that difficulties and challenges are often best faced with increased effort. A message regarding the issue of responsibility is sent as well. Ultimately, the client has a central role in making increased and continued efforts to reduce anger experiences and expressions.

❖ *Maintaining Gains as Treatment Ends*

As mental health professionals well know, ending treatment is best handled as a carefully considered stage of the change process. An abrupt end to treatment sessions, for almost any reason, is not recommended. The decision to end treatment is best made collaboratively when specific goals have been achieved and the client is well prepared to deal with ongoing triggers likely to produce anger in the future.

For example, in Ryan's case, treatment took place over the course of 30 sessions. One of his treatment goals was to reduce the frequency and intensity of his anger experiences at work. He was asked to keep a daily log; and when he began his anger management program Ryan reported approximately eight work-related experiences or episodes per week. In sessions 20 through 30, his weekly reported anger episodes dropped to around two. Given the large number of potential triggers associated with his work, the goal of zero anger episodes on the job was not viewed as realistic. Thus, a second and perhaps more important goal, especially given the verbal altercation reported in session five, was for Ryan to learn new ways to express himself assertively when he did experience customer- or supervisor-triggered anger. Ryan and the therapist focused on developing new responses to criticism through a combination of exposure and role-playing. Once he was proficient using the new skills in the simulations rehearsed in the office, it was decided that he could use the previous disagreement at work as a reason to discuss his current job performance with his supervisor. This, of course, required that Ryan request, hear, tolerate, and respond reasonably to criticism. In addition to the benefit of real-life exposure, Ryan also used this opportunity to clarify specific goals that he was expected to reach in order to be considered for promotion. This provided him with a better sense of control regarding his career path. The therapist and Ryan also went through problem-solving steps regarding the possibility that he might want to leave his current position in search of a better environment. It was agreed that he would update his resume and quietly begin exploring other employment options. It was at this point that Ryan and the therapist made the decision to begin concluding treatment.

As part of the termination process, the therapist had Ryan generate a list of high-risk situations likely to trigger strong anger responses at work. He was asked to generate known situations from the past and, using his imagination, possible novel triggers that could develop during the next month. Four sessions were then conducted to identify and rehearse strategies that could be applied to each trigger on his list. For example, Ryan anticipated difficulties if a customer simply asked to "go over his head" and speak with his supervisor. Ryan typically "awfulized" about such a request. He imagined this always meant the customer was unhappy, as opposed to simply seeking information from a more experienced person. Alternative cognitive responses to this trigger were discussed and rehearsed. Through problem solving, it also became clear that the best choice in this situation was to "act" graciously and cooperatively, and immediately put the client in touch with the supervisor. Then, he could follow-up with the supervisor to determine if there was anything more he could do to assist the customer. This scenario was rehearsed several times, using role-play in which the customer acted with less or more unhappiness. Ryan had little difficulty following his plan of action.

Once similar plans were developed and rehearsed for each trigger, the decision was made to taper off treatment by spacing sessions to once every two weeks for the next two months. Further reduction of treatment frequency would be implemented depending on progress. If progress was maintained, sporadic booster sessions could be scheduled at intervals to be agreed on later. It was also agreed that Ryan would call the therapist for an appointment if he believed that he was slipping into old anger patterns and not utilizing the skills learned in treatment.

Ryan's case represents an example of treatment conducted under optimal conditions. He was intelligent and motivated, and he established a productive working relationship with the practitioner. In addition, there were few barriers in terms of the structure of treatment (i.e., the number of sessions was not limited by an HMO and there was freedom for the client and therapist to make decisions together). We realize that many readers may work in institutional settings or in managed care frameworks that impose limitations on the number of sessions clients may receive. Also, anger treatment in institutional settings is often conducted in a group rather than an individual format. Groups differ in how they function; some have rolling admissions (new members may be placed in the group at any time) while others have a clear start and ending point for all participants. Certainly, considering ways to end treatment and prevent setbacks from developing into treatment failure are important issues for anger management programs regardless of how treatment is delivered.

Client Information Sheet

Anger Relapses: Causes and Remedies

Anger may reappear when you become overwhelmed with new problems such as increased debt, a car accident, emerging conflict, an illness, etc. Anger may also reappear when "good" things occur such as buying a house, receiving a promotion at work, or even winning the lottery. These can be very stressful. Preventing a relapse to anger involves a lifetime of active and thoughtful planning. Here are some causes and remedies for anger relapses.

1) Becoming overwhelmed. This may occur by: (a) over-scheduling daily activities, leaving no time for unexpected events; (b) not allowing time for exercise, sports, and other enjoyable leisure activities; and (c) not directly facing life's problems and allowing minor unresolved annoyances to build up. *Remedy:* We are all prone to anger when new stressors appear and there is little time to solve problems. Anticipate and plan accordingly. Don't take on new demanding responsibilities without significant forethought. Consult with others, for an objective opinion, about how the new responsibility is likely to impact on your life. Practice relaxation skills. Manage your life so that there is free time for exercise and leisure activities. When possible, avoid situations and people likely to lead to conflict.

2) Relying on old angry ways. Remember, acting with anger has short-term payoffs. Children, your spouse, or co-workers may temporarily obey your requests. It sometimes feels so good to yell at others and blow off steam. And, old angry patterns are likely to feel natural in times of challenge and difficulty. *Remedy:* Recognize that anger expression has long-term costs and that developing new more effective responses requires focus and discipline. Delay the immediate gratification you may experience with an anger outburst. Stop looking for a "quick fix." Decide what is "best" to solve the problem for the long-term, rather than simply doing what you "want" to do.

3) Isolating yourself, not sharing your concerns, and being afraid of feedback. You may believe that it is best to keep up a good front, and not ask for advice or help from others. This may be especially true if you do not trust others. Although self-reliance has many advantages, it does not allow for the social interaction required for growth and change. *Remedy:* Stay in touch with supportive people every day. Admit publicly that you are fallible and sometimes don't know what to do. Ask for help. Seek a model you believe handles stress well. Ask yourself: "What would this person do in this situation?" Be trusting of others and seek negative as well as positive feedback. Recognize that, indeed, you *can* tolerate disapproval from others.

4) Being dishonest with yourself about your capabilities. Telling yourself that you can handle anything, over-exaggerating your anger management skills, and not listening to the advice of others can undermine progress. This includes missing treatment appointments and not doing assigned homework. Grandiosity is not consistent with good anger management! *Remedy:* Be realistic about your progress. Have a little bit of honest doubt about your skills. Listen to the advice of trusted others. Remember, progress is "up-and-down." Every situation may be challenging, and may end in failure. Increase contact with your anger management practitioner when times are difficult. Face difficulties with increased efforts.

5) Hanging on to old ideas. Maintaining certain ideas is likely to increase anger experiences. For example, telling yourself, obsessively, that the world "should" or "must" or "is supposed" to be fair, setting unrealistic goals for yourself or others, or dwelling on past hurtful behaviors won't help to reduce anger. In addition, exaggerating the importance of everything in your life, taking minor inconveniences way too seriously, and telling yourself that other people are "jerks" and that you "can't stand" what they do will only fuel your temper. Finally, ruminating about justice and revenge will only take up needless energy and not allow you to get on with your life. *Remedy:* Be willing to accept the reality that unfairness is part of everybody's life. Describe unpleasant situations and people realistically. Distinguish between what people do (their acts) and who they are. It is better to say, "I don't like that *behavior*" than to say "I don't like that *person*." Be willing to forgive the person, while seeking a change in behavior. Minimize judging, blaming, complaining, and resenting.

Perhaps the *most important remedy* for the reappearance of anger lies in your collaborative relationship with your practitioner. Schedule more interactions when the going gets tough. Your practitioner can help!

[Howard Kassinove, Ph.D. and Raymond Chip Tafrate, Ph.D. *Anger Management: The Complete Treatment Guidebook for Practitioners* © 2002]

WORKING ON OUR OWN ANGER
Anger Reduction for Practitioners

Observe all men, thyself most
— Benjamin Franklin

In previous chapters we presented a four-part plan (Preparing, Changing, Accepting, Preventing Relapse) that included a variety of strategies for reducing anger in clients. Clients, however, are not the only ones who experience anger. Anger is very common for all of us and practitioners are certainly not immune to the experience. And, when practitioner anger is frequent, intense, and enduring it can have a very negative impact on personal and professional life. Thus, we note that the techniques described in this guidebook can also be applied in a *self-management format* when anger begins to interfere with your own functioning.

Practitioners face a variety of anger triggers. As with clients, the most common triggers are likely to be related to interpersonal relationships with family members, friends, and colleagues. However, additional triggers may appear as a direct outcome of the requirements of the work environment, such as dealing with managed care preauthorization, session limits and paperwork, professional isolation, lack of institutional support and case supervision, long hours, and low pay. Anger triggers may also be directly related to the types of clients seen. For example, frustration may emerge when clients are unmotivated (e.g., adolescents referred by parents), forgetful (e.g., the elderly), or marginal in education or intelligence. This chapter focuses on applying anger management skills to your own life, especially to anger that occurs during sessions with clients.

❖ *The Effect of Practitioner Anger on Client Outcomes*

We have all experienced clients who have abrasive personalities, exhibit inflexible interpersonal behaviors, and possess ways of perceiving the world that make it difficult to conduct treatment effectively. Some common and noteworthy client characteristics that are a source of irritation and anger for practitioners include:

Lack of motivation, ambivalence, and *resistance.* Some clients seem to have no real interest in working with the practitioner. Others are unsure of their goals and some persistently resist our genuine efforts to help them, even in the face of overwhelming evidence that their current methods of dealing with life's difficulties are not working.

Hostility and *anger.* Other clients, due to their tendency to distort and misinterpret the intentions of others, become highly critical and verbally attack practitioners. They question our training, skill, experience and sincerity, and little that is said satisfies them.

Impulsivity and *destructive behaviors.* There are of course individuals who deviate from treatment recommendations and spontaneously act in ways that were previously agreed upon as likely to lead to trouble. Managing dangerous behaviors such as suicide and aggression toward others is also a major practitioner concern when dealing with some cases.

Needy, dependent, and *clingy behaviors.* A number of clients expect that the practitioner will solve all their life problems, while they themselves remain relatively passive in terms of taking actions to change their circumstances. They may frequently ask the practitioner for advice or reassurance, have difficulty staying within the agreed-upon time parameters of sessions, and persistently seek contact with the practitioner between sessions.

Manipulation and *lying.* Obviously, some clients do not genuinely want to reduce their anger and are involved in treatment only to satisfy some other agenda. Individuals who are coerced into treatment, especially those in criminal justice settings, may have an alternate reason for wanting to attend treatment (e.g., spouse will consider remaining in the relationship, parole board will look favorably on inmates who enroll in programs...). These clients may not be truthful about reporting their symptoms or engaging in between-session practice. Practitioners will also sense the lack of a productive working relationship.

Depending on the setting, practitioners may routinely encounter clients with one or more of these characteristics. They seem to be their own worst enemy. Their self-sabotaging actions, unresponsiveness, or direct thwarting of the practitioner's efforts can lead to exasperation. Although it may seem natural to feel anger when interacting with or thinking about these types of cases, practitioner agitation, rumination, and angry responses are of questionable value. In fact, keeping emotions in check may be crucial to working successfully with such difficult cases.

The experience of anger and the expression of anger toward a client/patient, in most instances, will interfere with successful treatment. As noted in chapter 6, the three basic components of the therapeutic alliance are *agreement on the goals* of treatment, *agreement on the tasks*, and *quality of the relationship bond*. If any one of these elements is missing, the likelihood of a successful outcome is diminished. The therapeutic alliance is a building block for treatment across a wide variety of forms of psychopathology, client groups, and mental health settings. Experienced and expressed anger are likely to diminish its strength. Also, the alliance is *dynamic*, meaning that once it is in place, it is not necessarily permanent. Alliances with clients can and do rupture and sometimes have to be rebuilt. Constant vigilance, in terms of monitoring practitioner anger, is required.

Practitioner anger is not functional. For example, it is not going to assist in attaining agreement on goals. It does not help negotiate tasks, and it certainly is not going to set the backdrop for a warm, respectful feeling between the practitioner and the client. If you, as the practitioner, are angry when you think of your client, or during a session, it is likely to thwart efforts to establish an alliance or cause a rupture within an existing alliance.

Except in the context of planned and agreed upon role-play exercises, expressing anger forcefully and directly at clients is not usually recommended. There are times when we do recommend an *assertive* statement such as, "John, I felt surprised and annoyed when you didn't show up last week." However, harsh confrontation (arguing, interrupting, insisting that the client is wrong, demanding change) or strong expressions of feelings (e.g., "John, I was furious with you last week. You know you have to call if you aren't coming. What the hell happened?") are associated with treatment failure. It may well be useful to respond to the client with occasional annoyance, or even anger, since that kind of realistic feedback is useful for personal development. However, repeated expressed anger by the practitioner, without therapeutic purpose, is to be avoided.

Some practitioners believe that harsh confrontation is necessary for difficult clients such as those with anger problems, or with clients who abuse substances, or those who are incarcerated. However, the typical reaction when confronted with practitioner anger is usually to respond with increased arguing, denying, and hostile verbal statements in an effort to defend and preserve one's own views. These types of interactions, where the practitioner expresses anger and the client responds defensively, further entrench clients in their original angry thinking and behavior patterns. They are rarely won over to the practitioner's point of view by the forceful expression of anger. More often than not, expressing strong anger directly at a client will erode the alliance and contribute to treatment failure.

On the other hand, practitioner *empathy* is associated with generally more successful outcomes. Being able to demonstrate patience and an understanding of the client's position even when a transgression has been committed against the practitioner is more likely to get treatment back on a productive course. Since it is hard to be empathetic when feeling angry or bitter, practitioners are in a bind. Feeling justified with one's own angry feelings when clients act poorly, while also recognizing that empathy is the best course of action, can be a difficult balance. Nonetheless, it is a problem to be recognized and solved by practitioners — not clients!

Dealing with challenging and irritating client behaviors is part of the job, even in the most favorable working environments, and definitely part of the landscape in more difficult settings, such as prisons. Angry practitioner reactions are not likely to be productive. Several steps that practitioners can take to reduce anger in response to clients are presented below.

❖ *Preparation*

As part of the preparation phase for anger self-management, consider how to *foster an awareness of your own in-session anger reactions and the associated consequences.* That is, to become aware of your own anger experiences as well as the overt-but-subtle angry verbalizations and behaviors you emit with difficult clients. For example, is your anger related to clients with specific types of pathology? Do you react more strongly to some types of client statements, behaviors, or body language? Does your anger produce lower motivation to think about specific cases and the best ways to intervene? That is, does your anger periodically lead you to "give up?" An awareness of the stimuli that trigger anger is necessary for good anger self-management.

We recommend several methods to build awareness of the effects of anger on practitioner-client interactions:

Engage in self-monitoring of anger episodes. Using the *Anger Episode Record* presented in chapter 3, or the *Self-Monitoring Forms* in chapter 7, practitioners can better understand the chain of events that leads to their anger at clients, and the consequences of such episodes.

Audio or videotape sessions. Periodically reviewing sessions, by actually hearing your words and seeing your body language, is highly recommended for personal development. Observe how your own anger is communicated to clients. Although direct statements are the most obvious method of communication, pay attention to subtle cues such as tone of voice, facial expressions, and body posture.

Supervision and feedback from other professionals. Discuss difficult cases with colleagues. Ask for an objective opinion about how you handled anger-provoking client behaviors. Of course, pick colleagues who are skilled and experienced practitioners, who are willing to accept different points of view, and who are themselves relatively comfortable with anger.

Consider outcomes. Reflect on client outcomes from your own caseload. Review those cases where you have experienced anger and negative attitudes toward the client. In addition, consider clients with whom you have had outright conflict. How do these cases usually end? How productive are the sessions? Consider whether or not anger works productively in the long run.

Experiment with different styles of responding to difficult client behaviors. Vacillate between forceful statements and empathic statements to see which style is more productive. For example, you might respond forcefully when a client does not complete between-session assignments (as illustrated in the first dialogue) or respond with more empathic listening and reflective statements (as illustrated in the second dialogue). Try different styles and notice the way clients respond. If clients react more positively to your interventions, they are less likely to trigger anger in you.

Practitioner style #1:

Client: *You know, I didn't do the relaxation exercise because I really didn't think that it was going to help much.*

Practitioner: *How can you be sure it would not help if you didn't even bother to try it?* (Practitioner used an annoyed tone of voice.)

Client: *I don't know. It just didn't feel right.*

Practitioner: *Well, if you don't give it a try it certainly won't work. What do you think will help?*

Client: *I don't know.*

Practitioner: *What comes to your mind as a possibility?*

Client: *I don't know.* (Notice how the client is uncooperative and unrevealing.)

Practitioner style #2:

Client: *You know, I didn't do the relaxation exercise because I really didn't think that it was going to help much.*

Practitioner: *Sounds like you didn't think the relaxation was on target for you.*

Client: *No, it wasn't. I don't see how spending 45-minutes by myself does anything to change the situation with my boss.* (Notice that the client reveals more information than in the previous example.)

Practitioner: *So, it's just not clear to you how doing relaxation could be useful in your present job.*

Client: *That's right. My trouble is dealing with my boss.*

Practitioner: *So you would like something that's directly related to the situation with your boss.*

Client: *Right.* (Notice that the client has agreed with the
                     previous two statements.)
Practitioner: *What do you think would be more helpful at this stage?*
Client: *Something that I can say to him, so that he doesn't keep
                     giving me everybody else's work.*
Practitioner: *So, it would be more helpful to you if we came up with ways
                     to talk directly with your boss this week.*
Client: *Yeah.* (Although relaxation was not accepted at this
                     time, the client worked productively on building verbal
                     skills at work.)

Vacillating between two different styles will make it obvious that
one style seems to lead to withdrawal and another approach allows for
a productive path to be discovered.

❖ Change Strategies

There are a number of change strategies that practitioners can use to
better manage their own angry reactions during sessions. These include the
following:

Manage in-session physical arousal. Reducing your own physical
activation during interactions with clients will help decrease anger and
allow you to respond more effectively. The relaxation strategies presented
in chapter 9 are easily modified for practitioners. And, given its central
role in the treatment for emotional arousal, we believe that it is wise for
all practitioners to become expert in developing the relaxation response.
Thus, while still attending cognitively to clients, it is wise to focus on your
own breathing, rate of verbal responding, and letting go of muscular
tension in the jaw, arms, stomach. You are very likely familiar with the
process; we encourage you to practice it regularly so it is at your disposal
as needed during sessions.

*Skill Building — Develop advanced in-session therapeutic skills and
techniques.* For whatever types of client interactions you find to be
challenging, there are skills that can help you maintain a productive
collaborative relationship. For example, you might find that you feel
especially angry in the beginning stages of intervention when clients show
a lack of motivation or are ambivalent about change. If that were true for
you, it would be worthwhile to develop increased proficiency in skills
designed to increase motivation and move clients toward change. Or,
perhaps you feel angry when clients are verbally hostile or insulting. In this
case, it may be beneficial for you to develop an increased variety of de-
escalation skills, allowing you to accept verbal barbs without reacting
strongly. Books such as this one, continuing education seminars, graduate-

level classes, and supervision can all increase skills. Unfortunately, as practitioners we sometimes put our own development at the end of the list. This is natural, given the other demands of the job and your personal life. Nevertheless, we strongly recommend that you make it a priority to increase your own competencies, especially in those areas where you tend to feel anger at clients. Continuing education for professionals is mandated in some states. Where it is not, it is up to the practitioner to find time for self-development.

Problem-Solving. When faced with challenging client situations, consider multiple actions and their corresponding outcomes. For example, one of the authors of this book has a small fee-for-service clinical practice and does not want to work within a managed care framework. Recently, a client who had just begun treatment revealed that she could no longer afford the weekly sessions and she insisted that her managed care policy be accepted. Since the client had never indicated previously that money was an issue, there was admittedly some annoyance and anger toward her demands. Initially, the situation was viewed in simplistic "black" or "white" terms — either work with the managed care company or end treatment. However, through problem-solving, a range of alternative responses and their consequences were formulated (see chart).

Potential Actions	*Consequences*
1) Work with the client in her managed care plan.	Satisfies responsibility to her. Lots of paperwork and phone calls around getting paid. I will become resentful.
2) Take the case *pro bono*.	Satisfies responsibility to her. However, I would likely become resentful over time.
3) Reduce fee.	Satisfies responsibility to her. Might be an acceptable compromise.
4) Reduce fee until client finds higher paying job. Seeking a better job is consistent with her goals.	Satisfies responsibility to her. Also, allows us both to benefit from her occupational success. It is a compromise for both of us.
5) Terminate treatment.	Does not satisfy responsibility to her since treatment already started.
6) Refer to another practitioner.	Not ideal, since we already started treatment. But, is a possibility if the middle positions do not work out.

Option number four seemed to be the most preferable. This compromise position was presented and accepted. This allowed treatment to go forward and both parties remained engaged and positive about the arrangement. Failure to consider the full range of possibilities would have most likely resulted in a much less satisfactory outcome.

Avoidance and Escape. There are a number of situations where planned avoidance and escape might be helpful for practitioners. For example, some anger and frustration could simply be avoided by deciding not to take on additional cases. This might occur because you've set limits in terms of the optimal number of cases with which you wish to work. Avoidance of excess work allows you to establish a balance in terms of devoting time to family and friends, and work. One of the authors of this book used to work seeing cases until 10:30 p.m., thus missing family interactions and feeling quite tired when seeing that last client of the evening. Resentment was building until an avoidance decision was made to see no cases that would end after 9:00 p.m. This allowed for less fatigue, more time to interact with family, and less resentment toward clients. Limits can also be set on the number of clients seen with particularly difficult problems, such as those with co-morbid anger difficulties and substance use. Since these clients may demand more time and practitioner skill, such limits allow for more thoughtful attention to their problems.

An escape procedure that can be used strategically is to refer cases to other practitioners when treatment has gone off track and efforts to make improvements have not worked. Gently suggest that a fresh opinion might be valuable. Have the client try a session with somebody else to see if a different style or approach may work. Such clients may continue with you until they feel comfortable making the transition to somebody new. There are times when the "chemistry" simply is not right and a new person or approach can sometimes move the case forward.

Escape procedures are also related to practitioner safety. If clients become particularly abusive, disorganized, or difficult to manage, it is best that the practitioner end the session. Although rare, there are situations where a client will try to draw a practitioner into some type of physical confrontation. In spite of what may be seen in movies, which sometimes glorify the power of a health care professional, leaving the situation is usually preferable to standing one's ground. Displays of machismo and courage usually backfire and are not recommended in a treatment context. When working with practitioners in criminal justice settings we routinely discuss the option of removing oneself from the situation. Often, the only thing separating practitioners from physical injury is their clinical judgment. Unfortunately, we do know of cases where practitioners have been assaulted. In every case, the practitioner ignored warning signs, continued to pursue the interview or treatment plan, and did not leave the situation until the client was out of control. Always put your safety first!

Use exposure to become skilled at handling difficult interactions. Perhaps the best way to increase your competence in handling problematic clients, and to ensure that you can carry out new problem-solving skills, is to engage in exposure practice (chapter 12). For example, let's say that you have a tendency to experience anger when clients are critical of you and/or others. Find one or two colleagues who are willing to help you work on developing skills for responding constructively to criticisms. Next, think of some of the worst statements that clients have said to you. Ask your colleagues, or a friend or trusted family member, to make these statements to you. Take turns playing the roles of therapist and client. Say the critical statements to each other and practice coming up with responses that are productive and strengthen the therapeutic alliance.

For example, a disgruntled client might say the following to a practitioner:

You don't give a shit about me. You are only here to earn a paycheck.

Although this type of statement is difficult to receive and uncomfortable for many practitioners, there are nonetheless several effective responses that could be used. The practitioner might respond by saying:

You sound really angry. Could you tell me what I did to give you the impression that I don't care about you?

This is not the only effective response, but it is one that moves toward re-establishing the alliance with the client. With your colleagues, practice generating several effective responses to harsh critical statements.

When doing an exposure exercise such as this one, it is important to mimic the language, tone of voice, and body posture of the client who says the actual statement. Remember the goals are (1) *habituation to the harsh criticism* and the *(2) development of new response skills.* It is important for you to hear the tough statements delivered in a strong manner and then to maintain your composure. You are not doing yourself or your colleagues a favor by being polite and soft-spoken. Also, *repetition is critical.* It is not enough to practice hearing such negative statements one or two times. We have found that weekly practice sessions during supervision, aimed at

Figure 17-1.

Practitioners also benefit from help.

responding to difficult client statements, are extremely helpful in building practitioner competence and confidence.

Unfortunately, practitioners may be reluctant or embarrassed to openly discuss difficult interactions or treatment failures. There may also be a concern that supervisors will judge a practitioner negatively if mistakes are revealed. This is unfortunate, since by facing these situations we learn, in the long run, how to deal with them more effectively.

❖ *Acceptance Strategies*

Conducting interventions of any sort is difficult and challenging work. Thus, a practitioner's *mindset* in thinking about clients, their progress, and in-session interactions can greatly influence the professional's emotional functioning. Thinking accurately and realistically, and fostering an accepting and flexible philosophical perspective, were covered in chapters 13 and 14. While we generally think of developing these skills in clients, they are also relevant for those of us who conduct clinical work. In addition, even in the best of circumstances, practitioners sometimes make mistakes and push clients too hard or fail to listen clearly. At those times, we believe there are advantages to accepting our own mistakes and apologizing to clients when appropriate. Acceptance-related strategies include the following:

Foster a realistic and accepting, flexible, and less demanding philosophical view of your clients. When practitioners are asked, "What do you want for your clients?" they often give answers such as "to reduce their conflicts, anger, and negative behaviors." In short, we want to *change* our clients. This is admirable! Unfortunately, as we have noted many times, clients often do not want to change. And, even if you use every trick in this guidebook, some clients will simply fail to make progress. So, you would be wise to develop an accepting and flexible attitude about the outcomes of intervention!

Of course, *acceptance is hard* when we find our clients engaging in self-defeating choices and being unresponsive to our interventions. We ask that you consider what may actually be obvious: the outcome of treatment is rather unpredictable. Although we may use all the tools at our disposal, have much clinical experience, examine the research evidence about specific interventions, and consult with colleagues, it is still difficult to know in the early stage of treatment which of our clients will do well. Both authors of this book have been humbled many times by making pessimistic predictions about certain clients, only to be pleasantly surprised that the case turned out quite well. Of course, the opposite has also been true. Other clients, despite appearing to possess many positive indicators of success early on, sometimes do poorly.

Unfortunately, strategies and technologies in the mental health field are not as precise as those in other trades and professions, and we cannot make the precise predictions that are hallmarks of other sciences, such as physics and chemistry. Thus, no matter how good we are, we are doomed to lots of failure and disappointment. This does not mean that we give up. It does mean, however, that we become accepting of the unpredictability of the outcomes of our work if we want to remain anger free and mentally healthy. (It is worth noting that physicists and chemists are often not able to predict outcomes with certainty either! Indeed, it was a physicist – Werner Heisenberg – who discovered that simply *observing* a physical phenomenon changes the outcome. Needless to say, that's true in human sciences and practitioner activities as well.)

Perhaps it was the Gestalt therapist, Fritz Perls (1969) who best recognized the independence of people. Although he was not particularly focused on practitioner-client interactions, he said:

I do my thing, and you do your thing.
I am not in this world to live up to your expectations,
    and you are not in this world to live up to mine.
You are you and I am I,
    and if by chance we find each other — it is beautiful.
If not it can't be helped.

Another way to think about what Perls was saying, in terms of practitioner-client interactions, is to remember that clients often "march to their own drummers" and *their* difficulties are *their* struggles. We as practitioners simply move along with them.

Unfortunately, some practitioners think of their clients almost like puppets. They wrongly believe that those with whom they work *must* surely and absolutely comply with the anger-reducing strategies suggested in sessions if they explain them carefully, develop them collaboratively, and promise social rewards for compliance. In fact, the practitioner may have done it all correctly and, yet, some percent of clients still don't respond. That is why you'll find an attitude of acceptance of reality helpful.

One of the best ways to develop this attitude of flexibility and the acceptance of reality is to practice rational thinking, according to Ellis' REBT model. Consider Frank, a practitioner in an outpatient clinic who was working with, Paul, an angry husband. Paul often flew off the handle, accused his wife of being sloppy and uncaring, and suspected her of having an extramarital affair. Frank had done everything right. He determined that Paul was at a stage of readiness to work on his anger. In the preparation phase, he focused on developing a strong alliance and helped Paul to increase his awareness of the components of his anger episodes. In terms of change strategies, Frank taught Paul relaxation skills and outlined appropriate uses of avoidance and escape at times when anger seemed imminent and potentially destructive. Yet, when Frank introduced the additional strategy of using imaginal exposure to help Paul deal more effectively with his ruminations, little progress was made. The client was resistant to rehearsing visualizations related to two very troubling scenarios: his wife's carelessness and his own intrusive thoughts about her alleged infidelity. After several sessions of trying to persuade the client to engage in the exposure practice, Frank became highly frustrated and angry. He accused Paul of not wanting to get better and of undermining the effectiveness of the treatment program.

The chart on page 269 shows the irrational thoughts that contributed to Frank's anger, as well as the rational thoughts that would lead to less anger and a realistic, flexible attitude about the treatment.

One way for practitioners to practice and ultimately internalize a more realistic and accepting philosophy is to utilize the *REBT Anger Analysis Form* and the *Modifying Anger-Related Automatic Thoughts Form* presented in chapters 13 and 14. Like other skills, repetition is most likely to lead to success. We recommend reviewing your caseload frequently and using these forms as guides to shift thinking away from distorted and inflexible beliefs to ones that will be more rational and productive.

Practice Forgiveness/Apologize to Clients. Since anger negatively affects interpersonal relationships, it is important to rebuild connections that have been damaged by bad feelings. This also applies to the therapeutic relationship.

Our clients do some pretty bad things and we may respond with annoyance, anger, or outright rage. We may not show our agitation directly. Nevertheless, it will affect the therapeutic alliance. Depending on the setting, practitioners may work with thieves, pedophiles, wife abusers, murderers, arsonists, drug dealers, or other disreputables. Such clients appear in all cities and their patterns of dishonesty and hurt to others often begin in childhood. Public school counselors, university mental health professionals, and practitioners who work in criminal justice settings all see very difficult cases. Cases of industrial theft are harmful to the general public since the costs are passed along in the price of the products. And, there are many cases where people have lost their life's savings because of the dishonesty of corporate executives (e.g., the Enron Corporation scandals uncovered in 2001). Such cases will naturally arouse angry feelings in practitioners. This is the time to practice some of the principles of forgiveness described in chapter 15.

We certainly believe that it is important for society to do its best to correct or punish maladaptive acts. It would be unwise to accept, or excuse, or forget, or even justify antisocial patterns of behavior.

Irrational thoughts which lead to anger	*Rational thoughts which lead to acceptance of reality and flexibility*
1) It's *awful* that Paul still gets angry when he imagines his home and wife. And, it's *terrible* that Paul is not even trying to do the exposure practice. How am I supposed to help him if he won't do what is asked?	It is *unpleasant* that Paul still gets angry when he thinks of his wife. And, it is *surprising* and *unexpected* that he has not been willing to do the exposure. Clients do not always respond to every intervention. This is one of those times.
2) I *can't tolerate* Paul's lack of progress and his unwillingness to try the exposure. I try really hard to help him. I really *can't take it* any more.	I like Paul and *wish* he were improving. But, even if he never gets better, I *can accept* the outcome. *I just won't like it.*
3) Paul *should* be better by now. I am doing everything right. Paul *ought* to be responding.	There is no reason why Paul should or ought to respond. However, I did *predict* he would respond. I guess I was wrong.
4) Paul is a *jerk*. Can't he see that his wife is just who she is, and that she has always been sloppy? And, can't he see that even if she does leave him, he will survive? He'll be able to tolerate the outcome. But, he acts as though the world will come to an end. *Paul is just plain stupid!*	Paul is a *complex guy,* like all of us. He is bright and has been quite responsive in some ways. In other ways, he has not responded to my intervention, even though he seems to agree with our collaboratively developed plan. Well, there is no way of rating his totality, only his response to each intervention.

Nevertheless, condemning the whole person would interfere with professional intervention. Thus, we recommend that practitioners think about the causes of such acts and perhaps even discuss difficult cases (with care to protect client confidentiality) with colleagues, students, and others. Forgiveness and letting go occur when it is recognized that clients are not "evil" in the larger sense of that word but, rather, they are pawns of their learning history, biology and genetics, as we all are. Letting go of any vestige of global condemnation we may have for their acts will allow us to develop a better anger management program for them, and this will ultimately better serve all of society.

We also note that practitioners are human. Right? Thus, you will undoubtedly make mistakes when conducting treatment (we do!). In addition, you may have difficulty living up to a client's expectations. You may be late or miss scheduled appointments, experience scheduling conflicts, have difficulty returning phone calls in a timely fashion, not listen carefully, or say something that shows a lack of sensitivity. When these types of events occur, practitioners may tend to minimize their own culpability, or believe that a client is overly sensitive regarding a mistake, or think that he or she is not entitled to judge the practitioner. Of course, these attitudes are often the same ones we are trying to modify in our clients. *A better way to handle your own mistakes is to make it a practice to apologize to clients when you know you have erred.* Apologizing communicates a number of important messages. First, it models taking responsibility for your own actions. Second, apologizing shows that you are a fallible person who accepts making mistakes. It also sends the message that you care about the client's concerns and are empathic, even when you might be at fault. Ultimately, apologizing prevents resentment from building up and repairs alliance ruptures.

Under some very unusual circumstances, of course, an apology could jeopardize your position should a future complaint be lodged against you with civil or professional authorities. The client who can say, "Dr. Jones knew he was wrong! He even apologized to me at the time!" makes a strong case for your liability, should it come to that in our litigious society. We suggest you consult with authoritative colleagues and consultants on the ethics of your profession to guide your own course of action at times when an apology appears to be in order.

❖ *Relapse Prevention*

As we have noted throughout this book, anger reduction is a long process that requires continued commitment to modifying thinking and behavior patterns that have often been entrenched from years of practice. Learning to better manage your own anger reactions on the job will not be a smooth and linear process. You are likely to experience the same ups and downs as do clients. Thus, even when progress is made, it is useful to accept slips and mistakes as normal.

As practitioners, recognizing our own individual high-risk situations is a first step in preventing future relapse and solidifying gains. Spend some time considering those scenarios most associated with anger and develop strategies to cope with each one. The chart below illustrates this process for one of the authors of this book. In this case, anger was elicited by client behaviors associated with not showing up for sessions or terminating treatment without explanation. In these situations, the practitioner usually tried to contact the client by phone to discuss the situation. This rarely brought about a productive resolution. Clients usually did not return to treatment and seemed less likely to call for future sessions once they had been confronted about their behaviors. Obviously, anger at the clients was not helping the situation and a new way to cope with these scenarios was required.

Finally, developing a supportive and accepting atmosphere among colleagues can be helpful in strengthening and maintaining improvements in anger reduction and handling difficult cases. This

Client behaviors that were associated with practitioner anger	*Better ways to cope with such triggers*
1) Client does not show up for the scheduled appointment; does not call to cancel.	Don't take it personally. Work on your own beliefs that demand that appointments must be kept. Instead of getting angry, develop a clear cancellation policy, such as this: "Clients are obligated to pay for appointments cancelled less than 24 hours in advance." Create a client information sheet that spells out the policy.
2) Client does not discuss treatment termination but, instead, stops coming without explanation.	Again, don't take it personally. Work on beliefs associated with competence. Instead of calling, send a thoughtful letter that emphasizes that the client would always be welcome if more treatment was desired.

applies to both new and seasoned practitioners. Weekly case conferences or supervision meetings are used in many settings. Unfortunately, there are some work environments that do not provide any type of supervision or feedback. Practitioners faced with a lack of collegial relationships sometimes find creative ways to create such supports. For example, we know of several independent practitioners who attend bi-weekly support groups for mental health providers. Others pay for occasional supervision sessions from more experienced colleagues.

Our work as mental health practitioners is challenging, with many potential anger triggers related to stressors that are "built in" to this occupation. Not attending to our own angry reactions will negatively impact our effectiveness and sense of self-efficacy. Thus, it is useful to think of the four components of the anger management program as they apply to you. Preparing yourself to *deal more effectively* with anger, thinking about ways to *minimize* it, engaging in *change and acceptance* strategies with regard to your own reactions to clients, and being aware that managing your own anger is likely to be a *lifelong task* will go a long way toward your growth as a mental health practitioner and as a person.

SAMPLE TREATMENT PROGRAMS

Anger Management Treatment Program Samples

When we mean to build we first survey the plot,
then draw the model

—William Shakespeare

We introduced in this book a descriptive and explanatory model of anger episodes to provide a shared knowledge base for practitioners and clients. This allows for a shared understanding of the components of anger, including the costs associated with anger experiences. The anger episode model forms the foundation upon which the treatment program is built. Treatment itself is conceptualized as having four distinct phases: *preparation, change, acceptance,* and *preventing relapse.* A variety of strategies and interventions were described in detail for each phase of treatment. Although the chapters were written with adult clients in mind, the strategies can be adapted to children and adolescents. For practitioners whose work focuses on younger clients we recommend also the work of Feindler and her colleagues (Feindler, 1995; Feindler & Ecton, 1986).

In recognition that one model is not likely to be appropriate for all clients, we did not put forward a session-by-session treatment approach. This decision was based on feedback we received as we presented our anger reduction program at various training seminars and professional meetings. It became obvious that practitioners work in a wide variety of treatment settings with vastly different goals and resources. Strategies seem to lend themselves to some environments and not others. In addition, variability exists in terms of practitioner education and training. Thus, practitioners may be more comfortable with certain types of techniques than with others.

Our program is offered as a framework from which practitioners can select strategies that best match their clients, the treatment setting, and their own individual preferences. Although we encourage practitioners to choose interventions that address the four phases of treatment, the question of which specific strategies to apply in a single case, and how much time is to be emphasized in each area is left to professional judgment. Using this guidebook, we encourage the development of individualized anger management programs for each client.

Naturally, selecting strategies and interventions for each case requires careful consideration. Thus, we now present suggestions for adapting this program to several different treatment situations or environments. Sample treatment outlines are provided, for illustrative purposes, based on our own experiences. We have attempted in this section to clarify some common questions that practitioners have when developing programs for their angry clients.

❖ *Group Treatment Applications*

The information presented in this manual was written primarily for practitioners who work with clients in a one-to-one treatment format. However, much treatment — especially in institutional settings such as prisons, hospitals, and schools — is delivered in a group format. Thus, a common question is, *"I am running an anger group and I want to put together an effective program. What kinds of things should I do?"*

The techniques described can easily be adapted to a group format and would follow the same basic treatment model: *preparation, change strategies, acceptance,* and *relapse prevention.* Underlying the program would be the same philosophy that motivation is enhanced by a shared base of knowledge and that change occurs as a result of reinforced practice. For example, *preparing* group members to actively change their anger reactions can be the focus of the first three or four group meetings. Topics of group discussion can consist of defining anger, understanding the components of anger episodes, self-monitoring (with the *Anger Episode Record, Self-Monitoring Forms,* and the *Life Experiences Questionnaire*), and building awareness of the consequences associated with anger reactions. In fact, group members are often helpful in providing feedback to each other about potential outcomes of anger episodes. In our own observations of group treatment we have found that the biggest mistake made by practitioners is to move the group too quickly into active interventions without spending enough time developing motivation and momentum for clients to change.

Several *change strategies* can also be selected as the focus of group meetings. Practitioners, of course, are wise to consider time constraints and how many interventions can be reasonably discussed, practiced, and reviewed during the life of the group. Therefore, we recommend, depending on the length of the group, selecting one or two interventions from this phase of treatment. We have found that the problem-solving model presented in chapter 11 lends itself well to a group format. Group members can individually identify ongoing situations that are associated with anger, and go through the problem-solving steps while receiving feedback from others. Managing and reducing physical arousal (chapter 9) can also be done in a group format, but is likely to be more successful with adults than with children or adolescents. Regarding exposure, we have had clients develop their own exposure scenes and tapes individually within a group context and share them with other group members for feedback. Rehearsal is usually left to the client to do at home. Reactions to the exposure practice are discussed in subsequent group meetings (Grodnitzky & Tafrate, 2000). We have not yet attempted to incorporate *in-vivo* (barb exposure) into a group setting where participants deliver verbal barbs to each other. Practitioners should carefully consider the potential risk of group members responding angrily to each other and creating an environment that increases the likelihood of an altercation. Research attention is needed on the application of systematic *in-vivo* methods as a specific group treatment with anger-disordered clients.

Acceptance strategies can also be handled in group sessions. Again, it is not necessary to cover all of them and the practitioner can select what seems appropriate depending on the composition of the group. Certainly, the topic of forgiveness provides for thought-provoking discussion as some members of the group have experienced the benefit of forgiveness and can share their personal experiences with others, who may still be focused on revenge and retaliation.

Relapse prevention is recommended for the final two sessions. Group members can identify high-risk situations and help each other develop plans to deal with them. Also, any arrangements for subsequent booster sessions or aftercare meetings can be put in place.

There is significant variability in terms of how groups are conceptualized. Some have a set starting and ending point for all participants (closed groups) while others have a rolling admissions policy and new members may be admitted at any time (open groups). Since the present program moves through four distinct treatment phases, it may be problematic to have group members working in these different phases at the same time. Thus, we favor the *closed* group format. However, once participants have learned some of the basic skills and have completed a treatment program that covers all four areas, an *open* aftercare group could be used to provide ongoing support and to cover additional interventions that were not presented the first time around. Structuring an anger reduction treatment group in a way that satisfies both clients' and agency needs is the first step.

A sample program is outlined below for a 12-session treatment group. For this example, each group meeting is one and one-half hours in length and there are ten participants per group. Obviously, with shorter group meetings or more participants the program would need to be modified to cover less material.

Session 1 *(Preparation)*
Define anger, hostility and aggression with group members. Share real-life examples of each. Focus on the effects of anger on motor behavior and perception of solutions to life problems (i.e., the Yerkes-Dodson Law). Use the *Anger Thermometer* (chapter 1) to help group members develop a common vocabulary for experiences of varying intensities.

Session 2 *(Preparation)*
Present the anger episode model. Ask group members to identify a recent episode of anger and to complete the *Anger Episode Record* in the group meeting. Consequences of each group members' anger are highlighted in the discussion. Completion of the *Life Experiences Questionnaire* and an *Anger Episode Record* is given for homework.

Session 3 *(Preparation)*
Review the completed *Anger Episode Records*, with emphasis on the costs associated with anger. Elicit additional costs of anger from group members and the practitioner. Again, completion of an *Anger Episode Record* is given for homework.

Session 4 *(Change)*
Review the *Anger Episode Records*, with an emphasis on the physical symptoms experienced. Discuss the role of physical activation in anger, as a rationale for progressive muscle relaxation (PMR). Teach clients PMR skills. For homework, give tapes that guide clients through PMR (these were made ahead of time using the script outlined in chapter 9).

Session 5 *(Change)*
Clients report on their experiences with progressive muscle relaxation. Then, conduct another group session of PMR. Present a rationale for imaginal exposure (visualization) to group members. Provide guidelines for imaginal scene development. For homework, ask clients to write the first draft of anger scenes.

Session 6 *(Change)*
Clients read their anger scenes and receive feedback from the practitioner and other group members. Suggestions are incorporated into the scenes. Individually, clients are asked to practice rehearsing, in imagery, their anger scenes. Then, they share their experiences with

group members. Homework is given to rehearse anger scenes in imagery and to apply PMR skills.

Session 7 *(Change)*
The group focuses on a discussion related to the exposure practice with PMR. The problem-solving model is then presented and demonstrated by applying the model to several ongoing anger situations. For homework, ask clients to write out the problem-solving steps as they relate to a personal ongoing anger situation.

Session 8 *(Change)*
Review and discuss the problem-solving homework. For clients who did not complete the homework, problem-solving is conducted in the group. *Anger Episode Record* is again given for homework.

Session 9 *(Acceptance)*
Review the *Anger Episode Records*, with an emphasis on the thinking portion. The role of cognitive errors and misinterpretations is discussed in relation to specific anger episodes. Review techniques for fostering accurate and realistic appraisals. The *Modifying Anger-Related Automatic Thoughts Form* (chapter 13) is given as homework.

Session 10 *(Acceptance)*
Review the *Automatic Thoughts* forms. Ask members to present their individual thoughts to the group and have others assist in generating alternative but more realistic ways of thinking about the situations presented. Ask members to complete an *REBT Anger Analysis Form* (chapter 14) for homework.

Session 11 *(Acceptance)*
Review the *REBT Anger Analysis forms*. Have each group member discuss the rational thoughts about each trigger, with a focus on reinforcing why the thoughts are rational.

Session 12 *(Relapse Prevention)*
Clients identify and discuss high-risk situations. Group members share ideas for dealing effectively with the potentially provocative situations presented. Relapse prevention plans are reviewed and the practitioner and group members provide feedback. An overview of the skills taught in the group is also performed. Plans for aftercare meetings are set.

Criminal Justice Settings: Prisons, Alternative to Incarceration Centers, Probation & Parole

❖ ━━━

Anger reduction programs are widespread across a variety of criminal justice settings. Most commonly, treatment is delivered in a group format so the suggestions given above regarding group therapy are also appropriate for these settings. However, in correctional institutions there is obviously an interest in maintaining security and reducing aggressive behaviors among inmates. Thus, anger reduction is often viewed as a worthy goal among prison administrators because helping inmates control their anger is likely to reduce inmate-on-inmate assaults as well as dangerous attacks on staff.

One concern for criminal justice practitioners is that effective techniques in outpatient counseling and therapy may not be easily implemented in correctional institutions or agencies. A common question is, *Can these interventions be used with offender populations?*

Criminal justice environments do pose a number of obstacles to productive treatment. For example, a larger proportion of clients in criminal justice settings may be coerced into treatment, or may choose to participate because parole boards look more favorably on inmates who complete programs, or may choose a program over another type of sanction. Thus, clients in criminal justice settings are likely to be less personally interested in anger reduction. Nevertheless, many of the strategies presented can be adapted to fit into the functioning of criminal justice agencies and their offender-clients.

Assessment, prior to admission into treatment programs, can be useful in determining whether or not a client possesses adequate motivation to change. We recommend making attempts to screen out offender-clients who are extremely unmotivated or, at least, to have separate groups for what appear to be motivated and unmotivated offender-clients.

Assessment is also crucial for identifying offender-clients with significant antisocial features and psychopathy, who are not likely to respond positively to treatment of any sort. In addition, since anger treatment in the criminal justice system is commonly conducted in a group format, psychopathic clients can be disruptive and interfere with other inmates who are genuinely motivated to change their anger reactions. Thus, clients who score high on psychometric measures of antisocial behavior (e.g., MCMI; MMPI) may best be screened out.

Adequate assessment is also useful in identifying offender-clients with significant co-morbid psychopathology. Individuals with psychotic spectrum disorders, serious mood disorders, and/or current substance use problems may not be good candidates for group anger treatment and require additional interventions targeted at these problems.

Even when good assessment and screening have been implemented, clients in criminal justice settings will still have a greater tendency to view practitioners with distrust (e.g., view mental health practitioners as part of the correctional system; question confidentiality protections as less stringent). Thus, it is particularly important to spend time in the preparation phase of treatment. We have observed many treatment groups in prisons and found that practitioners sometimes assume that offender-clients are willing to immediately engage in change strategies. When active interventions are presented in the first or second group meeting, a large proportion of participants seem unwilling to share information. It often appears that no one ever bothered to ask the basic question of whether or not the participants thought they had a problem with anger. Focusing the first few meetings on how offender-clients view their own individual anger experiences and exploring anger episodes creates a stronger foundation for moving into change strategies.

Again, we recommend placing a focus on only one or two change strategies. Too often practitioners in criminal justice settings focus on trying to complete a specific treatment curriculum, and the material is not adequately absorbed or practiced by the offender-clients. Since the present program emphasizes building new skills, clients need time to try the new approaches and to rehearse them. Regarding acceptance strategies, forgiveness can be discussed in one or two sessions; this is important because offenders often harbor grudges, which bodes poorly for adjustment after release. Developing new cognitive skills can be introduced in one or two sessions. Again, depending on the clients, ongoing practice will often be necessary to make more permanent changes in thinking patterns.

Although practitioners who work in probation and parole agencies are not likely to implement a full anger management program with offender-clients, they nonetheless may help clients create an awareness of the negative impact of their anger episodes. Therefore, preparation strategies are most applicable to the role of some probation and parole officers. In addition, since practitioners in these settings frequently refer clients to outside programs, they often need an understanding of the characteristics of successful treatment to know the programs to which to send their offender/clients, and which ones to avoid. While treatment programs do not have to adhere exactly to the interventions presented in this book, effective programs will utilize similar strategies (Bowman-Edmondson & Cohen-Conger, 1996; DiGiuseppe & Tafrate, in press; Tafrate, 1995). Thus, we recommend that probation and parole officers spend time understanding the components of treatment programs to which they are likely to refer clients.

The sample program below outlines a ten-session treatment group that can be administered in a correctional setting. In contrast to the previous example, the group meetings are only one-hour in length and there are twenty offender-clients. In addition, consideration is given to the fact that offender-clients do not have access to tape players and are less likely to use forms and do written homework assignments. As noted above, all group members have been screened for significant co-morbid psychopathology, active substance use, low motivation, and antisocial features.

Session 1 *(Preparation)*
Define anger and aggression and have group members share real examples of each from their lives. Use the *Anger Thermometer* to develop a common vocabulary between group members and practitioners.

Session 2 *(Preparation)*
Discuss the anger episode model. Ask group members to identify a recent episode of anger and to complete the *Anger Episode Record* in the group meeting. Highlight the negative consequences of group members' anger. Differentiate short-term from long-term outcomes. However, expect that given the size of the group, and the time limitations, that only a few group members will be able to share their episodes.

Session 3 *(Preparation)*
Ask other group members, who did not share their anger experiences in the last meeting, to now do so and relate them to the anger episode model. Again, the negative consequences of anger episodes are highlighted at this point.

Session 4 *(Change)*
Present avoidance and escape strategies. (The clients — and perhaps the correctional staff — will likely respond to this different concept of "escape" in some settings!) Relate the appropriate uses of avoidance and escape to ongoing real-life anger experiences of members of the group. Ask group members to try avoidance or escape (from anger!) between sessions and to identify an example where this strategy was used. Announce that this will be discussed in the next meeting.

Session 5 *(Change)*
Avoidance and escape examples are now discussed. Note the drawbacks of avoidance and escape as long-term strategies for dealing with anger. Thus, a rationale is presented for developing new skills.

Session 6 *(Change)*
Present the problem-solving model. Demonstrate its use by applying the model to several clients' ongoing anger situations. Complete a *Problem-*

Solving Worksheet (chapter 11). Ask clients to try to apply the problem-solving steps to an ongoing anger situation before the next session.

Session 7 *(Change)*
Again, discuss problem-solving strategies and skills as they relate to situations the clients are experiencing.

Session 8 *(Acceptance)*
Define and introduce the concept of forgiveness. Have clients share examples where they have used forgiveness. Discuss obstacles to forgiveness.

Session 9 *(Relapse Prevention)*
Ask offender-clients to identify and discuss their individual high-risk situations. Ask group members to share ideas for dealing effectively with the potentially provocative situations presented. Ask each client to consider a plan for each of his or her high-risk situations.

Session 10 *(Relapse Prevention)*
Clients' relapse prevention plans are reviewed and feedback is provided by the group members. An overview of the skills taught in the group is provided.

❖ ## *Substance Abusers*

There seems to be significant overlap between anger and substance abuse (Tafrate, Kassinove, & Dundin, 2002; Deffenbacher, 1993). Thus, practitioners working with substance abusing clients are likely to recognize that many have difficulty managing emotions, including anger. Conversely, angry clients will often have a significant history of addiction or even ongoing substance use patterns that are problematic. Given this overlap practitioners frequently ask, *"How can I incorporate anger management into substance abuse treatment?"*

First, assessing substance use history among angry clients or assessing for the presence of dysfunctional anger among substance abusers is recommended. Clients meeting the criteria for dependency may have to undergo a detoxification program as a prerequisite to anger treatment. We do not recommend that the anger program be used for persons who are actively abusing substances because substance use is likely to interfere with emotional reactions and the ability to learn new responses. Substance abuse can be conceptualized as a strategy to avoid uncomfortable feelings, painful thoughts, and difficult situations. Since the present program emphasizes learning new responses while facing life's challenges, substance abuse will undermine the process. In most cases, we recommend dealing with the substance use problem first.

Of course, another option is to consider administering substance abuse treatment and anger treatment concurrently. For many clients, emotional problems may surface when substance use is diminished. Thus, having both treatments at the same time may be productive. However, we have found that, for practical reasons related to efficiency, practitioners will often conduct one or two sessions around the issue of anger management embedded within a substance abuse treatment program. Unfortunately, this approach does not devote enough time to fully develop anger management skills. Thus, a commitment to two full treatment programs (e.g., anger and substance abuse) is often necessary.

A sample 12-session program is outlined below. This client also happens to be addressing alcohol dependence. Since he is highly motivated, less time is spent in the preparation phase and more change strategies are covered. Also, because of the individual treatment format, barb exposure is used. Reference to the substance abuse problem is made. However, as noted above, anger and substance abuse are conceptualized as two problems each requiring a focused plan. Thus, the anger treatment is delivered as a full package and does not attempt to cover the substance abuse problem in any depth.

Session 1 *(Preparation)*
Use the *Anger Thermometer* to develop a common vocabulary. Present and discuss the anger episode model. Then address the possible relationship between anger and substance use patterns. Ask client to complete an *Anger Episode Record* for homework.

Session 2 *(Preparation)*
Review the *Anger Episode Record*. Highlight the negative costs of anger, especially noting that anger can be a trigger for substance use. Again, ask client to complete an *Anger Episode Record* for homework.

Session 3 *(Change)*
Review the *Anger Episode Record*, with an emphasis on the physical symptoms experienced. Discuss the role of physical activation in anger and use this as a rationale for progressive muscle relaxation. Teach client PMR skills and create a tape to be used for practice between sessions.

Session 4 *(Change)*
Review PMR practice. Present avoidance and escape strategies. Relate the appropriate uses of avoidance and escape to both anger triggers and situations where alcohol use is likely.

Session 5 *(Change)*
Review PMR practice and the use of avoidance and escape strategies. Discuss the drawbacks of avoidance and escape. Present a rationale for

exposure. Ask client to develop a list with the most common statements (verbal barbs) that trigger anger and to bring this comprehensive list to the next meeting.

Session 6 *(Change)*
Review the rationale for exposure. Practitioner and client rank order the barbs, from highest to lowest, according to the level of anger they produce. Also, identify the tone of voice and body language of the person who usually says them. Several of the least anger-provoking barbs are practiced with the practitioner until they produce little anger from the client.

Session 7 *(Change)*
Practice more difficult barbs until the client feels little or no anger.

Session 8 *(Change)*
Continue practice with the barbs. In this session, however, they are delivered with more provocative and exaggerated body language and tone of voice. Again, ask client to complete the *Anger Episode Record* for homework.

Session 9 *(Acceptance)*
Review the *Anger Episode Record* with an emphasis on the role of demanding and inflexible thinking. Ask client to complete an *REBT Anger Analysis Form* for homework.

Session 10 *(Acceptance)*
Review the *REBT Anger Analysis Form*. Discuss alternative less demanding beliefs and write them on cards for the client to practice.

Session 11 *(Relapse Prevention)*
Ask client to identify high-risk situations for anger. Present and discuss some ways to deal effectively with the situations presented. For homework, ask the client to develop a formal written plan for each high-risk situation.

Session 12 *(Relapse Prevention)*
Review the client's relapse prevention plan. Provide an overview of the anger management skills covered in treatment. Schedule several booster sessions.

❖ *Concluding Remarks*

Although anger is a common emotion, it seems clear that intense, frequent, and enduring anger contributes to a good deal of loss and human suffering. Anger is certainly a clinical problem worthy of treatment.

In our judgment, good treatment is based upon a shared base of knowledge about anger and the progression of anger episodes. Then, an individually tailored management program can be developed. It would first prepare the client cognitively for the intervention program, would then teach skills for change and acceptance, and would then provide for the minimization of relapse. Depending upon the client, setting, and preferences of the practitioner, some or all of the strategies presented might be included. Throughout the book, our presentation has focused on adult outpatients who are generally monosymptomatic (i.e., angry) and who come willingly for treatment.

In this chapter, in order to emphasize flexibility, we have presented some possible programs for clients who might be seen in groups, who are part of the criminal justice system, or who are angry and also substance abusing. As we reported at the outset, we decided not to write a session-by-session manual for all cases. Rather, we trust that practitioners will continue to read, attend workshops, gain supervision, and develop their personal skills to make solid judgments about which techniques to apply to each case.

In the course of teaching and training we have discovered that anger is the emotional problem about which practitioners seem most confused. As a consequence, they are quite uncomfortable with anger disorders and episodes, and often avoid working on such problems with their clients. We hope the program we present in this guidebook provides specific techniques that practitioners can use with their clients, patients, inmate offenders, consumers, students, group therapy members, and other service recipients. If reading this guidebook has helped in the development of knowledge and skill to assist others reduce their anger, and lead happier and more productive lives, then we have fulfilled our mission. If some practitioner-readers learn to reduce their own anger that, as they say, "is icing on the cake."

References

Abelson, R.P. (1987). Conviction. *American Psychologist, 43, 276-275.*

Abramowitz, J.S. (1997). Effectiveness of psychological and pharmacological treatments for obsessive-compulsive disorder: A quantitative review. *Journal of Consulting and Clinical Psychology, 65, 44-52.*

Agras, W.S., Rossiter, E.M., Arnow, B., Schneider, J.A., Telch, C.F., Raeburn, S.D., Bruce, B., Perl, M., & Koran, L.M. (1992). Pharmacologic and cognitive-behavioral treatment for bulimia nervosa: A controlled comparison. *American Journal of Psychiatry, 149, 82-87.*

Alberti, R.E. & Emmons, M.L. (2001). *Your perfect right: Assertiveness and equality in your life and relationships* (eighth edition). Atascadero, CA: Impact Publishers.

Alexander, C.N., Rainforth, M.V., & Gelderloos, P. (1991). Transcendental meditation, self-actualization, and psychological health: A conceptual overview and statistical meta-analysis. *Journal of Social Behavior & Personality, 6, 189-248.*

Arnett. J.J., Offer, D. & Fine., M.A. (1997). Reckless driving in adolescence: "State" and "trait" factors. *Accident analysis and prevention, 29, 57-63.*

Attenborough, R. (1990). *The Words of Gandhi.* New York: Newmarket Press.

Aune, K.S. & Aune, R.K. (1996). Cultural differences in the self-reported experience and expression of emotions in relationships. *Journal of Cross-Cultural Psychology. 27, 67-81.*

Averill, J.R. (1982). *Anger and aggression: An essay on emotion.* New York: Springer-Verlag.

Averill, J.R. (1983). Studies on anger and aggression: Implications for theories of emotion. *American Psychologist, 38, 1145-1160.*

Averill, J.R. (1987). *The classification of emotions.* Unpublished manuscript, University of Massachusetts.

Averill, J., Chon, K.K., & Hahn, D.W. (1994). Emotions, Creativity, and Health: Some Confluences Between East and West. Presented at the meeting of the National Congress of Applied Psychology. Madrid, Spain.

Barefoot, J.C., Dahlstrom, W.G., & Williams, R.B. (1983). Hostility, CHD incidence, and total mortality: A 25-yr follow-up study of 255 physicians. *Psychosomatic Medicine, 45, 59-63.*

Barefoot, J.C., Dodge, K.A., Peterson, B.L., Dahlstrom, W.G., et al. (1989). The Cook-Medley Hostility scale: Item content and ability to predict survival. *Psychosomatic Medicine, 51, 46-57.*

Barefoot, J.C., Siegler, I.C., Nowlin, J.B., Peterson, B.L., et al. (1987). Suspiciousness, health, and mortality: A follow-up study of 500 older adults. *Psychosomatic Medicine, 49, 450-457.*

Barefoot, J., Larsen, S., von der Lieth, L., & Schroll, M. (1995). Hostility, incidence of acute myocardial infarction, and mortality in a sample of older Danish men and women. *American Journal of Epidemiology, 142, 477- 480.*

Beck, A.T. (1964). Thinking and depression: Theory and therapy. *Archives of General Psychiatry, 10, 561-571.*

Beck, A.T. (1976). *Cognitive therapy and the emotional disorders.* New York: International Universities Press.

Beck, A.T. (1999). *Prisoners of hate: The cognitive basis of anger, hostility, and violence.* New York: HarperCollins.

Beck, A.T., Freeman, A., & associates (1990). *Cognitive therapy of personality disorders.* New York: The Guilford Press.

Beck, A.T., Wright, F.D., Newman, C.F., & Liese, B.S. (1993). *Cognitive therapy of substance abuse.* New York: The Guilford Press.

Beck, J.S. (1995). *Cognitive therapy: Basics and beyond.* New York: The Guilford Press.

Beckfield, D. (1998). *Master your panic and take back your life* (second edition). Atascadero, CA: Impact Publishers.

Benson, H. (1975/2000). *The relaxation response.* NY: William Morrow.

Beutler, L.E., Engle, D., Oro'-Beutler, M.E., Daldrup, R., et al. (1986). Inability to express intense affect: A common link between depression and pain? *Journal of Consulting and Clinical Psychology, 54, 752-759.*

Biehl, M., Matsumoto, D., Ekman, P., & Hearn, V. (1997). Matsumoto and Ekman's Japanese and Caucasian Facial Expressions of Emotion (JACFEE): Reliability data and cross-national differences. *Journal of Nonverbal Behavior, 21, 3-21.*

Bordin, E.S. (1979). The generalizability of the psychoanalytic concept of the working alliance. *Psychotherapy: Theory, Research and Practice, 16, 252-260.*

Bruene-Butler, L., Hampson, J., Elias, M., & Clabby, J. (1997). The Improving Social Awareness-Social Problem Solving Project. In Albee, G.W. and Gullotta, T.P. (eds.). *Primary prevention works. (pp. 239-267).* Thousand Oaks, CA, US: Sage Publications, Inc.

Buntaine, R.L., & Costenbader, V.K. (1997). Self-reported differences in the experience and expression of anger between girls and boys. *Sex Roles, 36, 625-637.*

Bushman, B.J., Baumeister, R.F., & Phillips, C.M. (2001). Do people aggress to improve their mood? Catharsis beliefs, affect regulation opportunity, and aggressive responding. *Journal of Personality & Social Psychology, 81, 17-32.*

Bushman, B.J., Baumeister, R.F., & Stack, A.D. (1999). Catharsis, aggression, and persuasive influence: Self-fulfilling or self-defeating prophecies? *Journal of Personality & Social Psychology, 76, 367-376.*

Butler, G., Fennell, M., Robson, P., & Geldeer, M. (1991). A comparison of behavior therapy and cognitive behavior therapy in the treatment of generalized anxiety disorder. *Journal of Consulting and Clinical Psychology, 59, 167-175.*

Butow, P.N., Hiller, J.E., Price, M.A., Thackway, S.V. Kricker, A. & Tennant, C.C. (2000). Epidemiological evidence for a relationship between life events, coping style, and personality factors in the development of breast cancer. *Journal of Psychosomatic Research, 49, 169–181.*

Cannon, W.B. (1963). *Bodily change in pain, hunger, fear, and rage.* Harper Torchbooks.

Chon, K.K. (2000). Toward an improved understanding of anger: A control theory approach. *Korean Journal of Health Psychology, 5, 146-170.*

Clark, D.M. (1996). Panic disorder: From Theory to Therapy. In P.M. Salkovskis (ed.), *Frontiers of cognitive therapy* (pp. 318-344). New York: Guilford Press.

Clum, G.A., Clum, G.A., & Surls, R. (1993). A meta-analysis of treatments for panic disorder. *Journal of Consulting & Clinical Psychology, 61, 317-326.*

Coué, É. (1922). *How to practice suggestion and autosuggestion.* Kila, MT: Kessinger Publishing.

Darwin, C. (1872/1965). *The expressions of the emotions in man and animals.* Chicago and London: University of Chicago Press.

Davidson, I., Golub, A. & Kassinove, H. (2000, August). *Effects of Social Context on Experience and Expression of Anger.* Poster presented at the annual meeting of the American Psychological Association, Washington, DC.

Deffenbacher, J.L. (1993). General anger: Characteristics and clinical implications. *Psicologia Conductual, 1, 49-67.*

Deffenbacher, J.L. (1994). Anger reduction: Issues, assessment, and intervention strategies. In A.W. Siegman & T.W. Smith (eds.), *Anger, hostility, and the heart* (pp. 239-269). Hillsdale, NJ: Lawrence Erlbaum.

Deffenbacher, J.L., & Stark, R.S. (1992). Relaxation and cognitive-relaxation treatments of general anger. *Journal of Counseling Psychology, 39, 158-167.*

Deffenbacher, J.L., Oetting, E.R., Huff, M.E., & Thwaites, G.A. (1995). Fifteen-month follow-up of social skills and cognitive-relaxation approaches to general anger reduction. *Journal of Counseling Psychology, 42, 400-405.*

Deffenbacher, J.L., Oetting, E.R., Huff, M.E., Cornell, G.R., et al. (1996). Evaluation of two cognitive-behavioral approaches to general anger reduction. *Cognitive Therapy & Research, 20, 551-573.*

Deffenbacher, J.L. (1993). General anger: Characteristics and clinical implications. *Psicologia Conductual, 1, 49-67.*

Deffenbacher, J.L., Dahlen, E.R., Lynch, R.S., Morris, C.D., & Gowensmith, W.N. (2000). Application of Beck's cognitive therapy to general anger reduction. *Cognitive Therapy and Research, 24, 689-697.*

Deffenbacher, J.L., Huff, M.E., Lynch, R.S. Oetting, E.R., & Salvatore, N.F. (2000). Characteristics and treatment of high anger drivers. *Journal of Consulting Psychology, 47, 3-17.*

Deffenbacher, J.L., Story, D.A., Brandon, A.D., Hogg, J.A., & Hazaleus, S.L. (1988). Cognitive and cognitive-relaxation treatments of anger. *Cognitive Therapy and Research, 12, 167-184.*

DeRubeis, R.J., Gelfand, L.A., Tang, T.Z., & Simons, A.D. (1999). Medications versus cognitive behavior therapy for severely depressed outpatients: Meta-analysis of four randomized comparisons. *American Journal of Psychiatry, 156, 1997-1013.*

Diener, E. (1984). Subjective well-being. *Psychological Bulletin, 95, 542-575.*

DiGiuseppe, R. & Tafrate, R. (in press). Anger treatment for adults: a meta-analytic review. *Clinical Psychology: Science and Practice.*

Dua, J.K., & Swinden, M.L. (1992). Effectiveness of negative-thought-reduction, meditation, and placebo training treatment in reducing anger. *Scandinavian Journal of Psychology, 33, 135-146.*

D'Zurilla, T.J., & Goldfried, M.R. (1971). Problem solving and behavior modification. *Journal of Abnormal Psychology, Vol. 78, 107-126.*

Easterbrook, J.A. (1959). The effect of emotion on cue utilization and the organization of behavior. *Psychological Review, 66, 183-201.*

Ebbesen, E.B., Duncan, B., & Konecni, V.J. (1975). Effects of content of verbal aggression on future verbal aggression: A field experiment. *Journal of Experimental Social Psychology,11, 192-204.*

Ekman, P. (1992). Are there basic emotions? *Psychological Review, 99, 550-553.*

Eliaz, I. (2001). *Self-reported anger episodes in American, Russian, Israeli, and Indian college students.* Doctoral dissertation. Hofstra University, NY.

Ellis, A.E. & MacLaren, C. (1998). *Rational emotive behavior therapy: A therapist's guide*. Atascadero, CA: Impact Publishers.

Ellis, A.E. (1962). *Reason and emotion in psychotherapy*. New York: Lyle Stuart.

Ellis, A.E. (1973). *Humanistic psychotherapy*. NY: McGraw-Hill Paperbacks.

Ellis, A.E. (1994). *Reason and emotion in psychotherapy: Revised and updated*. New York: Carol Publishing.

Ellis, A.E., & Dryden, W. (1987). *The practice of rational-emotive therapy*. New York: Springer.

Ellis, A.E., & Harper, R. (1975). *A new guide to rational living*. North Hollywood, CA: Wilshire Books.

Ellis, A.E., & Tafrate, R. (1997). *How to control your anger before it controls you*. Secaucus, NJ: Carol Publishing Group.

Enright, R.D. (2001). *Forgiveness is a choice*. Washington, D.C.: APA Books.

Eppley, K.R., Abrams, A.I., & Shear, J. (1989). Differential effects of relaxation techniques on trait anxiety: A meta-analysis. *Journal of Clinical Psychology, 45, 957-974.*

Evans, D.R., Hearn, M.T., & Saklofske, D. (1973). Anger, arousal, and systematic desensitization. *Psychological Reports, 32, 625-626.*

Everson, S.A., Kaplan, G.A., Goldberg, D.E., Lakka, T.A., & Sivenius, J.S. (1999). Anger expression and incident stroke. Prospective evidence from the Kuopio Ischemic Heart Study. *Stroke, 30, 523-528.*

Ewart, C.K. (1990). A social problem-solving approach to behavior change in coronary heart disease. In Shumaker, S. A. and Schron, E. B. (eds.). *The handbook of health behavior change. (pp. 153-190)*. New York, NY, US: Springer Publishing Co, Inc.

Eysenck, H.J. (1994). Cancer, personality and stress. Prediction and prevention. *Advances in Behaviour Research and Therapy, 16, 167-215.*

Feindler, E.L. (1995). Ideal treatment package for children and adolescents with anger disorders. In H. Kassinove (ed.), *Anger disorders: Definition, diagnosis, and treatment*. Washington, DC: Taylor and Francis.

Feindler, E.L., & Ecton, R. (1986). *Adolescent anger control: Cognitive behavioral techniques*. New York: Pergamon.

Frankl, Viktor E. (1963). *Man's search for meaning. An introduction to logotherapy*. Boston, MA: Beacon Press.

Freeman, A. & Dolan, M. (2001). Revisiting Prochaska and DiClementes's Stages of Change Theory: An expansion and specification to aid in treatment planning and outcome evaluation. *Cognitive and Behavioral Practice, 8, 224-234.*

Freud, S. (1958). On the beginning of treatment: Further recommendations on the technique of psychoanalysis. In J. Starchey (ed. & trans.), *The standard edition of the complete psychological works of Sigmund Freud* (Vol. 12, pp. 122–144). London: Hogarth Press. (Original work published 1913.)

Freud, S. (1958). The dynamics of transference. In J. Starchey (ed. & trans.), *The standard edition of the complete psychological works of Sigmund Freud* (Vol. 12, pp. 99–108). London: Hogarth Press. (Original work published 1912.)

Gaskin, M.E., Greene, A.F., Robinson, M.E., & Geisser, M.E. (1992). Negative affect and the experience of pain. *Journal of Psychosomatic Research, 36, 707-713.*

Gaston, L. (1990). The concept of the alliance and its role in psychotherapy: Theoretical and empirical considerations. *Psychotherapy, 27, 143-153.*

Geen, R.G. & Quanty, M.B. (1977). The catharsis of aggression: An evaluation of a hypothesis. In L. Berkowitz (ed.), *Advances in experimental social psychology* (Vol. 10, pp. 1 – 37). New York: Academic Press.

Gorman, W. (2001). Refugee survivors of torture: trauma and treatment. *Professional Psychology: Research and Practice, 32, 443-451.*

Greenberg, L.S. & Webster, M.C. (1982). Resolving decisional conflict by Gestalt two-chair dialogue: Relating process to outcome. *Journal of Counseling Psychology, 29,* 468-477.

Greenberger, D., & Padesky, C.A. (1995*). Mind over mood: Change the way you feel by changing the way you think.* New York: Guilford Press.

Grodnitzky, G.R., & Tafrate, R. (2000). Imaginal exposure for anger reduction in adult outpatients: A pilot study. *Journal of Behavior Therapy and Experimental Psychiatry, 31, 259-279.*

Heider, F. (1958). *The psychology of interpersonal relations.* New York: Wiley.

Henderson, C. (1986). *God and science.* John Knox Press.

Herman, J.L. (1992). *Trauma and recovery.* NY: Basic Books.

Hermann, C., Kim, M., & Blanchard, E. B. (1995). Behavioral and prophylactic pharmacological intervention studies of pediatric migraine: An exploratory meta-analysis. *Pain, 60, 239-255.*

Hill, W. (1985). *Learning: A survey of psychological interpretations.* (4th. ed.). New York: Harper and Row.

Hiller, J.E. (1989). Breast cancer: A psychogenic disease? *Women & Health, 15, 5-18.*

Holahan, C.J. & Moos, R.H. (1990). Life stressors, resistance factors, and improved psychological functioning: An extension of the stress resistance paradigm. *Journal of Personality & Social Psychology. 58, 909-917.*

Horvath, A.O., & Symonds, B.D. (1991). Relation between working alliance and outcome in psychotherapy: A meta-analysis. *Journal of Counseling Psychology,38 ,139-149.*

Iribarren, C., Sidney, S., Bild, D.E., Liu, K., Markovitz, J.H., Roseman, J.M., & Matthews, K. (2000). Association of hostility with coronary artery calcification in young adults: The CARDIA study. *JAMA: Journal of the American Medical Association, 283, 2546-2551.*

Ivey, A.E. (1999). *Intentional interviewing and counseling.* Pacific Grove, CA: Brooks/Cole.

Izard, C.E. (1992). Basic emotions, relations among emotions, and emotion-cognition relations. *Psychological Review, 99, 561-565.*

Jacobson, E. (1925/1987). Progressive relaxation. *American Journal of Psychology, 100, 522-537.*

Jacobson, E. (1938). *Progressive relaxation.* Chicago: University of Chicago Press.

Jacobson, E. (1977). The origins and development of progressive relaxation. *Journal of Behavior Therapy & Experimental Psychiatry, 8, 119-123.*

James, W. (1984). What is an emotion? In C. Calhoun & R.C. Solomon (eds.), *What is an emotion? Classic readings in philosophical psychology (pp. 127-141).* New York: Oxford University Press.

Johnston, M., & Voegele, C. (1993). Benefits of psychological preparation for surgery: A meta-analysis. *Annals of Behavioral Medicine, 15, 245-256.*

Kabat-Zinn, J. (1990). *Full catastrophe living.* NY: Dell Publishing.

Kassinove, H. & DiGiuseppe, R. (1975). Rational role reversal. *Rational Living, 10, 44-45.*

Kassinove, H. & Fuller, J.R. (November 2000). *The experience, expression and treatment of clinically angry men.* Paper given as part of a symposium on Anger: Implications in community and clinical populations, at the annual meeting of the Association for Advancement of Behavior Therapy, New Orleans, LA.

Kassinove, H. & Fuller, J.R. (August, 1999). *Anger disorders: frequent, ignored, and possibly/absolutely universal.* Paper presented as part of a symposium on Cultural Universals in Psychopathology, at the annual meeting of the American Psychological Association, Boston, MA.

Kassinove, H. & Sukhodolsky, D.G. (1995). Anger disorders: Basic science and practice issues. In H. Kassinove (ed.). *Anger disorders: Assessment, diagnosis, and treatment* (pp. 1-26). Washington, DC.: Taylor & Francis.

Kassinove, H. (ed.). (1995). *Anger disorders: Definition, diagnosis, and treatment.* Washington, D.C. Taylor and Francis.

Kassinove, H., Roth, D., Owens, & Fuller, J.R. (2002). Effects of trait anger and anger expression style on competitive attack responses in a wartime prisoner's dilemma game. *Aggressive Behavior, 28, 117-125.*

Kassinove, H., Sukhodolsky, D.G., Tsytsarev, S.V. & Solovyova, S. (1997). Self-reported constructions of anger episodes in Russia and America. *Journal of Social Behavior and Personality, 12, 301-324.*

Kelly, G. (1955). *The psychology of personal constructs.* New York: Norton.

Keltner, D., Capps, L. Kring, A.M., Young R.C. & Heerey, E.A. Just teasing: A conceptual analysis and empirical review. *Psychological Bulletin, 127, 229-248.*

Kiekolt-Glaser, J. Malarkey, W., Chee, M. Newton, T. Cacioppo, J., Mao, H. & Glaser, R. (1993). Negative behavior during marital conflict is associated with immunological down-regulation. *Psychosomatic Medicine, 55, 395-409.*

Komahashi, T., Ganesan, S., Ohmori, K., & Nakano, T. (1997). Expression of depressed mood: A comparative study among Japanese and Canadian aged people. *Canadian Journal of Psychiatry, 42, 852-857.*

Kowalski, R.M. (2001). Aversive interpersonal behaviors: on being annoying, thoughtless, and mean. (pp. 3–78). In R.M.Kowalski (ed.). *Behaving badly.* Washington, DC: APA Books.

Kune, G.A., Kune, S., Watson, L.F., & Bahnson, C.B. (1991). Personality as a risk factor in large bowel cancer: Data from the Melbourne Colorectal Cancer Study. *Psychological Medicine, 21, 29-41.*

Lambert, M.J. & Bergin, A.E. (1994). The effectiveness of psychotherapy. In A.E. Bergin & S.L. Garfield (eds.), *Handbook of psychotherapy and behavior change* (4th ed., pp. 143—189). New York: Wiley.

Leahy, R.L., & Holland, S.T. (2000*). Treatment plans and interventions for depression and anxiety disorders.* New York: Guilford Press.

Levi, P. (1959). *Survival in Auschwitz.* NY: McMillan.

Lewin, K. (1948). *Resolving social conflicts.* New York: Harper and Brothers.

Lewin, K. (1935). *A dynamic theory of personality.* New York: McGraw-Hill. Pp. 180-193.

Linden, W., & Chambers, L. (1994). Clinical effectiveness of non-drug treatment for hypertension: A meta-analysis. *Annals of Behavioral Medicine, 16, 35-45.*

Luborsky, L. (1976). Helping alliances in psychotherapy. In J.L. Cleghhorn (ed.), *Successful psychotherapy* (pp. 92—116). New York: Brunner/Mazel.)

Marlatt, G.A. & Gordon, J.R. (ed.). (1985). *Relapse prevention: Maintenance strategies in the treatment of addictive behaviors.* New York: Guilford Press.

Marlatt, G.A. & Parks, G.A. (1982). Self-management of addictive disorders. (p. 443-488). In *Self-management and behavior change* In P. Karoly and F.H. Kanfer, (eds.). New York: Pergamon Press.

Martin, D.J., Garske, J.P., & Davis, M.K. (2000). Relation of the therapeutic alliance with outcome and other variables: A meta-analytic review. *Journal of Consulting & Clinical Psychology, 68, 438-450.*

Martin, R. (1997). "Girls don't talk about garages!": Perceptions of conversation in same- and cross-sex friendships. *Personal Relationships, 4, 115-130.*

Matsumoto, D., Kudoh, T., Scherer, K., & Wallbott, H. (1988). Antecedents of and reactions to emotions in the United States and Japan. *Journal of Cross-Cultural Psychology, 19, 267-286.*

Miller, L. (1999). Workplace violence: prevention, response and recovery. *Psychotherapy, 36, 160-170.*

Miller, S. & Rollnick, W.R. (1991). *Motivational interviewing: Preparing people for change.* New York: Guilford Press.

Mittleman, M.A., Maclure, M., Sherwood, J. Mulry, R., Toffler, G., Jacobs, S., Friedman, R., Benson, H., and Muller, J. (1995). Triggering of acute myocardial infactions onset by episodes of anger. *Circulation, 92, 1720-1725 .*

Morris, D. (1998). *Forgiving the dead man walking.* New York: Harper Collins.

Nezu, A. & D'Zurilla, T.J. (1989). Social problem solving and negative affective conditions. In Kendall, P.C. and Watson, D. (eds.). *Anxiety and depression: Distinctive and overlapping features. (pp. 285-315).* San Diego, CA, US: Academic Press, Inc.

Nisbett, R.E. (1993). Violence and U.S. regional culture. *American Psychologist, 48, 441-449.*

Nisbitt, R.E. & Wilson, T.D. (1977). Telling more than we can know: Verbal reports on mental processes. *Psychological Review, 84, 231-259.*

O'Donnell, C.R., & Worell, L. (1973). Motor and cognitive relaxation in the desensitization of anger. *Behaviour Research and Therapy, 11, 473-481.*

Parks, G.A. & Marlatt, G.A. (1999). Relapse prevention therapy for aubstance-abusing offenders: A cognitive-behavioral approach in what works: Strategic solutions (pp.161- 233). In E. Latessa Lanham (ed.). *The International Community Corrections Association examines substance abuse*: American Correctional Association.

Parks, G.A., & Marlatt, G.A. (2000) Relapse prevention therapy: A cognitive-behavioral approach. *The National Psychologist, 9.*

Perls, F.S. (1969). *Gestalt therapy verbatim.* New York: Bantam Books/Real People Press.

Pinto, D. (2000). Driving anger, articulated cognitive distortions, cognitive deficiencies, and aggression. Doctoral dissertation. Hofstra University.

Plutchik, R. (1980). A general psychoevolutionary theory of emotion. In R. Plutchik & H. Kellerman (eds.), *Emotion: Theory, research, and experience, Volume 1: Theories of emotion* (pp. 3-31). New York: Academic Press.

Plutchik, R. (1994). *The psychology and biology of emotion.* NY: Harper Collins.

Plutchik, R. (2000). *Emotions in the practice of psychotherapy.* Washington, D.C.: APA Books.

Prochaska, J.O. & DiClemente, C.C. (1982). Transtheoretical therapy. Toward a more integrative model of change. *Psychotherapy: Theory, Research, and Practice, 20, 161-173.*

Prochaska, J.O. & DiClemente, C.C. (1983). Stages and processes of self-change of smoking: Toward an integrative model of change. *Journal of Consulting and Clinical Psychology, 51, 390-395.*

Prochaska, J.O., DiClemente, C.C., & Norcross, J.C. (1992). In search of how people change: Applications to addictive behaviors. *American Psychologist, 47, 1102-1114.*

Riebel, L. (1985). Usurpation: Strategy and metaphor. *Psychotherapy: Theory, Research, and Practice, 22, 595-604.*

Rimm, D.C., DeGroot, J.C., Boord, P., Heiman, J., & Dillow, P.V. (1971). Systematic desensitization of an anger response. *Behaviour Research and Therapy, 9, 273-280.*

Rogers, C.R. (1957). The necessary and sufficient conditions of therapeutic personality change. *Journal of Consulting Psychology, 21, 95-103.*

Rollnick, S., & Miller, W.R. (1995). What is motivational interviewing? *Behavioural & Cognitive Psychotherapy, 23, 325-334.*

Rosenberg, E.L., Ekman, P., Jiang, W., Babyak, M., Coleman, E., Hanson, M., O'Connor, C., Waugh, R., & Blumenthal, J.A. (2001). Linkages between facial expressions of anger and transient myocardial ischemia in men with coronary artery disease. *Emotion, 1, 107-115.*

Russell, J. & Fehr, B. (1994). Fuzzy concepts in a fuzzy hierarchy. Varieties of anger. *Journal of Personality and Social Psychology, 67, 186-205.*

Safran, J.D. & Muran, J.C. (eds.) (1995). The therapeutic alliance [Special issue]. In Session: *Psychotherapy in Practice, 1.*

Salter, A. (1949). *Conditioned reflex therapy.* NY: Creative Age.

Scherer, K.R. (1997a). The role of culture in emotion-antecedent appraisal. Journal of *Personality & Social Psychology, 73, 902-922.*

Scherer, K.R. (1997b). Profiles of emotion-antecedent appraisal: Testing theoretical predictions across cultures. *Cognition & Emotion, 11, 113-150.*

Schopen, A., & Freeman, B. (1992). Meditation: The forgotten Western tradition. *Counseling & Values, 36, 123-134.*

Schwartz, G.E., Weinberger, D.A., & Singer, J.A. (1981). Cardiovascular differentiation of happiness, sadness, anger, and fear following imagery and exercise. *Psychosomatic Medicine, 43, 343-364.*

Shaver, P., Schwartz, J., Kirson, D., & O'Conner, C. (1987). Emotion knowledge. Further exploration of a prototype approach. *Journal of Personality and Social Psychology, 52, 1061-1086.*

Skinner, B. (1953). *Science and human behavior.* New York: MacMillan.

Skinner, B. (1968). *The technology of teaching.* New York: Appleton-Century-Crofts.

Skinner, B.F. (1974). *About behaviorism.* New York: Knopf.

Smith, M.L., Glass, G.V. & Miller, T.I. (1980). *The benefits of psychotherapy.* Baltimore: Johns Hopkins University Press.

Speca, M., Carlson, L.E., Goodey, E., & Angen, M. (2000). A randomized, wait-list controlled clinical trial: The effect of a mindfulness meditation-based stress reduction program on mood and symptoms of stress in cancer outpatients. *Psychosomatic Medicine, 62, 613-622.*

Spielberger, C.D. (1988). *Professional manual for the State-Trait Anger Expression Inventory.* Odessa, FL: Psychological Assessment Resources.

Spielberger, C.D. (1999). *Manual for the State Trait Anger Expression Inventory - 2.* Odessa, FL: Psychological Assessment Resources.

Stiles, W.B., Shapiro, D. & Elliot, R. (1986). Are all psychotherapies equivalent? *American Psychologist, 41,* 165-180.

Stosny, S. (1995). *Treating attachment abuse. A compassionate approach.* New York: Springer.

Suinn, R.M. (2001). The terrible twos – anger and anxiety. *American Psychologist, 56, 27-36.*

Sukhodolsky, D.G., Golub, A. & Cromwell, E.N. (2001). Development and validation of the anger rumination scale. *Personality and Individual Differences, 31, 689-700.*

Tafrate, R., & Kassinove, H. (1998). Anger control in men: Barb exposure with rational, irrational, and irrelevant self-statements. *Journal of Cognitive Psychotherapy, 12, 187-211.*

Tafrate, R., Kassinove, H., & Dundin, L. (in press). Anger episodes in high and low trait anger community adults. *Journal of Clinical Psychology.*

Terry, P.C., & Slade, A. (1995). Discriminant effectiveness of psychological state measures in predicting performance outcome in karate competition. *Perceptual & Motor Skills, 81, 275-286.*

Tystsarev S.V. and Grodnitsky, G. (1995). Anger and criminality. In H. Kassinove (ed.). *Anger disorders: Assessment, diagnosis, and treatment* (pp. 91-108). Washington, D.C.: Taylor & Francis.

Underwood, G., Chapman, P., Wright, S., & Crundall, D. (1999). Transportation Research. *Traffic Psychology and Behavior, 2, 55-68.*

Wade, J.B., Price, D.D., Schwartz, S.M, et al. (1990). An emotional component analysis of chronic pain. *Pain, 40, 303-310.*

Walen, S., & DiGiuseppe, R., & Dryden, W. (1992). *A practitioner's guide to rational emotive therapy (2nd. ed).* New York: Oxford University Press.

Wessler, R. (1992). Constructivism and rational-emotive therapy: A critique. *Psychotherapy, 29, 620-625.*

Williams, J.E., Paton, C.C., Siegler, I.C., Eigenbrod, M.L., Nieto, F.J., & Tyroler, H.A. (2000). Anger proneness predicts coronary heart disease risk. Prospective analysis from the Atherosclerosis Risk in Communities (ARIC) Study. *Circulation, 2034-2039.*

Wolfe, B.E. & Goldfried, M.R. (1988). Research on psychotherapy integration: Recommendations and conclusions from an NIMH workshop. *Journal of Consulting and Clinical Psychology, 56, 448-451.*

Wolpe, J. & Lazarus, A. (1966). *The practice of behavior therapy.* Pergamon Press, New York, NY.

Wolpe, J. (1958). *Psychotherapy by reciprocal inhibition.* Stanford, CA: Stanford University Press.

Wolpe, J. (1990). *The practice of behavior therapy.* (4th ed.) NY: Pergamon.

Xu, Z, Li, X., Han, B., & Liu, J. (1995). Effects of psychological factors on the development of stomach cancer. *Acta Psychologica Sinica, 27, 263-267.*

Yerkes, R.M., & Dodson, J.D. (1908). The relation of strength of stimulus to rapidity of habit formation. *Journal of Comparative Neurology of Psychology, 18, 459-482.*

Index

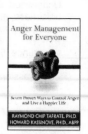